Patience, 1979

The Yeomen of the Guard, 2004

D0636266

The Mikado, 1979

Bitter Sweet, 1944

Me and My Girl, 2002

Romberg to Rodgers, 2005

IF YOU WANT TO KNOW WHO WE ARE...

RATHMINES & RATHGAR MUSICAL SOCIETY
1913–2013

IF YOU WANT TO KNOW WHO WE ARE...

RATHMINES & RATHGAR MUSICAL SOCIETY
1913–2013

MYLES DUNGAN

GILL & MACMILLAN

For Nerys and Gwyneth Owen Williams

Gill & Macmillan
Hume Avenue, Park West, Dublin 12
with associated companies throughout the world
www.gillmacmillanbooks.ie

© Myles Dungan 2013
978 07171 5712 9

Index compiled by Eileen O'Neill
Design and print origination by Design Image
Printed by Printer Trento Srl, Italy

This book is typeset in 10pt Adobe Caslon on 14pt.

The paper used in this book comes from the wood pulp of managed forests. For every tree felled, at least one tree is planted, thereby renewing natural resources.

The R&R and publishers have made every effort to trace all copyright holders, but if any has been inadvertently overlooked we would be pleased to make the necessary arrangements at the first opportunity.

A CIP catalogue record for this book is available from the British Library.

1 3 5 4 2

R&R

CONTENTS

PREFACE

'Will you write a few words about the R&R?' said Pat Campbell. A few words? I could write a book! I'll try and be brief, but I am half Irish.

The book would be about the years that I directed for the society. Years of joy, anxiety, anger, despair, remorse and moments of sheer elation. In retrospect, with some sense of satisfaction I can say, 'Yes, well we did do that rather well', thinking also, 'We could have done that better!'

The book would have potted biographies of some of the people involved in those productions. I have treasured memories of some performances. Louise Studley… surely the best Merry Widow *ever* and of the seven productions of *My Fair Lady* that I have directed elsewhere, *she* was the best Eliza Doolittle. I remember, too, Brendan McShane as Tevye in *Fiddler on the Roof*. He was also in *Gigi*, well supported by Pat Campbell – who also made me laugh in *The Desert Song*. The duet with Louise Studley and Lucy Lane in *The Dancing Years*; the duet with Joe Lane and Mary O'Callaghan in *South Pacific*; and Mary alone on the open stage singing of her love for Emile. And who could possibly forget Paschal Walsh in that show? (Who could forget Paschal, anyway?) And how could I have managed without Dodo O'Hagan at my elbow and my wonderful colleague and musical director Gearóid Grant?

I was reluctant to direct anything without the late Heather Hewson in it. Only once did she miss being in a show of mine – and how I missed her then! And now I miss her in real life.

I would like to thank all the actors/actresses, choreographers, musical directors, chorus masters and set designers who have worked with me and particularly I want to thank the many members of the chorus (the backbone of any musical society), who put up with my tantrums (I am half Irish) and yet still gave of their all.

Pat Campbell and I are of an age. We are not quite as old as the R&R but my Dublin-born mother would have been around at the time of the society's conception and if she hadn't met my English father on a blind date on the Portobello Bridge, Rathmines in 1920, I wouldn't be the 'me' that I am. And if the late Australian singer Laurie Payne had not recommended me, someone else would have directed all those shows for the R&R at the Gaiety Theatre. Pat Campbell, perhaps.

In 1969 when my agent called to see if I would be interested in directing the Irish premiere of *My Fair Lady* for the R&R but under the aegis of the Eamonn Andrews organisation at the Dublin Gaiety Theatre, I thought: 'Why not?' I had never directed a musical before and had always wanted to. I could have a 'paid for' six weeks with my Irish relations and if I made a hames of it no one would know. Little did I know how professional an amateur society the R&R were and still are! It was a wonderful cast. I was vastly helped and taught by the choreographer, Alice Dalgarno. I had great assistance from the adorable Terry O'Connor, who was the musical director at that time. A sweet man and a real pro, Bob Heade, did the scenery. I couldn't fool any of them! The first night was on my birthday. During the performance a piece of scenery broke in view of the audience but was magically whisked away by the backstage staff in an unscheduled five-second blackout. Despite that hiccup, the show was very successful. It was attended by then President of the Irish Republic Éamon de Valera. In the interval, I was photographed being introduced to him. A newspaper copy was sent by an aunt to my mother in England, who wouldn't speak to me for a month after: my mother knew Michael Collins, or so she would have us believe!

Unseen by audiences, however, are a group of people, including those who work backstage, unheralded, but without whom the R&R would not function. The officers of the society give hours of their time with little reward, other than the satisfaction of a job well done. Without them at the helm, there would not have been a society to celebrate. Sadly, many of those dedicated workers are no longer with us but their efforts on behalf of the R&R are evident. I take my hat off to them, and raise a glass to the future of the R&R in these troubled times.

Congratulations on achieving your century – not out!

Jimmy Belchamber
London, April 2013

James Belchamber directed the following shows for the Rathmines and Rathgar Musical Society:

My Fair Lady (twice)	March and November 1969
The Desert Song	1970
Fiddler on the Roof (twice)	1972 and 1988
South Pacific	1973
The Dancing Years	1974
Showboat (twice)	1975 and 1987
The Merry Widow	1977
Gigi (twice)	1978 and 1986
Hans Andersen	1985
Hello, Dolly!	1989

INTRODUCTION

It could almost be an examination question: 'Account for the survival and continued artistic success of the Rathmines and Rathgar Musical Society between 1913 and 2013' (Leaving Certificate, History, 2013).

In his or her response on why this organisation has outlived two world wars, a war of independence, a civil war and a cold war, the discerning and well-informed student might be expected to refer to *the three C's* – not the notes on a piano keyboard, but 'continuity, competence and camaraderie'.

Readers who persevere to the end of this volume will come across a number of recurring names. It would be tedious now to anticipate their introduction into the narrative, but it was their constant presence and guidance that gave the R&R the kind of continuity that secures permanence.

What this commemorative record sets out to establish is that it was by no means inevitable that the fledgling musical society that began its life in Rathmines on 20 April 1913 was destined to last at least a hundred years. Had a number of dedicated people not brought the professionalism of their workplace into their hobby, the R&R (as it soon became known) would have gone the way of the Austro-Hungarian Empire.

However, no amount of administrative stability or aptitude would have sustained the R&R had the whole project not been approached with a certain *joie de vivre*. Companionship and laughter have been at the heart of this hundred-year odyssey. Continuity and competence may have shaped the structure and the engine of the vehicle, but camaraderie provided the propulsion.

Up to the date of publication, and including the centenary *Mikado* at the National Concert Hall in November 2013, the R&R has staged 293 separate productions, compilations or entertainments at the Queen's, Olympia and Gaiety theatres, and at the National Concert Hall. That *oeuvre* has included critical and financial flops, flawed productions that have still managed to avoid deficits, as well as a plethora of acclaimed and exceptional shows worthy of many professional companies.

What follows is an attempt to record the triumphs, failures and occasional disasters, and to convey some sense of why the Rathmines and Rathgar Musical Society remains in existence and continues to offer outstanding entertainment and the (very) occasional let-down. While it has become an institution on the Dublin music scene, it has refused to atrophy and has always managed to reinvent itself when the urgent need for change has arisen.

I would like to record my thanks to a number of people.

Nora O'Rourke, who knows more about the history of the R&R than anyone, has been extremely generous in allowing me access to her memorabilia, personal records, opinions and recollections. She has been available at the end of a computer any time I needed to call upon her expertise, which has often been the case. She is the personification of 'institutional memory' and the R&R should be, and is, grateful for her hard work, dedication and total recall.

Michael Forde and Lewis Clohessy[1] were the first to ask me to examine the history of the R&R from an outside perspective. They have, on occasion, been surprised by what the society's archive has revealed. I thank them for their faith in my capacity to mine that archival mother-lode. The fiftieth anniversary booklet cost a mere £550 to produce. I apologise to both gentlemen if we went a little over that sum fifty years on. Nora, Michael and Lewis were joined in checking my excesses by a fourth Musketeer: Eamonn Beale, a man with a high regard for, and a true sense of, the early history of the society.

I am grateful also to my son Ross, a far more accomplished writer than myself, for conducting some of the interviews while I was pretending to be a San Franciscan yet again. Sorry for keeping you away from writing wonderful plays, Ross.

While a history such as this must, of necessity, be based on verifiable and *bona fide* records, room must also be made for the more subjective approach of long-standing servants of the R&R. Accordingly, my thanks are due to those who agreed to be interviewed for this book, among them Jackie Curran Olohan, Brendan Galvin (Junior), Camillus Mountaine, Gearóid Grant, Joe and Lucy Lane, Noel McDonough, Peter Nolan, Stephen Faul, Nora O'Rourke, Shay Gibson, Michael Forde and president Pat Campbell. Kindest regards also to those shadowy fact-checkers (other than the Four Musketeers) who have run the rule over each of the chapters and corrected or redirected this interloper.

Finally, the customary caveat: the opinions expressed herein are entirely my own. The mistakes are mine also.

Happy 100th birthday R&R and thank you for letting me in.

Myles Dungan
Kells, October 2013

R&R
ACKNOWLEDGMENTS

The R&R gratefully acknowledges the permission of the following people for use of their photographs:

- Jas. D. O'Callaghan
- Paul Timon
- Darren Johnson
- Gordon Poff.

We also wish to thank all of the members, and the families of past members, who contributed photographs and other memorabilia.

SPONSORS

This Book is Generously Sponsored by

Michael Forde
Nora O'Rourke
Clodagh Foley Martin
Wendy Thompson
Lewis Clohessy
Gordon Poff
Maeve Binchy
Gordon Snell
Caroline Murphy
P.J. Murphy
Gerry Maher
Joan O'Shaughnessy
Stephen Faul
Dodo O'Hagan
Dympna Bevan
Dympna Egar
Lucy Lane
Joe Lane
Maura Sweeney
Paschal Walsh
Donal Galvin
Jonathan Bewley
Glynis Casson
Jimmy Dixon
James Dent
Eamonn Beale
Basil Holland
Denis Leahy
Louise Studley Chalker
Howard Kilroy
Meriel Kilroy
Robert Daly
Daphne Millar
Paul Kelly
Clodagh Dooney
Fred Graham
Barbara Graham
Pat Campbell
Joan Campbell
Imelda Bradley
Eileen Gildea
Deirdre Connolly
Dorothy Kilroy
Ernest W. Smythe
Michael Foley
Cedric Bailey
Margaret Dickson
Arthur Salmon
Louise Stynes
Sylvia Tennant
Patricia Pasley
Des Byrne
Camillus Mountaine
Frans H. van der Lee
Michael Feighery
Gerard Prior
R. Graham Heather
Sally Young
Raymond Barror
David Humphries
Lynn Branagan
John Sweetman
Margaret Timoney
Padraig O'Rourke
Joan Brittan
Roger Brooks
Alan Cullinan
Noel Kenny
Celeste Kenny
Brighid Kehoe
Sean Slattery
Tom McGrath
Tony Sweeney
Ig Lyons
David Cox
Noel Magee
Mary Magee
Gerry McKnight
Barbara Bouch
Jim Treanor
Patricia Grant
Sandra Kelly Wade
Ted Ryan
Noel McDonough
Niamh McDonough
Jackie Curran Olohan
Barney Gorman
Ann Gorman
Michelle Foynes
Bernard Hurley
Helen Hurley
Seán Hogan
Marina Kealy
Gearóid Grant
Desmond O'Sullivan
Garrett Reynolds
Megan McGrath
Shay Gibson

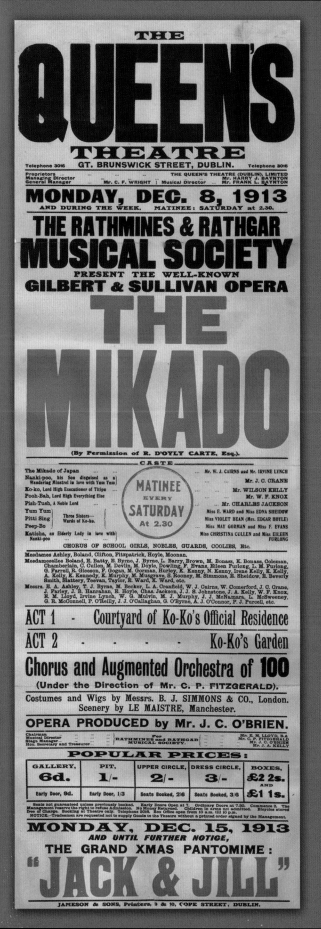

CHAPTER ON

'If you want to know who we are

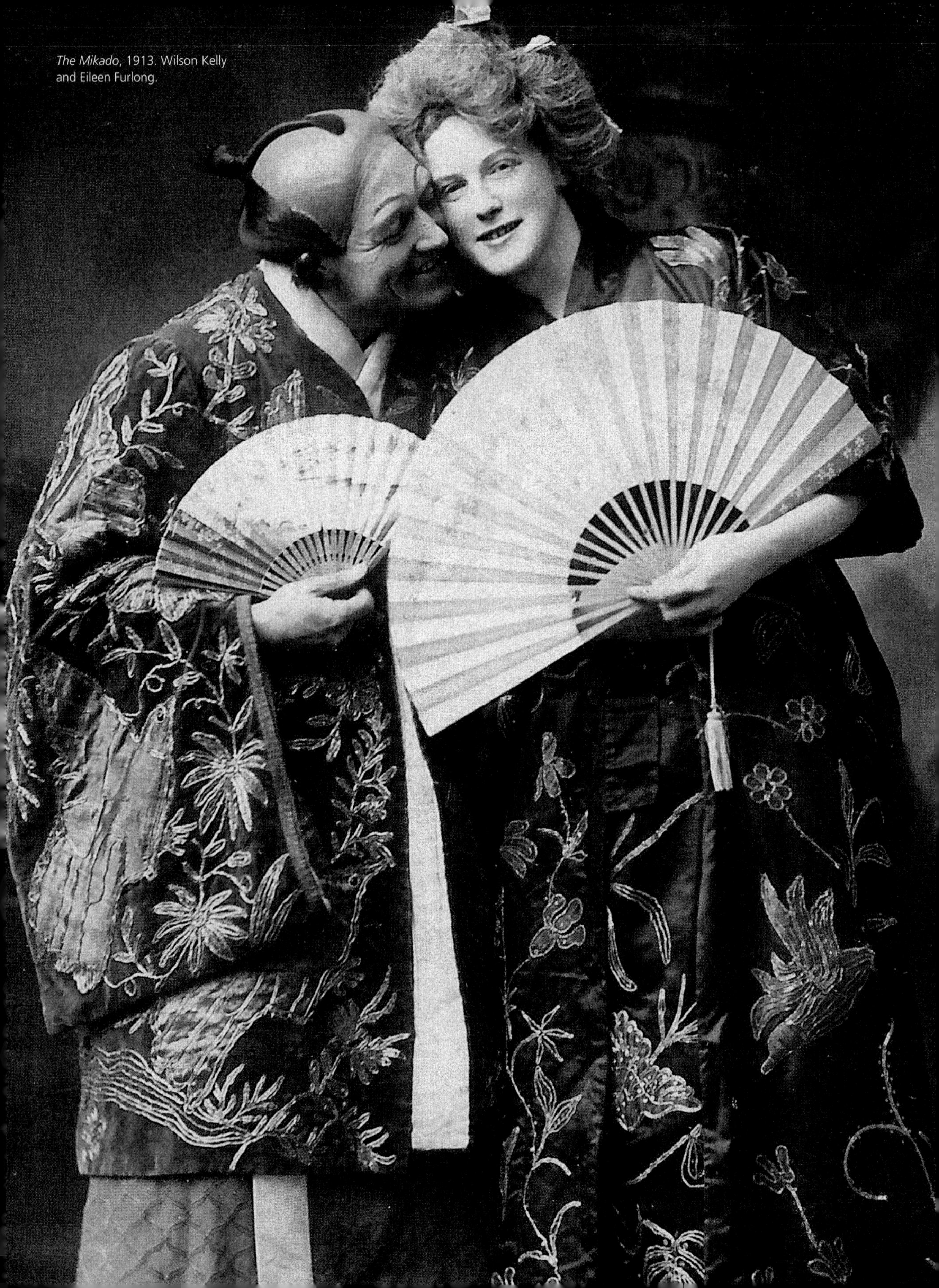

The Mikado, 1913. Wilson Kelly and Eileen Furlong.

CHAPTER ONE

'If you want to know who we are...'

If you want to know who we are,
We are gentlemen of Japan.
On many a vase and jar –
On many a screen and fan,
We figure in lively paint:
Our attitude's queer and quaint –
You're wrong if you think it ain't.

Not, perhaps, an introduction on a par with 'It was the best of times, it was the worst of times.' It certainly lacked the elegance of 'It is a truth universally acknowledged…'. But in life you take the openings you get – and the words of W.S. Gilbert have served this particular ensemble and their lineal descendants well this past century.

Of course the gentlemen in question were not from Japan. They were not even vaguely Oriental. They mostly hailed, not from the hazardous town of Titipu, but from the rather more anodyne township of Rathmines, a prosperous unionist-controlled enclave in an increasingly nationalistic Dublin. In the Sinn Féin landslide of 1918 Dublin Rathmines was the only constituency – outside of Trinity College – in what is now the Republic of Ireland to elect a unionist MP, Sir Maurice Dockrell.[1]

Rathmines included within its political bailiwick the nearby village of Rathgar. Hence, when it came to choosing a name for a musical society dedicated primarily to the performance of the comic-operatic works of Gilbert and Sullivan, both suburbs were given the same sort of equal billing as the composers that inspired them.

The borough of Rathmines was considerably more affluent than the city of Dublin, across the Grand Canal to the north-east. It boasted a higher proportion of wealthy Protestants and middle-class Catholics residing in an area governed by its own independent town hall. The township, where housing was well-constructed and relatively expensive, included few manual workers and no factories. The local council was, by and large, composed of prosperous businessmen, many involved in property construction and management. The 1901 census shows that Rathmines had grown considerably in population in the two prior decades. Just under 25,000 contented souls had lived there in 1881. By 1901 that figure had grown to 32,600, an increase of 30 per cent. The population of greater Dublin at the time was 390,000.

Rathmines jealously guarded its independence against encroachment by the city of Dublin. The city fathers in the municipal council regularly cast envious glances at the more affluent suburbs, whose prosperity would have yielded much-needed local government revenues. Townships like Rathmines strenuously resisted any such threats of annexation, the more so because they emanated from a city council dominated by nationalist representatives who appeared to be more concerned with issues of Home Rule and Empire (embracing the former and repudiating the latter) than sewage and street cleaning. Not that the suburbanite citizens of Rathmines and Rathgar denied themselves the pleasure of utilising, and thereby effectively degrading, the infrastructure of their larger neighbour. They continued to travel in and out of the city to work five and a half days a week. When Dublin city councillors pointed out the injustice of this they were imperiously ignored.

. . . .

GENESIS

It could be said that 1913 was an auspicious year in the history of Ireland in general and in Dublin in particular. It witnessed the most robust assertion of rights by the Irish trade union movement since its inception, the growth of potentially violent unionist activism in Ulster, an associated nationalist response in southern Ireland and the continued passage of the contentious 1912 Home Rule legislation

Christopher P. FitzGerald.

through the Houses of Parliament. Of enduring social significance was the successful conclusion by the Gaelic Athletic Association[2] of an eight-year fundraising drive designed to erect a fitting memorial to its first patron, Archbishop Thomas William Croke, who had died in 1902. The monument to the celebrated nationalist Roman Catholic archbishop of Cashel was a nine-and-a-half-acre site off Jones Road in Dublin purchased for £3,500. This was developed as a football/hurling pitch and renamed Croke Park.[3]

Less noteworthy, at least in the context of the momentous events that would help shape the Ireland of the early twentieth century, was the appointment in February 1913 of one Christopher P. FitzGerald as organist and choirmaster of the Roman Catholic Church of Three Patrons on Rathgar Road.[4] FitzGerald, a music teacher, accomplished pianist and violinist, and native of Limerick, had been organist in the Cathedral in Derry for twelve years before moving to Dublin.[5] It was at his suggestion that a meeting was held on 20 April 1913 at 48 Summerville Park, off Upper Rathmines Road, 'to consider the feasibility of forming a musical society in the township of Rathmines and Rathgar'.[6] The meeting was attended largely by 'residents of the district' and it was agreed that a society would be formed 'having for its object the study and production of Operatic, Choral, and other high-class musical works'. No reference was made to any bias towards the *oeuvre* of the idiosyncratic librettist W.S. Gilbert and his erstwhile musical collaborator Arthur Sullivan, but the first work chosen for production was their enduring composition *The Mikado*. Amateur companies and societies had been performing the works of Gilbert and Sullivan, under licence from Richard D'Oyly Carte and his estate, since 1887. It would be six years and fourteen shows before the society would stage any production unconnected with those doyens of light opera. There was but one exception:

a French aberration called *Les Cloches de Corneville* by Robert Planquette, written in 1877, which had, in translation, outlasted *H.M.S. Pinafore* on its 1878 London run. The new society opted to perform this French operetta in May 1915 before returning to its Gilbertian last in December of that year.[7]

While FitzGerald was the motive musical force behind the tyro society, Edwin Lloyd, a local solicitor from a musical family,[8] became its first chairman, and Charles Jackson and W. Gerald Mulvin its joint honorary secretaries. Mulvin was a committed aesthete. A civil servant who had worked in England for some years, he was also a leading member of the Dublin branch of the British Empire Shakespeare Society, which had been founded in 1907. He conducted a long rearguard action to prevent that society from dropping its imperial associations and becoming, merely, the Dublin Shakespeare Society. The more conservative members of the society finally succumbed to the reality

Edwin Lloyd.

of the inconvenient existence of the Irish Free State in 1933 and changed the group's name.[9] Mulvin assumed the chair of the fledgling Rathmines and Rathgar Musical Society in succession to Edwin Lloyd in 1915.[10]

The R&R, as it has been known affectionately for many years, was thus founded just at the cusp of profound and tumultuous political upheaval in Ireland and across Europe. It could not, and would not, remain untouched by the cataclysmic Great War, nor by the disruptive contending forces of the six-year struggle for Irish independence. The timing of its birth was hardly fortuitous and it might well have succumbed rapidly to irrelevance in the period of profound darkness that followed that inaugural meeting on 20 April 1913. That it managed to survive and thrive is a tribute to its founders and their successors. It flourished early and has had a long and productive existence since that Sunday meeting in Upper Rathmines.

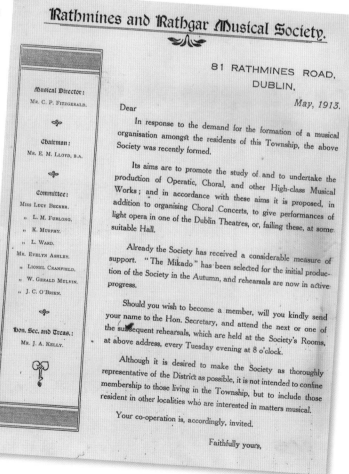

Rathmines and Rathgar Musical Society.

81 RATHMINES ROAD,
DUBLIN,

May, 1913.

Musical Director:
MR. C. P. FITZGERALD.

Chairman:
MR. E. M. LLOYD, B.A.

Committee:
MISS LUCY BECKER.
„ L. M. FURLONG.
„ K. MURPHY.
„ L. WARD.
MR. EVELYN ASHLEY.
„ LIONEL CRANFIELD.
„ W. GERALD MULVIN.
„ J. C. O'BRIEN.

Hon. Sec. and Treas.:
MR. J. A. KELLY.

Dear

In response to the demand for the formation of a musical organisation amongst the residents of this Township, the above Society was recently formed.

Its aims are to promote the study of and to undertake the production of Operatic, Choral, and other High-class Musical Works; and in accordance with these aims it is proposed, in addition to organising Choral Concerts, to give performances of light opera in one of the Dublin Theatres, or, failing these, at some suitable Hall.

Already the Society has received a considerable measure of support. "The Mikado" has been selected for the initial production of the Society in the Autumn, and rehearsals are now in active progress.

Should you wish to become a member, will you kindly send your name to the Hon. Secretary, and attend the next or one of the subsequent rehearsals, which are held at the Society's Rooms, at above address, every Tuesday evening at 8 o'clock.

Although it is desired to make the Society as thoroughly representative of the District as possible, it is not intended to confine membership to those living in the Township, but to include those resident in other localities who are interested in matters musical.

Your co-operation is, accordingly, invited.

Faithfully yours,

R&R recruiting letter.

The Mikado flyers and playbill.

The musical and dramatic performing landscape into which the R&R was launched was not one in which amateur companies had any absolute guarantee of success. While groups like the National Literary Society and the CYMS Choral Society staged either *conversaziones* or recitals, there was also a thriving professional and semi-professional music, drama and variety 'scene' in Dublin, as there was in all major provincial centres of what then constituted the United Kingdom of Great Britain and Ireland. The work of local companies was supplemented and augmented by frequent annual or biannual visits from illustrious British performers. Enthusiastic amateurs often found themselves squeezed out. A few weeks before the R&R was established the *Freeman's Journal* had drawn attention to what it described as 'a musical crisis' when the flourishing Dublin Oratorio Society found itself unable to secure a suitable venue for its Holy Week concert. The society was, accordingly 'forced to abandon their second concert of their tenth season, and meanwhile the work of the Society comes to a standstill'.[11] On the very day on which the curtain rose on *The Mikado* at the Queen's Theatre, a letter to the editor of the *Journal* bemoaned the fact that 'there is no Orchestral Society for amateur players in the city' because of 'the difficulty of obtaining a suitable hall for rehearsals and concerts'. The correspondent, using the *nom de plume* Tarisio, also decried as 'somewhat astonishing the facility with which picture houses arise all through the city'. He concluded with the rather over-optimistic thesis that 'the present unrest in our city could not exist side by side with cheap facilities of hearing good music'.[12]

The 'founding fathers' of the Rathmines & Rathgar Musical Society were somewhat unusual in their relative youth (Mulvin was 33; another motive force, A.E. Glynn, was in his early twenties; one of the first secretaries, Lionel Cranfield, was 31) but not in their mentality or their capabilities. They came from a social class where the piano was often a focal point within the house and where musical talent was something to be nurtured. They were also from managerialist backgrounds and brought their business and administrative skills to the table. They would be succeeded by generations with similar capacities – a vital ingredient in the survival and success of the society they inaugurated. They had a certain sense of priority. It was only when 'the details as to membership, management, subscription, etc. having been arranged, and having secured the premises'[13] [81 Rathmines Road] that arrangements began for the first production.

Among the other early members and performers was an English couple, Edgar and Violet Hoyle (née Bean). He was an electrical engineer from Kent; she had been a prominent member of the Middlesbrough Operatic Society. Violet Hoyle may well have been instrumental in sowing the seed that would become the R&R. She and her husband were friendly with Lionel Cranfield.

R&R in 1913. First photograph, including Edwin Lloyd (chairman) and C.P. FitzGerald (musical director) with members of the committee and cast of *The Mikado*.

At a Rathmines soirée one evening in 1913 a number of guests were gathered around a piano for a sing-song. Violet Hoyle remarked on 'how beautifully their voices blended'.[14] She enquired if they had ever considered staging light opera. That conversation may have begun the process that led to the inaugural meeting in April 1913.

The Mikado was rehearsed in 81 Rathmines Road[15] and 48 Summerville Park and 'after some vicissitudes' was performed at the Queen's Theatre on Pearse Street during the second week in December 1913. Some of the proceeds of its debut production went to charities like the Dublin Skin and Cancer Hospital in Hume Street.[16] Thus began a long tradition of benefit nights and an enduring affiliation between the R&R and a variety of benevolent organisations. By its tenth anniversary the R&R had channelled more than £1,500 towards charitable causes, which equates to €50,000 today. The royalty fee payable to the D'Oyly Carte Opera Company was £10 for each performance.[17]

The society's first choice of venue had been the more opulent surroundings of the Gaiety Theatre in South King Street but it had been solidly booked for the autumn/winter season. The old Queen's (formerly the Queen's Royal Theatre) had been refurbished in 1909 and, at the time of the R&R's only engagement there, was a venue associated with comedy and variety acts such as 'Alfredo, the Vagabond Violinist' or 'Le Dair, the Conjuring Comedian assisted by a Protean Lady'.[18] The Gaiety was more salubrious and decidedly more upmarket, rising regularly to performances of Shakespeare by the likes of the F.R. Benson company and to French drama performed in French.

The society magazine *Irish Life* heralded the debut of the R&R with the prediction that it was an 'enterprise that should be capped with success' and pointing out that 'in England amateur presentations of the Gilbert and Sullivan operas have been wonderfully successful, and there is no reason why they should not be equally so in Dublin'.[19] And so it proved, though not without the negotiation of a number of hoops first. Between the decision to stage *The Mikado* and the actual production itself one of the great antagonisms of Irish history intervened. This was the struggle between Jim Larkin of the Irish Transport and General Workers Union, and the businessman William Martin Murphy. Cork-born Murphy would later (in 1916) become President of the R&R.[20] Murphy lived on the Rathgar–Milltown border, was a former nationalist (anti-Parnellite) MP, *Irish Independent* proprietor, transport entrepreneur and owner of Dartry House, which also happened to be adjacent to the terminus of one of his own tramlines from Dublin city centre. Much of his fortune had been made in the development of railways in the colony of South Africa. Having weathered the cantankerous Boers he was not about to be out-manoeuvred by a syndicalist who boasted that he was on a 'divine mission of discontent'.

On 26 August 1913, in a move timed to inconvenience devotees of the Dublin Horse Show and cause maximum embarrassment to Murphy, members of the ITGWU working for his Dublin United Tramways Company, abandoned their trams in protest against moves by the city's employers to dismiss more than 300 workers who had joined Larkin's union. What followed was the great 1913 Dublin Lockout, which did not formally end until January 1914. Larkin's highly personalised struggle with Murphy polarised opinion in Dublin. The bulk of the membership of the R&R, natives of middle-class suburbia, might reasonably be expected to have had little sympathy with the trade unionists. The staging of *The Mikado* was seriously affected by what the Minute Book for 1914 euphemistically describes as 'a very serious deadlock in labour circles in Dublin [which] involved a great deal of anxiety and extra work'.[21]

Jack O'Brien.

With labour ferment as a backdrop, the society was also forced to come to terms with the social and economic realities of staging high-quality light opera in an unsettled environment. Apart from the psychological toll of staging even an amateur presentation of Gilbert and Sullivan, there was clearly some naivety among the early membership of the R&R about the cost of such a venture. This was especially onerous in the case of the sumptuous and relentlessly oriental *Mikado*. The *Irish Life* had congratulated the society on its decision to opt for 'the production of so difficult and expensive an opera'. That was akin to a latter-day civil service manager congratulating his minister on making a 'courageous decision'. The subtext in both cases is: 'You're on your own.' In addition to funding the expensive Japanese-style sets and the elaborate costumes (provided by Simmons and Company of London), the society had to augment the Queen's Theatre orchestra and spend an unexpected sum of money on advertising.[22]

The curtain went up on *The Mikado* on 8 December 1913. FitzGerald was musical director for the eccentric piece of oriental whimsy and J.C. (Jack) O'Brien produced.[23] Their partnership was compared at the time to that of Gilbert and Sullivan themselves. It was, however, of shorter duration (two years)[24]

THE MIKADO (1913)

Eileen Furlong
as Katisha.

Joseph Crane
as Nanki-Poo.

Wilson Kelly
as Ko-Ko.

Charles Jackson
as Pish-Tush.

Walter Knox
as Pooh-Bah.

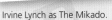

Irvine Lynch as The Mikado.

Wilson Kelly as
Sword-Bearer.

Edgar Hoyle as Go-To.

Violet Bean (Mrs Edgar Hoyle), Lizzie Ward and
May O'Gorman as the Three Little Maids.

The Mikado, 1913. Full company on stage at the Queen's Theatre, including: C.P. FitzGerald (musical director), Jack O'Brien (producer and stage manager) and Edwin Lloyd (chairman).

and must have been considerably less fractious. The two men did lay down solid foundations upon which the R&R was successfully built. Although the rehearsal schedule was, necessarily, that of the amateur, the dedication required of principals and chorus was of the professional standards to which FitzGerald and O'Brien themselves aspired.[25] FitzGerald made his living from music and O'Brien was an accomplished actor and singer as well as a committed theatre-goer in both Dublin and London. He had been attending Gilbert and Sullivan operettas at the Savoy Theatre since at least 1901.[26]

O'Brien had been recruited by Edwin Lloyd. According to the *Evening Telegraph*, his involvement in the R&R's first project was 'sufficient guarantee that the work will be properly staged'.[27] A few weeks before beginning rehearsals with the R&R, he had played the part of the fiery Welsh trade union activist David Roberts in a staging of John Galsworthy's *Strife* in a newly re-opened Gaiety Theatre. Written in 1909, the play was set in a strike-bound tin-mining village on the Welsh–English border. It was an ironic choice of material given what was about to commence barely a fortnight later in the city in which it was being staged. In his notice, the critic of the *Irish Independent* (Murphy's newspaper) looked to the day when 'a serious drama will give us the true picture of modern industrial strife – the strike-monger rising from obscurity to the possession of a fat salary with increments'.[28] While praising the performance of O'Brien as Roberts, the polemical tone of the review was worthy of the newspaper proprietor himself.

The part of the 'wandering minstrel' Nanki-Poo in this inaugural R&R production was taken by Joseph Crane; Irvine Lynch was the Mikado and Ko-Ko, the Lord High Executioner, was played by Wilson Kelly.[29] All three would reprise the roles twelve months later. Lynch was to remain with the company for another decade, logging almost twenty appearances before his final bow as Wilfred Shadbolt in *The Yeomen of the Guard* in 1923.

The ageing and statuesque Katisha was played by Eileen Furlong. Furlong, an accomplished *chanteuse*, had been recruited by Jack O'Brien after they had worked together on concerts and recitals in the Abbey and the Rathmines Town Hall. Though it was the first of many occasions on which she would take the role, she was chronically miscast on her debut – at the tender age of 19! Her frame had to be artificially fleshed out to match expectations.

In their first and last appearances with the R&R, Violet Bean and Edgar Hoyle took the parts of Pitti Sing and Go-To. By the autumn of 1914, Edgar (a member of the Territorial Army) had been called up for service on the western front and Violet, who had just given birth to their only child, Joy, insisted on being taken back to England. Among the audience on the opening night were the Lord Lieutenant, the Liberal peer Lord Aberdeen and his wife. Lady Aberdeen was presented with a bouquet after the performance. The lavish flower arrangement cost the society a guinea, rather more than the average weekly wage of an unskilled labourer at the time.

One of the chorus members in that first production, Evelyn Ashley had an interesting theatrical pedigree. Ashley was one of the directors of the Dublin Repertory Company, along with Casimir Markievicz, the *soi-disant* ennobled husband of Countess Constance Markievicz. The new company, formed from the ashes of the Independent Theatre Company – a vehicle for the writing of Casimir and the acting of Constance – had staged *Strife* at the Gaiety. Ashley had directed the piece. The Dublin Repertory Company would go on to produce Shaw's *John Bull's Other Island* and *Mrs. Warren's*

Advertising hoarding, Church Street, 1914.

Profession.[30] R&R mythology has it that the Count himself was briefly employed by the society in the 1914 production of *The Yeomen of the Guard* in the pivotal task of ringing the Tower Bell, sounded to herald the execution of Colonel Fairfax. The neophyte campanologist used a bell that was suspended in the flies of the Gaiety and was said to have originated in the old parliament building (now the Bank of Ireland) in College Green.

The choice of a Gilbert and Sullivan operetta for its debut performance was never going to be entirely unproblematic for the R&R. Only the previous March, on Easter Monday, the celebrated D'Oyly Carte Opera Company (the London source of all things Gilbert and Sullivan) had offered Dubliners a professional production of *The Mikado*. This was as part of the company's annual stint in the Gaiety Theatre, featuring its Repertory Company (previously Company 'C') rather than the established Savoy Theatre troupe. The following April, with stars like Fred Billington and Leicester Tunks in the cast, they would return with a similar repertoire. Dublin theatre-going audiences were well aware that if they missed one D'Oyly Carte rendering of Gilbert and Sullivan there would be another one along soon.

It was for this reason that *The Irish Times* review of the first night opened with the ominous line, 'The Rathmines and Rathgar Musical Society are to be congratulated on their belief in themselves.' The review went on to contend that 'when all due allowances are made for a first attempt, even the captious critic must admit that the performance in many respects compared very favourably with its predecessors'.[31] The *Freeman's Journal* described the production as 'in every manner meritorious' and predicted a 'hugely successful week'.[32] The performances in the 'heavy' roles by Wilson Kelly as Ko-Ko and Eileen Furlong as Katisha (his 'daughter-in-law elect') were singled out by both the *Irish Times* and *Journal* reviewers. The 'sweet notes and expressive vocalism' of Joseph Crane was praised by *The Irish Times* but this was qualified by a sting of wonderment as to why he had been unwilling to share his perfect pitch with the entire theatre. He was described as being 'self-conscious', with a delivery that 'favoured the more fortunate portion of the audience who were seated nearer to the stage'. Coverage in the *Irish Independent* was terse but positive.[33]

The society's assessment of its debut was self-congratulatory. In oracular style the minutes of the 1914 annual general meeting record that 'although it is perhaps hardly necessary to dilate at any length on the success attained in its initial venture it is pardonable to record as a matter of congratulation to the Society that a very high level of excellence was reached and that the public by its attendance and applause endorsed its appreciation of the Society's work'.[34] The R&R came out of the Dublin Lockout and its performing debut with a debit of £9 for its first financial year, which the committee judged to be 'very creditable'.

Despite having emerged relatively unscathed and comparatively solvent from its first musical venture, the Rathmines and Rathgar Musical Society might well have been consigned to oblivion within months – not through any artistic or financial failure but arising out of the desire of certain members to abandon the troupe's suburban name. At the annual general meeting in September 1914 a proposal came from the company's first Nanki-Poo, Joseph Crane, 'that the Society be known as "The Dublin Operatic and Dramatic Society"'. The minutes give no indication as to Crane's motivation. This may have involved a principled assault on parochialism or it may have been prompted merely by overweening hubris. The issue was discussed at length but, after a vote, Crane's motion was defeated and the R&R was spared the unfortunate acronym DODS.

In 1914 the society migrated, as had been the original intention, to the Gaiety Theatre for a revival of *The Mikado* and its first production of an enduring favourite, *The Yeomen of the Guard*. It was the beginning of an abiding association with the Gaiety that was to continue, almost uninterrupted, for seventy years.[35] For decades the tradition was a week of shows by the R&R followed by the annual Gaiety pantomime. The theatre was then forty-three years old, having opened on 27 November 1871. It accommodated almost 2,000 people: 700 in the pit and stall, 200 in the balcony, 210 in the upper circle and a further 700 in the gallery.[36]

Playing the part of Colonel Fairfax in *Yeomen*, the darkest of the Savoy operettas, was one of the society's first *bona fide* operatic stars, Arthur Lucas. Lucas, aged 25, was a consummate performer who monopolised tenor lead parts such as Nanki-Poo in *The Mikado* (1916) and Marco in *The Gondoliers* (1916) from his arrival in 1914 until his departure for the London stage in 1918. There, with the D'Oyly Carte company, he occupied similar roles until 1920 when he left for a career in Australia, taking with him as his wife the company's principal soubrette of the time, Catherine Ferguson.[37]

Before a single note had been heard in the society's second season, the *Freeman's Journal* was prepared to declare that 'the Society can rightly claim to be regarded as amateur in name only, their performances of *The Mikado* at the Queen's Theatre last year being quite on a par with the best professional representations of an opera by no means easy to stage'.[38] That professionalism was no doubt encouraged by the officially designated one-man 'vigilance committee' of the society. In addition to the regular officers of the R&R (chairman, treasurer, etc.) there existed a figure designated as the registrar. His lot, whether or not it was a happy one, appears to have been to monitor attendance at rehearsals and report back to the committee. For example, when one Una O'Loughlin failed to turn up for rehearsals for *The Yeomen of the Guard* the registrar reported her absence to the committee and she was committed to the musical equivalent of the Tower of London. It was 'ordered that her name be struck off the roll'.[39]

Yeomen, 1914: J.C. O'Brien as Jack Point, with Lena Munro, Joan Burke and Gertrude Farrell.

Members were also kept guessing as to exactly who would occupy the principal roles. More than one candidate would rehearse a leading part almost up to the opening night, at which point a choice was made. One contender would 'be selected as principal and the other as understudy'.[40] Much like county football and hurling, up to the advent of the omnipotent manager in the 1980s, a five-person Cast(e) committee, which included the musical director and producer, would make the final decisions.[41]

Of course, in the interval between the debuts at the Queen's and the Gaiety the small matter of a pan-European conflict had intervened. It was called neither the 'Great War' nor 'World War I' at the time, because by early December 1914 it was neither. Although it was no longer expected to have run its course by Christmas it was still, by and large, being fought by professional soldiers. The cast-lists of the two productions for December 1914, run in repertory from 7–12 December, reflect this to some extent. The same principals took part in both 1914 shows as had dominated the cast-list of *The Mikado* the previous year. There appears to have been no huge rush on the part of the society's male leads, at least, to join the armed forces. The same might not have been true of the more anonymous male chorus. An obvious exception was Edgar Hoyle, recently departed for service in Belgium with his two brothers. Wilf Hoyle, one of his siblings, was killed in March 1915. Three weeks later, Edgar succumbed. He left Violet a widow with a 9-month-old child, Joy. Almost half a century later, Joy Hoyle, daughter of Edgar, visited Ireland and was introduced to Lal Cranfield, son of Lionel. In her own words, he was 'able to tell me all kinds of things about my father which I hadn't experienced or known'.[42]

Souvenir of *Yeomen*, 1914: Jack Point's Mascot painted by Joe Brooke-Kelly, makeup artist to the R&R for many years.

Rathmines and Rathgar
Musical Society

PLANQUETTE'S
Charming Opera Comique,

Les Cloches
de Corneville

(By permission of Joseph Williams, Ltd.)

WILL BE PRODUCED IN THE

GAIETY THEATRE

DURING THE

Week commencing 17th May

Under the direction of
Mr. C. P. FitzGerald, Musical Director, and
Mr. Jas. C. O'Brien, Stage Manager.

Full Chorus and Augmented Orchestra
of over 100 Performers

ORDINARY THEATRE PRICES

The first annual general meeting of the society, held on 24 September 1914, while expressing retrospective concern about the impact of the Lockout, is oddly bereft of even a single reference to the European war that had begun on 28 July. Clearly it was proving far less inconvenient to the society than had the activities of the ITGWU. However, the society was not entirely detached from events in Europe. Proceeds from the benefit nights of the December 1914 Gaiety productions of *The Mikado* and *The Yeomen of the Guard* were designated for the national relief fund and the Belgian relief fund.[43]

In fact the R&R was able to profit from the political unrest that had beset the country since the establishment of the Ulster Volunteer Force in 1912. The following year, under the aegis of Professor Eoin MacNeill and Sir Roger Casement, an equivalent nationalist body, the Irish Volunteers, had been formed. That organisation had split in 1914 after the declaration of war. Irish party leader John Redmond had advised the membership of the Volunteers to enlist in the

Les Cloches de Corneville billboard.

Les Cloches de Corneville, 1915.

British armed forces and to go 'wherever the fighting line extends'.[44] His policy caused a rift in the Irish Volunteers with 140,000 of the 150,000-strong force siding with Redmond and forming a new paramilitary body, the National Volunteers. In October 1914 the R&R received a letter from the National Volunteers seeking the use of the society's Rathmines rooms for meetings. The committee agreed to the request and charged the National Volunteers three shillings a night for the privilege.[45]

By the following autumn, however, the society was having the same sort of recruitment difficulties that His Majesty's armed forces would encounter in Ireland from 1916 onwards. The committee had proposed the staging of *Iolanthe* and *The Yeomen of the Guard* at the Gaiety in

Kathleen Gahan as Phyllis, *Iolanthe*, 1915.

Wilson Kelly as Lord Chancellor, *Iolanthe*, 1915.

December 1915, and it was left up to FitzGerald and O'Brien to 'dispose'. However, it proved difficult to assemble a cast for both productions and the musical director and producer suggested that one of the operas simply be abandoned. Financial commitments already entered into with the Gaiety meant that this rather obvious solution was not acceptable to the society's committee. A resolution was passed to the effect that 'Mr FitzGerald and Mr O'Brien were to be given any help they required so as to enable them to produce the two operas in the time'.[46] In other words, the production of two operettas was mandatory and, once again, the artistic directors were on their own.

Despite the European conflict and U-boat activity in the Irish Sea, the R&R continued to face stiff annual competition from the D'Oyly Carte Opera Company. This may have dictated the decision in April 1915 to deviate from Savoyard orthodoxy. For its spring production that year, the society abandoned G&S and chose instead to stage Robert Planquette's 'charming' *Les Cloches de Corneville*. *The Irish Times*, for one, was unimpressed, maintaining that the production did not live up to the high standards established over the previous two years. It would be four years before the society next staged a production not associated with either Gilbert or Sullivan,[47] when it premiered two works by Edward German and Basil Hood, *A Princess of Kensington* and *Merrie England*.

In December 1915, at a time when three battalions of the Royal Dublin Fusiliers (1st, 6th and 7th) were being evacuated from Turkey along with the rest of the ill-fated Gallipoli expeditionary force, the R&R reprised the quasi-militaristic *Yeomen of the Guard* and launched its first production of the 'topsy-turvy' fantasy *Iolanthe*, with Lucas as the dim-witted Earl Tolloller, contralto Eileen Furlong as the Queen of the Fairies and Wilson Kelly in the comic baritone role of the Lord Chancellor. As late as October doubts had been expressed as to whether the two shows could be produced due to the reportedly lackadaisical approach of the membership in rehearsal. FitzGerald and O'Brien wrote

May Doyle.

to the committee indicating their preference for a single production but refusing to accept any financial liability for the show that would have to be cancelled.[48] In the end, both productions went ahead after the Rathmines Town Hall was booked for four rehearsals a week as opposed to the normal twice-weekly booking.[49]

The fears of FitzGerald and O'Brien, after a lot of hard work, proved groundless. *The Irish Times* reviewer commented of the *Yeomen* production that 'it could favourably compare with many professional performances that have been given in Dublin… the opera is one which is eminently suitable for amateurs but it is doubtful whether it has ever been given a better presentation than last evening'.[50] Jack O'Brien, who also produced the show 'made an admirable Jack Point'. Making her debut was a young May Doyle, as Elsie Maynard. The reviewer observed that she was 'an artist who appears to have a brilliant future before her'. These were the days of the running encore and Doyle had responded to audience demands for an instant reprise of her solo ''Tis done! I am a bride'. Doyle would perform in more than twenty productions, monopolising the role of Elsie Maynard in three of those, before bowing out after her third appearance as Patience in the eponymous operetta in 1929.

THE VOLUNTEERS V *THE GONDOLIERS*

In 1916 the society, having moved into new premises in 36 South Frederick Street, had booked the Gaiety Theatre for an entirely new production in June.[51] The setting would be the aqueous Venetian playground of Marco and Giuseppe Palmieri (the gondoliers of the title) and the visiting dignitary, the Duke of Plaza Toro. *The Gondoliers* had been the last great success of a warring Gilbert and Sullivan. It had premiered in December 1889 but during the run Gilbert had fallen out with Richard D'Oyly Carte over money. Sullivan, already profoundly sick of comic opera and looking forward to Carte's promotion of his grand opera *Ivanhoe*, sided with the impresario. The partnership had come to a temporary end and its subsequent revival for two further collaborations – *Utopia Limited* and *The Grand Duke* – had been either largely (the former) or entirely (the latter) unsuccessful.

With numerous celebrated stirring choruses and melodies of the quality of 'Take a Pair of Sparkling Eyes' the R&R was almost guaranteed packed houses and a probable financial

The Gondoliers flyer, 1916.

bonanza. Unfortunately, at almost the last moment, insurrection intervened in the shape of the Easter Rising of 1916. While rehearsals were set to intensify as the 5 June opening date approached, Patrick Pearse, Tom Clarke and Joseph Plunkett took the Irish Volunteers onto the streets of Dublin and into some of its more strategic buildings, accompanied by James Connolly and the Irish Citizen Army. On 24 April, around the corner from the Gaiety Theatre, far from the canals and piazzas of a fictional Venice, Countess Markievicz and Michael Mallin of the Citizen Army were issuing instructions for the digging of trenches in St Stephen's Green and the fortification of the Royal College of Surgeons. Even closer to the stamping ground of the R&R, a Volunteer unit led by Thomas MacDonagh and Major John MacBride, had moved into the Jacobs Biscuit factory in Bishop Street. With the city under martial law, and O'Connell Street being shelled by the gunboat *Helga*, times were not conducive to the frivolous celebration of the good fortune of the brothers Palmieri. After one rehearsal it was noted that members had been 'trapped' in the Shelbourne Hotel by the Easter week hostilities. There are, however, worse places to be temporarily incarcerated, and the

Poster for *Gondoliers* and *Iolanthe*, 1916.

Shelbourne was, thankfully, well out of range of the revolver prominently sported and rebelliously employed by the excitable Countess.[52] At least the R&R was only in rehearsal. The D'Oyly Carte had arrived in force for their traditional Easter week shows at the Gaiety. As fortune would have it the players and stage crew had been booked into the Gresham Hotel in Sackville Street for the week. Discretion proving to be much the better part of valour the company members never left the building.[53]

However, the indefatigable Rathmines and Rathgar Musical Society was, relatively, undeterred by such potentially crippling setbacks. In the wake of the executions of the leaders of the Rising, and with the British military in control of a city under curfew throughout the month of May, it was virtually impossible to rehearse and organise the logistics for a brand new production. In addition, according to *The Irish Times*, some members of the cast had 'suffered bereavements' through what it euphemistically described as 'the disturbances in the city'. It was deemed unwise to proceed with the production of *The Gondoliers*. Instead the 'old reliable' *Mikado* was disinterred. Some of the proceeds from the Gaiety run went to a fund that had been raised 'for the benefit of persons thrown out of employment by the recent fires',[54] the Mansion House Fund for the Relief of Distress in Dublin.[55]

Not long thereafter, in the latter half of 1917, the society parted company with its first motive force Christopher P. FitzGerald. Jack O'Brien had already begun to disengage from a committee disposed to take the contributions of both men for granted. O'Brien had sought payment for his work in 1916 and had been informed that none was possible. However, when he withdrew from the production of one of the two December 1916 shows, *The Gondoliers*, the services of a professional 'coach' E.A. White, were engaged at a cost of £20. *Iolanthe*, performed at the Gaiety from 4–9 December was O'Brien's personal curtain call. He never produced, 'stage managed' or 'coached' another show for the R&R. In March 1917 London-based 'coach' Arthur Cullin was hired to direct *Haddon Hall*, by Sullivan and Sidney Grundy. He was paid £40 for five weeks' work.[56] At the AGM that year Mulvin proposed that a letter

Haddon Hall, 1917: Reginald Montgomery, A.E. Glynn, Lal Cranfield, Willie Comerford and Arthur Healy.

be sent to O'Brien thanking him for his past services. To the discredit of the society 'the meeting decided that as the matter was rather belated it should be allowed to drop'.[57]

FitzGerald was next to jump ship. He had indicated to a number of cast members that *Haddon Hall* would be his own swansong. He appears to have relented and agreed to work on *Ruddigore*, the proposed December 1917 production. However, FitzGerald was also beginning to place a monetary value on his services and had ambitions of his own unrelated to the R&R. Unbeknownst to the R&R, he entered into an arrangement with the Empire Theatre to produce shows there. In an entirely pragmatic move, viewed by the committee of the R&R as a development of '*et tu, Brute?*' proportions, he also offered parts in his new venture to some of the more talented R&R principals.

They were promised payment for their services. When they got wind of FitzGerald's ambitions, the R&R committee pounced. On 28 August he was summoned to a meeting where he was informed that 'it would be impossible to rehearse two operas concurrently'.[58] When he sought to reassure the society grandees, the supplementary issue 'as to how far inroads had been made on the society's membership in connection with the Empire enterprise' was then raised. He insisted that only half a dozen members had been approached. He then withdrew from the Star Chamber assembly. In his absence it was claimed that 'upwards of a dozen of the society's members' were taking part in Empire operas 'while nearly all the useful members had been circularised or approached on the subject'. As a consequence, the fulfilment of the R&R contract with the Gaiety had been jeopardised.[59]

Fifty-seven members were contacted in order to enquire whether they were available for the R&R winter production or whether they had committed to FitzGerald. Replies were sought on pre-paid postcards. Thirty-four committed to the R&R, five admitted to having defected and eighteen failed to respond. At first FitzGerald not only attempted to tough the matter out, but he muddied the waters still further by insisting, reasonably enough, on a fee comparable to that of the professional 'coaches' now being engaged. He was offered a derisory £15.[60] At a meeting on 7 September a letter from FitzGerald was read out announcing that he had accepted an offer to become musical director of the Pioneer Orchestral Society. The committee accepted his resignation and set about finding a successor.

A myth exists within the society that FitzGerald's departure was prompted by his desire to remunerate some of the R&R's principal players in society productions[61] probably with a view to improving standards. That received wisdom also holds that the committee at the time demurred because the R&R has never paid its performers. This is entirely untrue. In the society's founding rule-book, Rule 13(a) stated quite clearly: 'The Committee reserve the right to engage special Artistes for their performances when they consider it desirable.'[62] At the first committee meeting after the departure of FitzGerald the minutes inform us that: 'The Chairman raised the question of re-imbursement for members playing parts and it was generally agreed that if necessity arose, payments would have to be made in certain cases.'[63] By the following year a number of 'professional' performers were being paid three guineas for what was described as 'loss of engagements' brought about because of their commitment to the R&R.[64] In 1919 the Abbey actor Eric Gorman took the leading part of Sir James Fellicoe in *A Princess of Kensington* by Edward German and Basil Hood. Gorman was taken on after Lionel Cranfield had been given 'discretionary powers' to secure professional actors to fill a number of parts.[65] Gorman was 37 years old at the time and would have a long career in the Abbey. He was still performing with the company in 1964, seven years before his death. He also played a cameo role in John Ford's *The Quiet Man* in 1952, as Costello, the driver of the train that takes John Wayne to Inisfree.[66]

T.H. Weaving and Edwin Lloyd.

FitzGerald re-surfaced at the helm of the FitzGerald Opera Company. The new group, to the obvious chagrin of the R&R committee, was clearly a competitor. In 1918, for example, the Empire Theatre played host for two weeks to *The Chocolate Soldier* (the 1908 adaptation by Oscar Strauss of George Bernard Shaw's *Arms and the Man*) and *My Lady Molly* (a comic opera by Sidney Jones[67] and George H. Jessop). FitzGerald was both musical director and producer. Performances were twice nightly, at 6.45 and 8.45. *The Irish Times* advertisement for *My Lady Molly* promised 'a full operatic chorus and company of 100 performers'.[68] FitzGerald also continued to antagonise his erstwhile musical family by poaching some featured performers away from the society. There was, in fairness, always an inevitable overlap with other musical and/or dramatic societies in Dublin at the time. For example, in a 1932 revival of FitzGerald's production of *The Chocolate Soldier*, Irvine Lynch and Florence Howley – both R&R leads of long standing – assumed leading roles. Back in 1917, after FitzGerald's abrupt departure the R&R had toyed with the idea of banning members who participated in the 'Empire enterprise' but managed to concoct a diplomatic fudge to ensure that it did not lose some of its most talented members as a result.[69] The 1901 GAA 'ban' on participation in foreign sports was not about to be aped by the R&R.

FitzGerald continued to play some part in the Dublin music scene, as a conductor or teacher, until his death in 1961. There may well have been an abiding resentment between members of the original R&R committee and its first musical director. In 1932 one of the original R&R *burgomeisters*, Lionel Cranfield (who survived a 1918 power struggle with chairman Edwin Lloyd),[70] sketched out the origins of the society, as it approached its twentieth anniversary, in a lecture to the Dublin Rotary Club. It was uncontaminated by any references to FitzGerald or Jack O'Brien.[71]

FitzGerald's baton passed to Thomas Henry (T.H.) Weaving, professor of organ, piano and harmony at the Royal Irish Academy of Music. Weaving was one of three names suggested to the committee and was to be paid 12/6 per rehearsal and given a 'special fee' based on the success of the shows for which he was MD.[72] Born in Birmingham, Weaving had come to Ireland with his parents at the age of 12 in 1894. Weaving would retain the baton, virtually uninterrupted, for the next thirty-five years, until his retirement in 1952. He was musical director of 104 R&R productions during that period, a record yet to be emulated by any of his illustrious successors.[73] Weaving was, for a period, organist of Christ Church Cathedral, and right up to the time of his death in 1966 at the age of 84 he was organist of the Adelaide Road Presbyterian Church.[74]

KILMICHAEL AND TITIPU

T.W. Hall as King Paramount in *Utopia Limited*, 1920.

A.E. Glynn as Lord Dramaleigh in *Utopia Limited*, 1920.

In 1920 the society was scheduled to deviate again from its normally all-consuming commitment to Gilbert and Sullivan. Plans were laid to produce *The Rose of Persia*, an operetta written by Arthur Sullivan and Basil Hood in 1899. Their collaboration had been prompted partly by the conspicuous lack of success of the penultimate offering of the Gilbert and Sullivan behemoth, *Utopia Limited*, and the abject failure of their valedictory, *The Grand Duke*. In addition, Sullivan was seeking to distance himself from his habitual collaborator's desire to impale the aristocracy and the *haut bourgeoisie* on the *poignard* of his satire. Described in one recent review as more of 'an interesting curiosity than a forgotten treasure' whose Arabian setting is 'more *Road to Morocco* than *The Desert Song*',[75] *The Rose of Persia*, which ran for 211 performances in its original incarnation,[76] has received only one professional production since World War II. The piece comprises multiple cases of mistaken identity both inside and outside the over-populated harem of the chief comic character, Hassan. There are also four threatened executions, and the appearance of a recreational drug called *bhang*.

The production was expected to be 'a landmark in the history of the society'.[77] Unfortunately politico-military realities intervened and the ambitious plans were blighted by the introduction of a curfew by

The Rose of Persia cartoon of principals.

an administration increasingly being run ragged by the activities of the IRA in Dublin.[78] The society, however, was financially committed to *The Rose of Persia*. The show, of necessity, had to go on. Rehearsals took place 'under most trying conditions'. These included the defection of the nominated English producer when rehearsals coincided with Bloody Sunday in November 1920. In terror of his life he returned to England, only informing the society of his flight when he had arrived safely in London.[79] Rehearsals nonetheless continued in complete defiance of the military clampdown, as on at least one occasion the troupe was rounded up and one member was briefly taken into custody by the DMP. The wisdom of observing the curfew was borne out a couple of days into the run when the cast found themselves trapped in the Gaiety while a full-blown 'revolver and machine-gun battle' raged outside in South King Street. That was sufficient to cause *The Rose of Persia* to be pruned beyond recovery. The production had to be cancelled, at considerable loss to the funds of the society.[80]

The military situation had not improved in 1921. In the interim, Bloody Sunday, the Kilmichael Ambush and the Burning of Cork had traumatised either the beleaguered civilian population or the increasingly jittery Crown forces. In such a fraught environment the relatively ephemeral activities of the R&R once again fell victim to an increasingly bitter war. The losses sustained by the society, already financially committed to another Gaiety Theatre run, jeopardised its very future. In an era when indebtedness was the handmaiden of insolvency, it was imperative that the R&R dig itself out of that particular pit. The chosen instrument was a 'sweep' on the 1921 Derby (won by the colt *Humorist*, ridden by the great Steve Donoghue). Tickets, limited to 2,000, cost £1 each (about €40 today). With the promise of 75 per cent of the stake being distributed as prize money the issue was oversubscribed by £300 on the day of the draw. The society, whose output had been driven by the librettos of a lyrical humorist since its foundation in 1913, was probably saved from extinction in 1921 by the equine *Humorist*.

The successful sweep allowed members to gather (somewhat prematurely) to celebrate the society's tenth anniversary on 29 April 1922, in the same Shelbourne Hotel where the cast of *The Mikado* had been forced to take shelter from the Irish Republican Brotherhood and the Irish Citizen Army in 1916. Since its inception the R&R had weathered more vicissitudes than most musical societies might reasonably have been expected to face, and had done so with considerable aplomb. The politically divisive figure of William Martin Murphy had died in 1919 and his place as president of the R&R had been taken by another captain of industry – or robber baron, depending on your perspective – Sir Stanley Cochrane of the drinks firm Cantrell and Cochrane.

Tenth anniversary dinner, menu cover.

Cochrane, a lover of cricket and opera in equal measure, had built what was originally intended to be an indoor cricket pitch, in his Woodbrook home, near Bray, Co. Wicklow. Ultimately, however, he turned it into a concert venue instead. A committed patron of the arts, he was responsible for bringing the great Australian operatic performer Nellie Melba to Ireland. He also organised full orchestral concerts in his own home. However, Cochrane's involvement with the R&R, even on significant occasions like annual general meetings, appears to have been episodic. The honorary vice president, Dr Lombard Murphy, son of William Martin Murphy, regularly deputised for him.[81]

The members assembled for the tenth anniversary bash were disposed to applaud their own achievements and tenacity but allowed some distinguished guests, including the composer J.F. Larchet, to do the job for them. Proposing a toast of congratulations, Sir Robert Tate (the Trinity College academic) suggested that the society had solved a problem that had defeated men from the time of Euclid,

Rathmines and Rathgar Musical Society's Dinner

G.E. HALL (D'OYLY CARTE OPERA Cº & PRODUCER OF RUDDIGORE)

T.H. WEAVING BROUGHT HIS BATON

Dr ASHE

LIONEL CRANFIELD PROPOSES THE PRESS

"CHIDDY"

SIR HENRY McLAUGHLIN IN FACETIOUS MOOD

SIR ROBT TATE PAYING TRIBUTE

A.E. GLYNN

H.R.W. RESPONDS FOR THE PRESS SUPPORTED BY W. CHILLINGWORTH

PROF. O'DWYER

SIR JOSEPH GLYNN

W. TUNNEY

JOE ROCK (GEN. SEC MATER CARNIVAL)

DAVID TELFORD

EDWIN LLOYD

DR. J.F. LARCHET

JOE HOLLOWAY

DAVY OGDEN

Tenth anniversary dinner, caricatures of members and guests.

"RUDDIGORE" AT THE GAIETY

Old Adam (W.F. Comerford)

Irvine Lynch as Sir Despard

A J O'Farrell as Sir Roderick

Rose Maybud (May Doyle)

Alf Gaynor as Robin Oakapple

Mad Margaret (Mabel Horne)

Joseph O'Neill as...

Dame Hannah

Ruddigore cartoon of principals, May 1922.

that of perpetual motion. 'They had been given to understand that if they eliminated friction from the universe, everything would move entirely smoothly. This society seemed to have discovered the key to that enigma, and had eliminated all friction from its working, and for that reason [he was] perfectly safe in prophesying for it that perpetual motion, which meant perpetual life.'[82] The consensus at this understandably solipsistic occasion was that the wheels of the machine were being skilfully greased, musically by T.H. Weaving and administratively by Lionel Cranfield as honorary secretary. Thus far, Tate's prophecy of permanency appears eminently sound.

THE ROARING TWENTIES

As the United Kingdom of Great Britain and Ireland gave way to the Irish Free State in early 1922 the R&R might well have experienced some of the tensions that profound political change can bring. The struggle of one of its senior members, W.G. Mulvin, to hold the pass against the deletion of the words 'British Empire' from the title of the local Shakespeare Society has already been described. No such vestigial animosities appear to have riven a musical society essentially dedicated to the performance of works by two quintessentially English collaborators. At the tenth anniversary dinner Weaving, a Presbyterian, pointed out that the society 'was very mixed in its membership [but] they worked so well together, despite differences in politics and religion that he thought that on a foundation of art they might be able to build up a united Ireland'.[83] Thus far, Sir Robert Tate's prophecy is faring better than Weaving's.

For the R&R the transition to political independence for the twenty-six-county Free State meant little more than a change in the status of the guest of honour on its opening nights. Instead of welcoming the Lord Lieutenant,[84] the committee would now be laying out the red carpet for the British monarch's new representative in Ireland, the Governor General.[85] From December 1922 to February 1928 that meant offering hospitality to the former nationalist MP Timothy Michael Healy, scourge of Parnell, journalist, barrister, politician and a man who had once been horse-whipped by Parnell's nephew. By and large the advent of the Irish Free State went unnoticed in the annals of the society. While the stage productions of the Abbey Theatre or even the *conversaziones* of the National Literary Society might have been more reflective of social and political realities, the nature of musical comedy allowed the members of the R&R to escape from such realities into the 'topsy-turvy' world created by W.S. Gilbert.

The only intrusion of early Free State politics into the deliberations of the committee was a vote of sympathy 'with the Governor General and Mrs Kevin O'Higgins on the sad bereavement they had suffered'.[86] This was in the wake of the assassination of Justice Minister Kevin O'Higgins on 10 July 1927. The reference to the Governor General should not be interpreted as a slight on the President of the Executive Council, W.T. Cosgrave. Healy was included in the motion of sympathy as O'Higgins had been his nephew by marriage.

By 1924 *The Irish Times* was describing the R&R as 'the most vigorous musical organisation in Dublin'.[87] Ironically, the War of Independence, whose savagery had blown the society off course, ultimately proved fortuitous, if only by default. The society's main competition in the still-lucrative business of staging Gilbert and Sullivan, the D'Oyly Carte Company, temporarily abandoned its annual Dublin visit in the early 1920s. Unpleasant and off-putting experiences and indignities suffered by the storied professional troupe during the Anglo–Irish conflict, ensured its absence from Dublin stages during the formative years of the Irish Free State. The R&R, under the guidance of Weaving with J.J. Bouch as chorus master,[88] took full advantage. The society performed an extensive repertoire of operettas to packed houses over a four-year period and further re-vitalised their fortunes. So successful was the society that by 1924, when the D'Oyly Carte Company decided that it was safe to return, the professional Savoyards realised that the competition from the Corinthian Dubliners needed to

Lionel Cranfield as Jack Point, 1923.

be confronted. Accordingly, the R&R was denied a licence by Rupert D'Oyly Carte, son of the founder, to perform a Gilbert and Sullivan piece for the season.[89] Instead, Lionel Cranfield entered into an arrangement to stage *The Duchess of Dantzic* by Ivan Caryll and Edwin Hamilton.

Having established a benchmark for the production of light opera in Dublin, the R&R offered not just competition for the D'Oyly Carte: the society would also prove to be a useful recruiting zone. In the 1920s the R&R provided the Savoy Theatre with two highly capable performers: the aforementioned tenor Arthur Lucas and bass-baritone Sam Mooney. Mooney, 24 years of age when he made his debut with the R&R in the May 1930 Dublin premiere of *The Beloved Vagabond* by Adrian Ross and Dudley Glass, was rapidly head-hunted to the Savoy and spent the next six years working for Rupert D'Oyly Carte. His London career was, it has to be said, relatively undistinguished, comprising mainly understudy roles as Samuel in *The Pirates of Penzance* and the Mikado in *The Mikado*, while playing the Second Yeoman in his own right in *The Yeomen of the Guard* from 1933–6.[90] December 1936 saw him safely ensconced once again at the Gaiety with the R&R in the part of Florian in *Princess Ida*. He then went on to produce the next thirteen consecutive shows, a feat unique amongst the R&R's many accomplished producers.

Immediately prior to the introduction of Sam Mooney to the society, his more illustrious namesake Ria made a number of appearances at the outset of what was to become a long and distinguished career on the Irish and international stage. Although best-known for her lengthy association with the Abbey Theatre, between 1923–5 she appeared in eight R&R productions before being inveigled into the Abbey company by its playwright-manager Lennox Robinson.

Born in Ranelagh in 1903 Ria Mooney had been stage-struck from an early age and had been trained as a dancer. As a young girl, according to her biographer Joseph McGlone, she had been taken by

Ria Mooney.

her father to audition for the part of the Fairy Child in the premiere of the W.B. Yeats drama *The Land of Heart's Desire*. She had been uninspired by the 'drab and colourless' Abbey Theatre rehearsal space and unimpressed with its artistic director. After hearing her read, the eminent poet and playwright had instructed the young ingénue to go to the nearest mountain 'listen to the wind sighing through the trees' and return in a few days.[91] Oddly, she failed to do so. Instead she opted to audition for a part in the R&R's December 1922 production of *Patience*. It was the first staging of the popular piece by the company.

Mooney was cast in the mezzo role of The Lady Angela, one of the 'rapturous maidens' dizzily in love with the affected and ineffectual Bunthorne, a character based on the young aesthete Oscar Wilde. She was given the responsibility of leading the first chorus, 'Twenty Love-sick Maidens We', along with another debutante, Renee Flynn. While May Doyle attracted most of the critical accolades in the title role, Mooney was described by *The Irish Times* as 'singing sweetly' and as 'a Burne-Jones Lady Angela'.[92] She reprised the role the following year when the society revived the show at the Gaiety in December 1923.

Of her eight appearances on the Gaiety stage with the R&R, one of the most notable was her portrayal of Renee de Saint Mezard in the December 1924 production of *The Duchess of Dantzic*. This light opera, based on the 1893 play *Madame Sans-Gêne* by the French writer Victorien Sardou, had been highly successful in its original run at the Lyric in London. Mooney appeared alongside Abbey Theatre co-founder Frank Fay, guesting for the society, appropriately enough, in the role of Napoleon Bonaparte. Mooney was described by *The Irish Times* as 'good in song and dance',[93] while Fay, a professional of long standing, was complimented, in the best *infra dig* tradition of theatre criticism, for his 'good diction'. According to Joseph McGlone, Fay invited Mooney to study with him but, having her heart set on a career as a singer and dancer, she declined his offer.

Patience postcard flyer, 1923.

Her other notable achievement with the R&R before turning professional was in the December 1925 production of *Merrie England* by Edward German and Basil Hood. Their first collaboration had been on the libretto by Hood for *The Emerald Isle (or The Caves of Carrig-Cleena)*, the score of which had been left incomplete on the death of Sullivan in 1900. This, on the face of it, might have seemed a more apposite vehicle for the society in preference to a comic opera featuring such notable friends of Ireland as Queen Elizabeth I, Sir Walter Raleigh and the Earl of Essex. However, Sullivan's entirely ephemeral valedictory was more in the nature of a revenge on the land of his bandmaster father than an *homage*. Replete as it was with characters bearing names like Dr Fiddle D.D., Black Dan and 'a chorus of Irish peasants', it was perhaps wiser for the committee to have opted to depict the halcyon days of Elizabethan England. Mooney played the major part of the unfortunate Jill All-alone, accused of witchcraft and imprisoned in the Tower of London (from which she escapes in Act 2). The *Irish Independent* praised her performance as: 'ever elfish and never witch-like. She acted well and wisely used her sweet voice.'[94]

While performing with the R&R Mooney also became involved in drama productions for the United Arts Club in the mid-1920s, playing alongside a young man whose actual name was William Shields but who would later adopt the stage name of Barry FitzGerald. Her career in musical theatre ended in 1926 when she was invited by Lennox Robinson to join the Abbey Theatre Company.[95]

Alongside Mooney in the 1925 production of *Merrie England*, in the tiny part of a royal page, was the 15-year-old Betty Chancellor, making her sole appearance for the R&R. At the age of 21, Chancellor played opposite the 16-year-old prodigy Orson Welles who had conned Hilton Edwards into casting him in the Gate Theatre production of *Jew Suss*. Welles later told his biographer, Barbara Leaming, that Chancellor was 'the sexiest thing that ever lived'. Leaming describes him as having been 'wildly

27

Mabel Home as Mad Margaret, *Ruddigore*, 1922.

infatuated' with Chancellor. 'She was one of those absolutely black-haired girls, with skin as white as Carrara marble…and eyelashes you could trip on', Welles had enthused.[96] Later Chancellor would play Ophelia to Micheál Mac Liammóir's Hamlet. In March 1945 Chancellor became the second wife of playwright Denis Johnston, with whom she had two children. She appeared with Jack Hawkins in Johnston's play *The Moon in the Yellow River* in London in 1947. Chancellor moved to the USA with Johnston and their two sons in 1948.[97] She died in 1984.[98]

In addition to a steady stream of performers who would go on to professional or semi-professional careers in music or on the stage, in those early years of the twentieth century many of the more prominent 'gifted amateurs' of the R&R acquired committed local followings of their own. Often in its advertising the society, rather than simply identifying its latest show, would highlight the involvement of certain principals. For example, in its newspaper advert for the spring 1921 production of *The Yeomen of the Guard* the names of a dozen members of the cast were featured just below the title.[99] These included Irvine Lynch and May Doyle, and a relatively new 'star' Mabel Home. She had made her debut in the spring 1918 production of *Utopia Limited* as The Lady Sophy.[100]

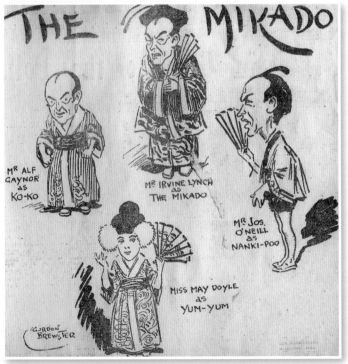

The Mikado caricatures, 1923.

Given the parsimonious nature of the committee and the 'line by line' cost of advertising, there was a clear assumption that the R&R should mimic the promotional methods of professional companies and, so to speak, stand on its principals. The society saw its featured players as having 'box office' potential. Audiences encouraged this by often reacting to individual performers as if they were matinee idols. One of the society's favourite comic performers of the twenties and thirties, Alf Gaynor, 'was recalled again and again' after the final curtain of the winter 1923 *Mikado* in which he played the lugubrious Ko-Ko. While Gaynor was taking his bows 'scores of presents were handed up to the principals. Miss May Doyle, Miss Florence Howley, Miss Ria Mooney and Miss Mabel Home all had piles of boxes of chocolates in front of them when the presentations ceased.'[101] Local heroes being applauded by a parochial claque, perhaps, but heady treatment nonetheless.

The Barley Mow Group in *Tom Jones* (1925): Mabel Home, Margie Hall, Mida O'Brien, P.A. Delany, A.E. Glynn and E.M. Healy.

There is little doubt that the R&R viewed and represented itself as a company that merely happened to be amateur. Weaving and his collaborators – often London-based directors like Avalon Collard and Phillip Howley – were intensely ambitious in the scale and values of their productions. Once the travails of the War of Independence were left in the past, the society came out with its own guns blazing. With the Civil War at a virtual end – the fighting around Dublin had subsided months before – in the spring of 1923 *The Yeomen of the Guard* and *The Gondoliers* were staged at the Gaiety. They were reprised in December with the addition of *The Mikado* (in a new production by F.W. Patrick) and *Patience* (also directed by Patrick). All four shows were well-supported, prompting Weaving to express his thanks from the stage 'to the musical people of Dublin, who had given the society such tremendous "houses" during the fortnight'.[102] Clearly a portion of the population had forsworn the subversive appeal of the cinema for a couple of weeks at least.

Three further productions followed in the spring of 1924 before Rupert D'Oyly Carte inserted a well-placed spoke in the wheels with the refusal of a licence for a G&S show the following December. While that policy continued, until December 1926, the society still managed three productions in 1925, of *Tom Jones*,[103] *Merrie England* and a reprise of *The Duchess of Dantzic* with Mabel Home in one of the leading roles.

THE DUCHESS OF DANTZIC (1924)

Cicily Chancellor as Caroline Murat.

Queenie Shea as Lisette.

Mack Glynn as Papillon.

With the society progressing into early adolescence in the mid-1920s, as with any teenager there was the need to push boundaries. *The Duchess of Dantzic*, staged thanks to D'Oyly Carte's injunction, was described as 'experimental' by *The Irish Times* but pronounced 'entirely successful'.[104] As with any teenager, there were the hormonal highs and lows. Occasionally the frightening pace of production appears to have resulted in a measurable diminution in quality. One of the four December 1923 shows, *The Yeomen of the Guard*, was criticised by *The Irish Times* for a 'lack of professional experience…to a degree not evident in the opening performances this week'.[105] However, reviews of R&R shows – 'the triumphant Rathmines musical combination'[106] – throughout the 1920s and 1930s were almost universally positive, often emphasising that they were 'produced on a scale and in a manner able to compare with professional productions'[107] or 'beyond the usual amateur standard'.[108] An ecstatic *Irish Times* review of the June 1932 production of *Monsieur Beaucaire*[109] with a young Robert McCullagh in the title role concluded with the observation that: 'one feels just a little touch of pride that visitors to Dublin have this opportunity to judge just what these accomplished amateurs can accomplish [*sic*]. They have reached a standard of musical performance which can be equalled – certainly not surpassed – in any other city.'[110]

The visitors in question were, of course, those attending the Eucharistic Congress that summer. Not that many of them strayed too far from the main event. It was an unusually hot summer that year, more appropriate for a series of major outdoor set pieces than a period musical. Robert McCullagh recalls that 'we perspired as we made up in the dressing rooms and perspired again as we saw the sparse attendances each night. I counted seventy people in the whole theatre for the matinee…'.[111]

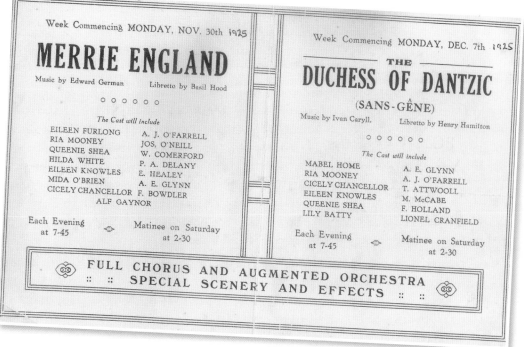

Flyer for *Merrie England* and *The Duchess of Dantzic*, 1925.

'NO, NO, CRANFIELD'

The 1930s in Europe was a decade of polarisation, conflict and tension. Democracy was threatened and former allies went their separate ways. While the affairs of the R&R were distinctly more harmonious, issues arose between the society and two of the main factors in its outstanding success, namely the D'Oyly Carte Theatre Company and the Gaiety. These pivotal relationships became problematic largely for commercial reasons, although personalities did play a significant part in both disagreements.

Sixteen of the twenty-six R&R productions presented at the Gaiety in the 1930s were traditional Gilbert and Sullivan favourites. On the face of it this does not suggest the existence of any major tensions between the professional rights-holders and the perennial amateur supplicants. However, if the figures for the first half of the decade alone are considered the picture is somewhat more stark and revealing. During that period, the society produced thirteen shows, only four of which were penned by G&S. Why was this the case with a musical society for which the Savoy repertoire had been central?

The principal reason was by way of a back-handed compliment to the R&R. The D'Oyly Carte touring company was still a frequent visitor to Ireland in the 1930s. Even elements within the Savoy Theatre could see that certain operas 'were thought to be played out'.[112] As the Gilbert and Sullivan *oeuvre* was the Comstock Lode of the D'Oyly Carte it was deemed unwise to allow a popular and talented amateur society to work the seam in one of the major 'provincial' touring centres. This was especially so in the 1930s when London theatres themselves were experiencing the worst of the Great Depression. In the middle of 1932 twelve West End theatres were dark and others had been reduced to showing films.[113] The situation in Dublin was not quite so bad, as a result of the abolition of an entertainment tax on 'live' theatre by Finance Minister Ernest Blythe, a future director of the Abbey Theatre.[114]

Lionel Cranfield had approached Rupert D'Oyly Carte in the autumn of 1929 for permission to restore Gilbert and Sullivan to their rightful place in the R&R repertoire with productions of *Patience* and *H.M.S. Pinafore*. It is clear that a negative response was anticipated. When D'Oyly Carte gave his *imprimatur* the committee was caught unawares but deemed that 'it would not be politic to refuse the offer now made'.[115] However, similar permission was not forthcoming in 1930. It was not until 1932, when the society wished to celebrate its twentieth anniversary with *Iolanthe* and *The Mikado* that D'Oyly Carte gave the green light again.[116] This was subsequently extinguished again and it wasn't until December 1935 that the R&R entered into a run of D'Oyly Carte licensed productions that lasted, almost uninterrupted, until the outbreak of World War II.

During this period there was also a subtle change in the relationship between the Gaiety Theatre and the R&R. After doing some disappointing business with some of the shows produced at the end of the 1920s, the Gaiety management intervened. When the two 1930 shows, *The Beloved Vagabond* by Adrian Ross and Dudley Glass (a Dublin premiere) and *A Country Girl* by James Tanner, Adrian Ross and Lionel Monckton, brought in a combined box-office total of just over £1,000[117] – about half of what might have been expected – Hugh Hyland, the Gaiety Theatre manager intervened. He proactively suggested a change in direction on the part of the society with the intention of improving box-office figures. In a letter to Cranfield, Hyland 'conveyed his feelings that a very modern production would be the best business proposition if the society was equal to the task, but as he felt there would be a failure to secure the requisite speed in the musical numbers, he was disposed to vote for a safer medium for the society's capabilities and suggested *The Arcadians*'.[118] It was to be presented at the beginning of May 1931. So successful was the outcome of Hyland's suggestion of the Edwardian musical comedy by Lionel Monckton and Howard Talbot – which concerns an attempt to transform a perfidious London into a sylvan nirvana – that it was brought back for a second week at the end of the month and netted total receipts of over £1,300, leaving the R&R with a healthy surplus of £286 as opposed to the normal average of around £100. The added dates included a gala performance to celebrate the founding of the Irish Hospitals Sweepstake on 30 May 1931.

Not unnaturally, Hyland's next recommendation, a December 1931 production of *A Waltz Dream* by Oscar Strauss and Basil Hood, was accepted with alacrity. The musical – by the composer of *The Chocolate Soldier* – was another notable success, garnering receipts of £870. Hyland, it seemed, had the Midas touch. It was not long, however, before trouble broke out in paradise. At the centre of the maelstrom were Hyland and the R&R's very own alpha male, Lionel Cranfield. The two men fell out spectacularly over the sort of extra-curricular activity that Cranfield had been wont to criticise in fellow members of the R&R: those not content to restrict their musical activities to the cloisters of the society.

In October 1933 Cranfield, and the R&R chorus-master J.J. Bouch, put together a company of players and produced *No, No, Nanette* by Irving Caesar, Otto Harbach and Vincent Youmans at the Olympia Theatre. The musical (which included such popular songs as 'I Want To Be Happy' and 'Tea For Two') was, according to *The Irish Times* 'presented…to an appreciative audience'.[119] It was also something of a family affair. Cranfield directed his son Lal and his daughter Maisie, the latter in the title role. Taking the female lead in this 'excellent amateur company' would have done no harm to the confidence of Maisie Cranfield who had, in 1929, pulled out of playing the title part for the R&R in the operetta *San Toy* by Sidney Jones and Edward Morton. As her father had put it to the committee at the time, 'she had not been giving [producer – Fred] Mr Payne satisfaction and as she could do no better she preferred to give it up'. She had been replaced by her understudy, a youthful Eileen Clancy, who would go on to play many similar parts in the years ahead. Cranfield's Olympia production was described as 'a personal venture'.[120] Hugh Hyland decided to take it very personally indeed.

In late December 1933 the R&R received correspondence 'related to the intention of the Gaiety Theatre to debar members of the society from appearing at any other theatre in Dublin as a basis for entering into future engagements'.[121] Rather shell-shocked at what was clearly Hyland's reaction to Cranfield's 'personal venture', the issue was long-fingered and referred to a specially formed sub-committee. In January the Gaiety's London manager, Selby, was approached and asked to withdraw 'the restrictive clause proposed for future contracts'.[122] He declined to do so. At a hurriedly convened special general meeting

Twentieth anniversary dance.

Cranfield intervened. His intransigence was absolute. He informed the meeting, which had proposed sending a deputation to Hyland, that he had no intention of negotiating with the Gaiety whose 'antagonism…was directed at him personally'. He went on to unburden himself of what appeared to be years of frustration in dealing with the Gaiety. He pointed to 'the harsh measures generally which theatre people imposed on the society and the way they interfered generally with the progress of the organisation'. He read a number of letters purporting 'to show the hectoring dictatorial methods employed by theatre'. He concluded with the, by now blatantly obvious, observation that, if disposed to negotiate the society would require a new honorary secretary 'as antagonism would undoubtedly be in the forefront in negotiations conducted by him'.[123]

At another hastily convened annual general meeting Alf Gaynor, one of the R&R's most talented comic players, adopted a deadly serious mien and proposed a radical course of action 'to find a way out of the deadlock'. This involved a legislative *coup d'état*, the negation of the standing committee and the creation of a four-person emergency committee mandated to act as plenipotentiaries in discussions with the Gaiety. This was clearly an essential manoeuvre designed to bypass the immovable and immoderate Cranfield. The society, in keeping with the spirit of much of the Europe of the 1930s, duly opted for elective autocracy. However, this miniature 'committee of public safety' (which included Gaynor, Lombard Murphy, Arthur Healy and George Hewson) had no Robespierre and, unlike fascist Europe, was prepared to hand back power once its task was completed.[124]

In the end it was the R&R who blinked. The so-called 'emergency committee' reported back in April 1934 to another special general meeting. Dr Lombard Murphy outlined the stark choices that the uncompromising attitude of Hyland had generated. The society had two options: (a) to agree to be bound by the Gaiety's restrictions or (b) to reject and disband 'which was Dr Murphy's view as to what rejection of the proposals would mean'. The society found itself, rather invidiously, in a living production of *Hobson's Choice* by Harold Brighouse. The members chose discretion. It was pointed out that a 'letter from theatre wound up by expressing the hope that friendly harmonious relations which existed in the past might be renewed'. Accordingly 'it was generally agreed to let the matter rest there…so that there might be a clear path for a renewal of work at the Gaiety if necessary and desirable'.[125] The committee of public safety immediately liquidated itself without the intervention of the guillotine and a new standing committee was elected. The only obvious casualty of the entire affair was Lionel Cranfield. Having dominated the politics of the R&R since 1916, Cranfield was replaced as honorary secretary by Arthur Healy.

The R&R resumed its association with the Gaiety in December 1934 after a twelve-month gap with a production of the Edwardian musical comedy *Florodora* and T.H. Weaving, in a speech from the stage on closing night, remembered to thank Hugh Hyland profusely. So too did Healy.[126] Although the society had not yet begun to grapple with the modern American musical, the members had certainly grasped the reality of one American axiom: you can't fight city hall.

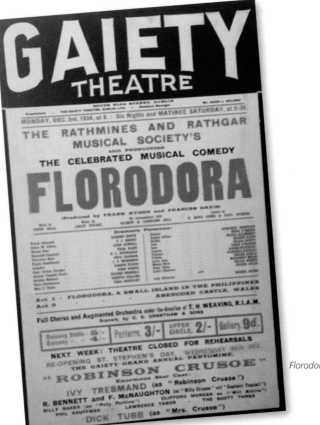

Florodora poster, 1934.

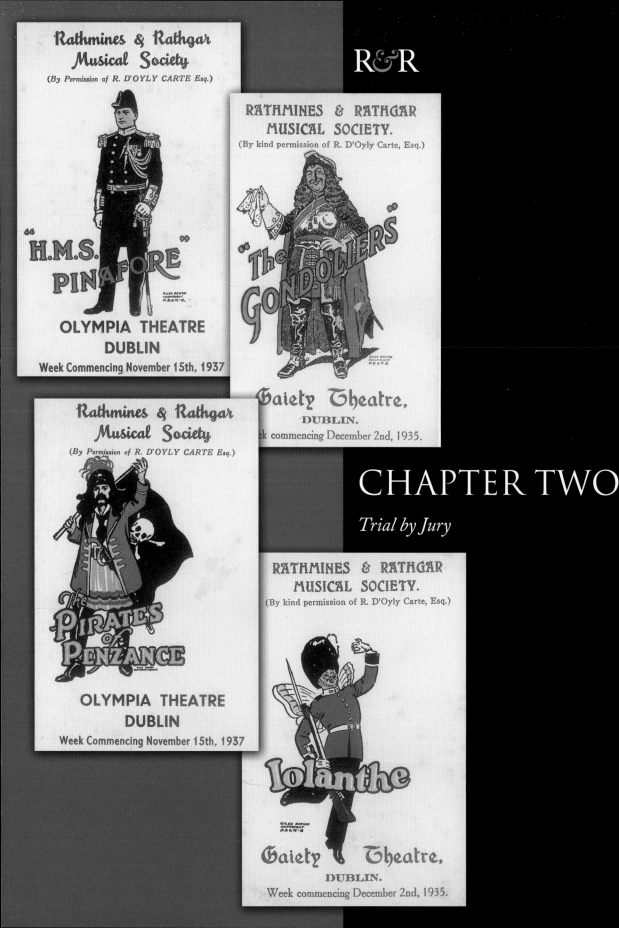

R&R

CHAPTER TWO

Trial by Jury

CHAPTER TWO

Trial by Jury

Here is a bouquet to the members of the Rathmines and Rathgar Musical Society for their work. They bring us a comfort that is not worn by the years, a comfort that spreads out beyond the actual moments of pleasure in theatre. They encourage us to hum while waiting for that overcrowded bus on the way home, that simple song that tells of love being like a flower that fades within the hour…'.

Maxwell Sweeney, *The Irish Times*, 14 November 1942.

. . . .

THE HUNGRY THIRTIES

From its coming of age in 1934 to the end of 'the Emergency' (Irish-speak for the carnage of World War II), the Minute Books of the Rathmines and Rathgar Musical Society lack references to domestic contemporary events. Neither the debut in office of Fianna Fáil nor the introduction of Fascism-lite to the streets of Dublin by the Blueshirts was deemed worthy of consideration in the parallel universe and appropriately 'topsy-turvy' world of the foremost amateur musical society in Dublin. However, despite confining its organisational discussions to the stultifyingly germane, the R&R could not help but be buffeted by the political and economic cyclones of the 1930s and 1940s. While one would be entirely frustrated in any search for overt or far-reaching allusions to societal malaise, nonetheless the *zeitgeist* haunted the committee room. The society's twentieth anniversary publication, which appeared in December 1932, had confidently forecast that the R&R had at least another two decades in it. There were times in the 1930s when that prediction looked very much like hubris.

It was 'the hungry thirties', the era of the Great Depression. Ireland was not immune to massive unemployment rates and depressed global economic circumstances and the R&R was not invulnerable to financial reality. But just as many made their escape from the austerity of the 1930s via the picture palace and the conjurors of Hollywood, a dedicated cadre of Dublin thespians entered instead the quaint world of serendipity and outrageous good fortune created by two Victorian gentlemen.

Patience, 1966. Victor Leeson and Heather Hewson.

By early 1935 'amicable relations [were] re-established with the Gaiety management'[1] but, despite this, no spring production took place. While the society's December 1934 production of *Florodora* (from the book by Owen Hall –pseudonym for Dubliner Jimmy Davis – also writer of *A Gaiety Girl*) appears to have been an artistic success and 'had served the purpose of restoring the society to what might be justly termed the forefront of musical activity in Dublin',[2] it suffered a loss of £35 mainly because of the need to hire special scenery for the Edwardian musical, set on a fictional Filipino island. Largely because only three productions had been staged between January 1933 and December 1934 the R&R found itself in the red and officers of the society had been required to 'dip deep[ly] into their own pockets during this financial difficulty and help the society to meet its commitments'.[3] The committee was forced to organise another member's sweep (this time on the 1935 Royal Hunt Cup at Ascot in June) to clear off the deficit. The sweep raised £80, which would have cleared the running deficit at that time of £59.[4]

This pattern continued through much of the late 1930s with, for example, a significant loss of £90 on *Princess Ida* in December 1936 cancelling out the profits made on the productions of *The Mikado* and *The Yeomen of the Guard* in May of that year. This particular operetta had been chosen in order to complete the G&S repertoire as the society approached its twenty-fifth year. *The Irish Times* observed, 'it has been very much of a mystery why they did not present this work before, as it is one of the brightest and most amusing of the series'.[5] *The Irish Press*, however, noted that 'the house was not as well filled as it should have been'.[6] The reason adduced by the committee for the relative failure of *Princess Ida* was the coincidence of the abdication crisis in Britain![7] Just as likely a cause was the subject matter of the opera, which concerns a princess who founds a women's university and advocates the supplanting of male dominance of the known universe by the leadership of women.

Flyer for *The Yeomen of the Guard* and *The Mikado*, 1936.

The cast was, in R&R terms, *non pareil*. Without the distraction of any other show running in repertory all the society's considerable musical resources were ploughed into the production. The three male leads were taken by three of the undoubted stars of the 1930s: Joseph Flood (Hilarion), Robert McCullagh (Cyril) and Sam Mooney (Florian). The title role was played by an imperious Eileen Clancy, with Mabel Home as Lady Blanche, Hilda White as Lady Psyche and Mida O'Brien as Blanche's daughter, Melissa.

The reviews could hardly have been better. *The Irish Times* was happy that 'everything down to the last detail is presented in the best tradition of the opera'.[8] *The Irish Press* was equally enthusiastic. *The Irish Times* lauded Eileen Clancy in the title role, deeming the R&R 'fortunate to have in their ranks such a fine soprano' while she got 'first rate support' from Mida O'Brien, Hilda White and Mabel Home in particular 'who gave an impressive study of the Lady Blanche'. But in the opinion of the *Irish Times* reviewer 'the male principals were even a stronger team'. Flood played Hilarion 'in sprightly fashion' and with his 'helpmates' McCullagh and Mooney 'they were a clever trio…all singing with rare charm'. The return of Mooney from the D'Oyly Carte was also welcomed as one whose 'acting and singing had the stamp of the real artist'.

But the positivity of *The Irish Times* and *The Irish Press* was not reflected in the box office. *Princess Ida*, despite its Savoy origins, was an unknown quantity launched on a Dublin theatre-going audience pinched by a worldwide economic depression. This was more likely to have been the reason why it lost £33 based on total receipts of only £458, rather than the fanciful notion that it was damaged by the abdication crisis.

Whatever the cause, the Dublin public absented themselves in droves. In order to mitigate the loss, members were asked to organise whist drives in their homes for the benefit of the R&R. Discussions took place on how to extract subscriptions from members in arrears. Some things never change! Efforts were made to secure broadcasting engagements from Radio Éireann until it was realised that 'the scale of remuneration offered was too low to prove either attractive or beneficial to the society'.[9] As already observed, some things never change!

The straitened circumstances of the society may also have contributed to the resignation of its largely absentee president, Sir Stanley Cochrane, the man who had brought the phrase 'apologies for absence' to new heights. It was announced at the annual general meeting in March 1937 that 'continued absence from Ireland prevented Sir Stanley Cochrane from taking any active interest in the society'. His non-presence seems to have had no material effect on his continuation in the role prior to 1937, but it was also flagged that he was no longer in a position 'to contribute to the society's funds'.[10]

Exit Cochrane, enter Dr William Lombard Murphy, son of former president William Martin Murphy. Already a significant presence in the society, his presidency would be far more 'hands on' in nature than that of either of his predecessors. Dr George Hewson, organist of St Patrick's Cathedral and husband of contralto Mabel Home, became vice president.

Dr Lombard Murphy, president (1932–1943).

George Hewson, vice president (1942–1947).

After the restoration of a relative state of calm in the arrangements with the Gaiety Theatre, that relationship returned to a state of flux in 1937 when the Gaiety management succeeded in double-booking its own theatre for the autumn season. While the London-based Selby had promised to accommodate the R&R, Hyland had made a prior commitment elsewhere. The week beginning 13 December was offered as an alternative but its proximity to Christmas caused the R&R committee to reject the offer. The search began for alternative venues; the Mansion House and Rathmines Town Hall were mentioned. A return to the Queen's Theatre was canvassed. Finally, after a special meeting of active members on 31 August, the Olympia (primarily a professional 'variety' theatre venue) was settled on. Although, as a 'twice-nightly' house, this involved the amateurs of the R&R performing at 6.45 and again at 9.00.[11] The reaction of some of the regular Olympia aficionados to Gilbert and Sullivan was somewhat discouraging. There was an element in the audience that had little appreciation for the finer dramatic arts. Their affiliation to theatre was based solely on their ability to secure a drink in one of the theatre bars after the city's other establishments had closed.[12]

Selby was asked to be sure to reserve Spring Show week 1938 for the R&R's next production. This he failed to do, adding insult to injury by offering the date (25 April) to the Dublin Operatic Society. Negotiations began, once again, with the Olympia. Because there were difficulties in obtaining permission to perform many modern musicals twice-nightly it was considered likely that the R&R would have to revert to Gilbert and Sullivan. But eventually a licence was secured for bi-nightly performances of the Broadway musical farce *Mercenary Mary*, with music by William Friedlander and Con Conrad, and lyrics by Irving Caesar. The accomplished Mabel Home was cast in the title role with one of the R&R's comic leads, P.J. 'Paddy' Henry, as her 'brainless husband'.[13] Mary's *raison d'être* is to devise a series of stratagems in order to ensure that her feckless spouse is not stripped of his annual allowance by his censorious parents.

Dublin, unfortunately, decided not take Mary to its bosom, although the reviews in *The Irish Times* and the *Irish Independent* were relatively positive. The latter described the production as 'very humorous with a good blend of delightful singing and pleasing choruses'.[14] The portents had not been good. As opening night approached cast members were asked, where possible, to provide their own costumes to keep costs down. No extra musicians were to be hired except 'where absolutely necessary'.[15] 'Several of the members…promised to advance small sums to the society should occasion demand'.[16] T.H. Weaving decided *Mercenary Mary* was not his cup of tea and he declined the role of musical director. In December 1936 he had become a Fellow of the Royal Irish Academy of Music, although there is no suggestion that this influenced his decision to pass on *Mercenary Mary*. The society was forced to rely on the resident conductor of the Olympia, Robert Bolton, to carry the baton. Weaving's wasn't the only defection, either. A number of society members had chosen to take parts in a production by Lionel Cranfield of *Lilac Time* in, of all places, the Gaiety Theatre. They were, as a consequence, asked to stand down for the R&R's Olympia run.

Mercenary Mary gave the lie to the financial resourcefulness of the main character, and lost a hefty £90. At the first post-production committee meeting a stark choice was proposed between God and Mammon. J.J. Bouch, concerned at the increasingly parlous state of the society's finances, suggested that he 'should send a letter to the clergy of the Dublin Diocese seeking subscriptions to the society'. A more practical proposal made at the same meeting was for a sweepstake on the St. Leger.[17] In the end the more diabolical option was chosen. The Dublin clergy were left untapped and instead a sweep was run on the outcome of the Goodwood Cup. Clearly the final classic of the season, traditionally staged in September, was too far distant. The financial outcome of the punt on *Mercenary Mary* forced the R&R to return, like the prodigal son, to the Savoy stable. It had been hoped to mount a production of *Showboat* by Jerome Kern and Oscar Hammerstein in November 1938. That project was abandoned (until 1955 as it transpired) in favour of the old reliables *Mikado* and *Gondoliers* because it was felt that royalties for *Showboat* would be too high.[18] At the 1938 annual general meeting Arthur Healy acknowledged that the R&R 'had passed through one of the most trying and difficult years in its history'.[19] The R&R was not alone, however. The music critic of *The Irish Times*, in February 1937 had delivered himself of 'some plaintive remarks about the decline of public interest in music as a means of entertainment'.[20]

The November 1938 productions of the society's two most popular Gilbert and Sullivan operas, and a return to the Gaiety from the twice-nightly tyranny of the Olympia,[21] seemed to have the desired effect. With Weaving in the musical driving-seat and Sam Mooney at the start of an uninterrupted thirteen-show reign as producer, the R&R regained some of its confidence and restored its fortunes. Perhaps the clear and present approach of European war persuaded Dubliners to part with some of their scarce financial resources in pursuit of frivolity, but the two shows made a clear profit for the R&R of a very welcome £140. It was to be almost four years

Arthur V. Healy, honorary secretary (1934–44).

T.H. Weaving, musical director (1917–52).

and twenty productions before the society would deviate from a partially Gaiety-inspired policy of following one G&S season with another. Gaiety Theatre management had decided that the R&R should deny itself the pleasure of performing anything other than a Savoy opera while the wider world was bent on destroying itself. But in that respect they were entirely *ad idem* with the society itself. The inescapable reality of World War II inevitably shaped R&R policy, given the restraints and strictures under which the country at large was forced to operate between 1939–45. Like a twenty-something who has flown the coop and seeks to return to the fold when he finds himself in financial difficulty, the R&R went back home to 'mother' for much of the war. The mother in question was the familiar, popular and (relatively) unproblematic *oeuvre* of Gilbert and Sullivan.

While the society's Minute Books are free of any reference to contemporary events in Ireland itself, they could not avoid alluding to the global war that profoundly affected the lives of those even in neutral Ireland. The first acknowledgment that anything untoward was happening in North Africa, the Far East or the continent of Europe between 1939–42 was a note in the minutes regarding the November 1939 productions of *Patience*, *Trial by Jury*, and *H.M.S. Pinafore*. The attention of the public was to be 'drawn to the time of commencing (8pm) and finish of the show. This was essential in view of the blackout precautions which might have a detrimental effect on attendance'.[22]

The Gondoliers, 1939. E.M. Healy, Joe Flood, Hilda White and Mabel Home.

At some point in the 1930s, the society also acquired two rather interesting and entirely fictional chorus members. In 1939 Flann O'Brien, aka Brian O'Nolan published his acknowledged masterpiece, the surreal *At Swim-Two-Birds*. A tour de force consisting of three narratives concocted by an unnamed Dublin-based college student, O'Nolan's work made some amends to the society for having missed out on James Joyce by a few years. The talented lyric tenor and author of *Ulysses* had, unfortunately, departed his native city a decade before the R&R became an inescapable fixture on the Dublin cultural scene. Had the society been formed before 1904, Leopold Bloom, his wife Molly or Stephen Dedalus might well have been included in its membership. As it was the R&R had to be content with nurturing the dubious talents of the uncle of the unknown narrator of *At Swim-Two-Birds*, and his friend Mr Corcoran. The novel describes how the uncle (a clerk in the Guinness brewery, who is highly suspicious of the lack of studious activity on the part of his nephew) and Corcoran, both of whom were members 'of an operatic society composed of residents of the Rathmines and Rathgar district', would meet in the uncle's house and listen to Gilbert and Sullivan songs on the gramophone. The uncle – a character said to be based on O'Nolan's own father[23] – had 'an indifferent voice of the baritone range' while Corcoran was 'likewise situated'.

The narrator described the practice of the two mediocre choristers as they put a recording on the gramophone and placed a needle finely on the revolving disc:

> The tune came duly, a thin spirant from the *Patience* opera. The records were old and not of the modern electrical manufacture. A chorus intervening, Mr Corcoran and my uncle joined in it in happy and knowledgeable harmony, stressing the beat with manual gesture.

My uncle, his back to me, also moved his head authoritatively, exercising a roll of fat which he was accustomed to wear at the back of his collar, so that it paled and reddened in the beat of the music.[24]

The uncle's reaction to the piece was one of barely controlled ecstasy, Corcoran's was to emit a tumultuous sneeze 'spattering his clothing with a mucous discharge from his nostrils'. The nephew beat a hasty retreat and left them to the exploration of Victorian light opera and the clearing of nasal cavities. The picture presented is less than edifying and the comedy is, of course, enhanced by the knowledge that no indifferent baritone would ever have passed the membership audition to gain entrance to the R&R!

In his primary alter-ego, that of Myles na gCopaleen in the celebrated 'Cruiskeen Lawn' column in *The Irish Times*, O'Nolan suggested that his affection for Gilbert and Sullivan went only so far. In a November 1944 column he made his first post-*At-Swim* reference to the society. It was less than gracious.

> I see that the Rathmines and Rathgar Musical Society is producing (positively 2,500th performance, I understand) 'I. O'Lanty' and 'Eamon of the Guards' and I should like to take this opportunity of congratulating this enterprising musical combination on their enterprise, not to say their daring in embarking on such ventures in war-time… There is, of course, nothing *wrong* with Gilbert and Sullivan. There are some damn lovely things in that stuff, if the truth were known. Indeed the modest pleasure that these works afford the people of Rathmines and Rathgar is a healthy thing. Whereby the simpler and lighter art-forms have a following, you have a firmly-seated middle class, a stable political regime and a bulwark against pests of the type, say, who copy French paintings. But here is my trouble. One of my London agents tells me that he can supply scores for about 200 light operas, mostly French and Italian in origin. Attractive stuff like, say, 'The Bells of Corneville'. New. Different.[25] Is the G&S feed re-hashed again and again because the customers know what they like and like what they know? Or for the sounder reason that the society has the wigs and the fans? Or just to try my Patience.[26]

He returned to theme again in a column in 1950. Here he is debating with himself the true meaning and usage of the word 'banal'. He concludes that it is frequently employed to describe something that is 'commonplace'.

> Where would we be without the commonplace?… I see that the Rathmines and Rathgar Musical Society threaten shortly to produce in public certain Gilbert the Sullivan 'operas' – the trashiest of all known pseudo-musical pap. Is THAT banal?[27]

O'Nolan copper-fastened his antipathy to the Gilbert and Sullivan repertoire in 1955 when he took a final swipe at the R&R in a piece decrying the extent of foreign infiltration of the Radio Éireann orchestra. He wrote on that occasion, 'one cannot expect the same single-mindedness as is evinced by

THE HOLE IN THE WALL

IF YOU KNOW OF A BETTER 'OLE. THAN THIS WE DON'T

BEGINNERS FOR ACT 2

Brooke.K.

A "Drinking Chorus" in full swing. (Not by Gilbert and Sullivan)

Cartoon of R&R members by Joe Brooke-Kelly, c.1947: The Peers from *Iolanthe* Queuing for a Drink. (The Gaiety did not have a green room until the 1950s.)

the Rathmines and Rathgar Musical Society, but how soon are we to have *The Yeomen of the Guard* again, I wonder? Or *The Mikado* perhaps?'[28]

There is, to say the least, a consistent line on the works of Gilbert and Sullivan and the pomps of the R&R through the *oeuvre* of Brian O'Nolan, aka Flann O'Brien, aka Myles na gCopaleen. His, however, was a highly personal and typically curmudgeonly viewpoint, fortunately not shared by the theatre-going public of Dublin.

• •

THE 'EMERGENCY'

In August 1940 a discussion arose as to which production to launch in the Gaiety that winter. In the committee chair the redoubtable P.L. 'Paddy' Forde, a prominent associate member,[29] offered the opinion that the society should restrict itself to Savoy operas for the foreseeable future 'as the times were inopportune for any other kind'. He pointed out that G&S was always considered to be 'a safe venture'. Others argued against such a conservative and apparently unadventurous policy but eventually Forde prevailed and the society decided to opt for *Trial by Jury*, *Iolanthe* and *The Pirates of Penzance* that winter.[30]

When it came to planning the spring production of 1941 Rupert D'Oyly Carte was approached by Arthur Healy, still honorary secretary,[31] to see if he would permit the production and presentation of more than two G&S operas in a single season. (Because of its brevity *Trial by Jury*, planned for the winter of 1940, was not considered to be a 'full' production. It was generally run in conjunction with shows like *Pirates* or *Pinafore*. They were both considered too short to be performed alone so *Trial by Jury* was added as a curtain raiser.) Healy had pointed out in a letter to Carte 'that it was due to the precarious times that such a request should be made as it was essential that the society should, so far as possible, keep to Gilbert and Sullivan for the time being'.[32]

Flyer, 1941.

There was, however, another compelling reason for adherence to a 'G&S only' policy. The R&R had, by and large, relied on British producers for both its G&S repertoire and its occasional forays into more modern forms of musical comedy. The difference was that while the society had within its ranks producers experienced and capable enough to tackle Savoy light opera, the same was not necessarily true when it came to taking on some of the contemporary Broadway or West End successes. The closest acknowledged professional experts in that field were in London, and a hostile Irish Sea, patrolled by German U-boats, lay between the West End and the Gaiety. Furthermore, had any potential producer even been willing to make the trip there was the added complication of the travel restrictions in place at the time between the UK and Ireland.

British diplomatic representatives were approached and enquiries were made as to the possibility of a West End producer obtaining a passport to travel to and work in Ireland. The response was non-committal. The society was advised that all requests should be addressed to the nearest passport office in England 'by the person in question for the facilities they were seeking'.[33] So, in the circumstances, it was considered wiser for the R&R to stick to what it knew best, assuming Rupert D'Oyly Carte was prepared to relax his own restrictions.

Fortunately he was. On 18 December 1940 it was noted that Rupert D'Oyly Carte, probably feeling the financial pinch brought on by the dearth of amateur musical shows in blitz-torn Britain, had given permission for the production of up to *four* Savoy operas in a season. The R&R decided to content itself with three and *The Yeomen of the Guard*, *The Gondoliers* and *Patience* were chosen for runs at the Gaiety in April/May 1941. When it came to the selection of a producer it appeared that the uninterrupted reign of Sam Mooney was at an end. Healy told the committee that in the three November productions a great deal of extra work had devolved on himself, and semi-professional singer Joseph Flood, 'due to the uncertain manner in which Mr Mooney had produced the recent operas'. He felt it was better to engage another producer. Flood confirmed that 'he personally had to instruct several of the principals as to the correct manner and method in which their lines should be delivered'. He felt that Mr Mooney 'had left himself short of time which caused him to be so uncertain and changeable in his methods'.[34] In the end Mooney was actually offered a contract on similar terms to that of November 1940. But when he sought an increase in payment the three operas were parcelled out between Flood, Healy (after numerous heavy hints on his part) and Eileen Clancy.[35]

In addition to its many other difficulties the R&R also faced competition for access to the Savoy operas. Failure to arrange for a G&S production in either the society's spring or autumn season

Eileen Clancy and A.E. Glynn, *Patience*, 1941.

jeopardised the long-standing arrangement between the R&R and Rupert D'Oyly Carte, which had previously given the R&R a virtual monopoly on the production of Savoy operas. In the late 1930s and early 1940s, one the society's main Dublin city rivals, the (Old) Belvedere Musical Society, referred to condescendingly at one committee meeting as 'the Belvedere people', had managed to obtain permission from D'Oyly Carte to stage some G&S productions. A 1940 Belvedere production of *Iolanthe* at the Jesuit Hall in Milltown had featured a young Ethna Barror (Ethna Graham at the time – she married Cecil Barror in 1942) in the part of the Queen of the Fairies. The previous year she had been understudy to Mabel Home in the R&R productions of *Patience* and *H.M.S. Pinafore*.[36]

However, Rupert D'Oyly Carte intimated in December 1940, much to the satisfaction of the R&R, that he was not prepared to licence two amateur companies for performances in Dublin within the same musical season.[37] When, in late 1941, the society felt confident enough to deviate from its 'G&S only' policy, and contemplate an ambitious production of the sumptuous Strauss-inspired *Waltzes from Vienna* the following spring, there was some conservative opposition to this *démarche*. The proposal was to 'give Gilbert and Sullivan a rest'. A.E. Glynn, a founder member of the society – who played Reginald Bunthorne in the 1941 production of *Patience* – counselled caution. He suggested the R&R should first ascertain Carte's reaction to this temporary cessation of its Gilbertian activity and should also 'ask Mr Carte to still allow the society to be their representatives in Dublin'.[38] Was Carte prepared to allow the R&R to have his cake and not eat it?

Carte was duly approached and his response was neutral. No undertaking could be given that permission would be withheld from any other society from presenting Gilbert and Sullivan. But no permit would be given in spring 1942 to any other society if the R&R sought a licence. Prudence won out on this occasion and the society divided its forces. *Waltzes from Vienna* was staged in May 1942 with the experienced Dublin producer Stanley Illsley at the helm and Ernest Broadhurst, conductor of the Gaiety Orchestra, wielding the baton. It was an elaborate project, requiring a hugely augmented orchestra, achieved with the assistance of the Royal Irish Academy of Music. But the previous month, as a hedge against an uncooperative Carte, Weaving had conducted revivals of *The Mikado* and *The Gondoliers* and a Healy-produced *Iolanthe*. As it transpired the Strauss piece proved to be so popular that it was, almost unprecedentedly for an amateur company, retained at the Gaiety for a second week.[39]

R&R Committee, 1942. Back: A.E. Glynn, J.H. Hutchinson, J.J. Bouch, Eileen Knowles, P.J. Henry, Michael McGreal. Front: Arthur V. Healy, Hilda White, P.L. Forde, Mida O'Brien, F.J. Holland.

STRAUSS, THE SPY AND THE SOLICITOR'S LETTER

The story behind how the R&R broke out of its own wartime siege mentality with *Waltzes from Vienna* revolves around the frustrating search for a producer. This involved a threatened lawsuit and an assignation with a future British poet laureate.

Conscious of the logistical difficulties that a return to musical comedy would present, the society was intent on procuring the services of the best possible producer. Hilton Edwards, partner of Micheál Mac Liammóir in the Gate Theatre, was the first to be approached.[40] Though describing himself as 'flattered' by the offer, he politely declined. Unsure that any other director of sufficient experience and *chutzpah* could be found in Ireland the R&R went back to London and secured agreement from the West End veteran Ed Royce to take on the show. Once again, however, the problem emerged of securing an exit visa along with a producer. After making his own enquiries in England, Royce had to inform the society in February that he had been unable to obtain the required permit to travel to Ireland.

Determined to get their man, Forde and Healy sought and secured a meeting with the UK Trade Commission assistant secretary J.D. Craig, with a view to charming him into making a recommendation that Royce be permitted to travel. Accompanying Craig at the meeting was a certain John Betjeman,[41] future poet laureate of England and, officially, press attaché at the Embassy since 1941. However, Betjeman was also close enough to the British intelligence community in Ireland to have been put on an IRA death list.[42] He was, apparently, removed from the list because, as IRA head of civilian intelligence Diarmuid Brennan wrote to him after the war, 'I came to the conclusion that a man who could give such pleasure with his pen couldn't be much of a secret agent. I may well be wrong.'[43] Quite what Betjeman hoped to glean by rubbing shoulders with the chairman and the honorary secretary of the Rathmines and Rathgar Musical Society is not known. Neither Paddy Forde nor Arthur Healy

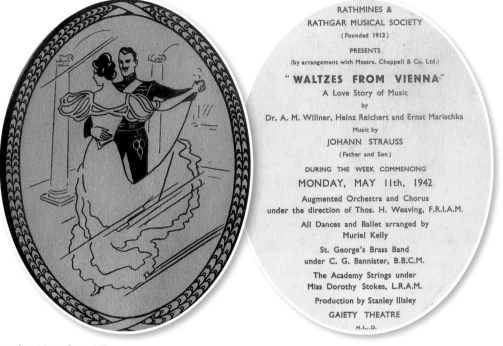

Waltzes from Vienna flyer, 1942.

were thought to have had any dealings with subversives, outside of a few spats with the Old Belvedere Musical Society (see below). It is highly likely that Betjeman took the opportunity, while based in Ireland, to attend the society's Gaiety productions. He was a fan of Gilbert and Sullivan. In 1975 he wrote the foreword for the Caryl Brahms book *Lost Chords and Discords*, an account of the relationship between the two composers. His poetry, heavily laced with wit, was probably influenced by the great Victorian satirist. The crusty Gilbert would, almost certainly, have empathised with Betjeman's desire to see bombs rain down on the ugly and increasingly industrialised town of Slough, immortalised by Betjeman in the poem of that name.[44]

Betjeman and Craig were sufficiently impressed by the case made by Forde and Healy to recommend that Royce be allowed to travel to Dublin. The approval, however, was not rubber-stamped in London and the R&R remained Royce-less. The search continued. Former R&R stalwart Ria Mooney was approached but her reply 'was not altogether satisfactory'.[45] When Lionel Cranfield became aware that the situation was vacant he immediately applied. This was evidence of a rather schizophrenic attitude on the part of Cranfield to the R&R. Only a few weeks previously he had been asked to contribute a photograph for a thirtieth anniversary almanac, then being compiled. His response had been to curtly decline, adding his wish, 'if mention of [my] name be made, that it should be done in the minutest manner'.[46]

The society passed on Cranfield and instead opted for an accomplished drama producer who had the advantage of not being required to seek an exit visa from the UK. Stanley Illsley was an actor/ director of some note. In his later years (he died in 1992) he was well known to TV viewers as Colonel Waterson in the long-running ITV soap *Crossroads* and Sir Valentine Knox in the 1980s TV adaptation

Waltzes from Vienna: Mabel Home, A.E. (Mack) Glynn, Maria Viani and Robert McCullagh, 1942.

of Somerville and Ross's *The Irish R.M.* In the spring of 1942 a rather sulky and unhappy Illsley was touring the country with Anew McMaster's company. He badly wanted to be elsewhere and leaped at the chance when approached by the R&R. He met members of the committee at the end of March and intimated that although he had never tackled musical comedy before he felt confident that he could do the job. He also informed them – and this was probably something of a white lie – that he was ready to start shortly as he had given Anew McMaster his notice because the current tour was 'uncongenial and unsatisfactory to him'.[47] He accepted a fee of £30 for five weeks' work (he was eventually paid £50 when the run was extended).

Illsley's engagement was rapidly followed by a solicitor's letter from a firm representing McMaster. The Great Man was threatening to sue the R&R 'for inducing Stanley Illsley to leave the McMaster company'. The intervention of a society member, Roderick J. Tierney, a lawyer in private life and a future honorary secretary,[48] smoothed things over and the threat was withdrawn. This was probably just as well as *Waltzes from Vienna*, despite being a critical and popular success, was not as lucrative for the R&R as it was for the Gaiety. It was an expensive production to stage. The hiring of a choreographer and, in effect, an extra orchestra, meant that the society made a profit of a paltry £3.6s.0d from the first week and £55 from the second.

Roderick Tierney.

The following year, 1943, was marked by the arrival (however brief) of a neophyte dramatic genius and the sad demise of a great and much-admired servant of the society.

The name John MacGowran appears on the programme of the spring production that year, *The Student Prince*. He played the part of Nicholas in the Romberg romp, and would have contributed to the famous 'Drinking Song' in the show, which premiered on Broadway in 1924. He is, of course, better known as the late Jack MacGowran, one of the foremost interpreters of the work of Samuel Beckett. From the wordiness of Gilbert to the sparseness of Beckett was quite a journey for the young actor. He did not get much of a chance to impress in the minor role of Nicholas, although he could be said to have shared in the accolade from the *Irish Independent* review, which declared that 'the smaller parts are all efficiently filled'.[49] MacGowran later remembered his time with the R&R as 'some of the happiest years of my life…I haven't worked with any professional company here or in England or America whose standards were higher, nor one with more integrity'.[50]

MacGowran had also appeared in the G&S show *Utopia Limited* the previous year when he would have been forgiven for having failed to notice one of the young pages. His name was David Kelly and he was 12 years old at the time. He had been recruited for the role by one of his teachers in C.B.S. Synge Street: Micheal McGreal, an R&R committee member. Kelly went on from those humble beginnings to

The Student Prince flyer.

The Student Prince: Denis Roe and Jack MacGowran, 1943.

forge a long and distinguished career as an actor, his most memorable performance probably being as 'Rashers' Tierney in RTÉ's adaptation of James Plunkett's *Strumpet City*, although there are those who prefer his interpretation of the cowboy builder O'Reilly in one of the episodes of *Fawlty Towers*. In a conversation with Pat Campbell in 2010, not long before his death, Kelly 'cursed' the R&R for introducing him to acting.[51]

The major loss in 1943 was of the society's president, Dr William Lombard Murphy, M.A., M.D., son of the R&R's first president William Martin Murphy and himself chairman of *Independent* newspapers. He died at the family home in Dartry on 9 January. In a medical context Murphy had been an ENT (ear, nose and throat) specialist. He was also a Great War veteran, having served in the Army Medical Service in Salonika, with the rank of Captain. While seconded to the French army he had won a Croix de Guerre and the Legion of Honour. On the death of his father, in 1919, he had abandoned the practice of medicine and taken control of the many businesses owned by Murphy Senior. Unlike his predecessor, Sir Stanley Cochrane, Murphy rarely missed an R&R AGM and was a huge supporter of the society in a variety of ways. Maintaining the link with the Murphy family, he was succeeded as president by his sister Eva. She would hold the office until 1958 when she was succeeded by Michael J. Campbell of New Ireland Assurance.

Two years later, the society was to lose another invaluable servant – J.J. Bouch. Joe Bouch, a 'tall and portly figure'[52] was an assistant librarian at the National Library. He had been Weaving's deputy for almost three decades. In addition to his musical interests Bouch, in his professional capacity, had spent many years researching the 1916 Proclamation. He had managed to establish that the original document had been written by Patrick Pearse, with amendments from James Connolly and Thomas MacDonagh. It had then been printed at Liberty Hall on Easter Sunday (23 April 1916) by three working printers under the protection of the Irish Citizen Army.

Michael Campbell, president (1953–1980).

Bouch married late in life, in 1940, after meeting a young American, Elizabeth Clark, on a bus tour of Switzerland in 1938. They had parted company at the end of the tour but Bouch, in a supremely romantic gesture, had intercepted her during a stopover in Cobh of her transatlantic return voyage. The following year he visited her in New York and proposed. She accepted. Their nuptials might well have been put on hold, due to the intervention of Adolf Hitler, had there not been a counter-intervention by the Irish consul in New York – Leo McAuley. He offered Elizabeth a timely visa to travel to Europe. But her route to J.J. Bouch was circuitous in the extreme. She landed in southern Europe, made her way to Free France and from there to Calais and on to Ireland. The couple had three children before J.J. Bouch died after a period of illness, in April 1945. A few years after his death Elizabeth Bouch returned to the USA with their three children, Brendan, Kevin and Barbara. She died there on 17 February 2013 at the age of 102!

Bouch had conducted in his own right on only one occasion, the November 1941 production of *Princess Ida* with Eileen Clancy in the title role. A few weeks before his death a testimonial variety concert had taken place in his honour at the Gaiety, in which the R&R had presented *Trial by Jury* with Weaving conducting the show as a gesture of esteem towards his long-time colleague.

Flyers from the
1940s.

Louis Elliman.

100 – NOT OUT!

In the winter of 1945 the world celebrated the end of a second global war and segued effortlessly into an ideological conflict that continued for forty-four years. The R&R, now a survivor of two world wars, celebrated a further landmark, its 100th production. Negotiations with Louis Elliman,[53] who along with Patrick Wall had acquired the Gaiety in 1936, had been left to Hilda White. She persuaded the theatre impresarios to agree to the staging of three shows over a ten-day period that November: *The Gondoliers*, *Patience* and *Ruddigore*. Elliman was unconvinced about the popularity and box-office potential of *Ruddigore*. In its original incarnation it had not proven spectacularly successful for the D'Oyly Carte either, but was not helped by being the follow-up to the triumphant *Mikado*.

However, rather than bury it on unfashionable nights Elliman counselled the opposite course of action. He suggested that the status of the opera should be enhanced by a public relations campaign, and that it should open the season. This meant that it was *Ruddigore* that would bring up a 'century – not out' for the Rathmines and Rathgar Musical Society. The committee went along with Elliman's suggestion to the point where the premiere was followed by a brief talk by the actor and Gaiety manager, Hamlyn Benson, who (prompted by the R&R) claimed that *Ruddigore* had only been reintroduced to the D'Oyly Carte repertoire 'because of the success attending the R&R's revival of it in 1917'.[54] *The Irish Times* review suggested that 'the occasion was obviously a little too trying, but the faults were very slight'. Roderick Tierney as Sir Ruthven Murgatroyd, Joseph Flood as Dick Dauntless, Hilda White as Rose Maybud and Eileen Furlong as Dame Hannah, were singled out by the newspaper. The latter had, of course, been involved in the very first R&R production in 1913.

As Quidnunc – Patrick Campbell, 3rd Baron Glenavy – of *The Irish Times* observed, 'if all the nights on which the society has played were put together, they would amount to a year and a quarter'. He also totted up the running score for each G&S opera and came up with 'twelve Mikados, nine Gondoliers, eight Yeomen, eight Iolanthes, four Pirates, four Trials by Jury, three Ruddigores, three Utopias, two Sorcerers, five helpings of Patience, two of Princess Ida, a couple of Cox and Box, and thirty-three musical comedies'.[55]

'THE BELVEDERE PEOPLE' AND THE DOGS

Despite its financial travails in the 1930s the R&R never lacked for self-regard. It considered itself, justifiably, to be *primus inter pares* when it came to the amateur musical and dramatic scene in pre- and post-war Dublin. At the 1946 AGM, then honorary secretary Roderick Tierney referred to the society's 'pre-eminent position in the world of light musical entertainment in this country'.[56]

Among its rivals, in different contexts, were the aforementioned Old Belvedere Musical Society[57] and the Dublin Grand Opera Society – both fellow members of the British-based National Operatic and Dramatic Association. (The only other Irish member in the 1940s was the Bank of Ireland Musical and Dramatic Society.)[58] Both provided stiff competition for worthwhile dates in the Gaiety calendar. 'The Belvedere people' (as mentioned earlier) also threatened at various times to move in on the Gilbert and Sullivan *oeuvre* and carve out a niche for themselves in that area. The R&R resisted and the D'Oyly Carte family remained loyal to the Dublin company that had performed Savoy operas since 1913. The Dublin Grand Opera Society or DGOS (unkindly but inevitably dubbed the DOGS) also had to be constantly watched as it attempted to siphon off some of the R&R's tenor and soprano principals into grand opera.

Both Belvedere and the DGOS were also in competition with the R&R, as all three effectively operated on a city-wide basis, for both chorus members and principals.[59] In 1943 the R&R, not for the first or last time, was forced to advertise in the daily newspapers because of a 'shortage of gentlemen in the chorus'.[60] This was an enduring phenomenon. In 1959 the society reported, in common with most other Dublin musical groups, a severe shortage of tenors. An unnamed R&R 'official' told *The Irish Times:* 'We are always short of tenors. So is everybody else. When we find a good one we treasure him. It just happens that in this country the tenor is the odd man out. There are lots of baritones – but never enough tenors.'[61]

The society also jealously guarded its relationship with the Gaiety Theatre – this, as we have already seen, waxed and waned over the years. Like a problematic marriage, on occasion the spouses were barely on speaking terms. At other times they would bill and coo like turtle doves. In 1941, for example, the R&R was asked by Louis Elliman, to contribute players to a review called *Hullabaloo* at the Theatre Royal. Although the committee expressed the opinion that the society had nothing to gain from such a venture, it was agreed to give Elliman what he wanted. When the sides were on terms of affection the Gaiety would be closely consulted as to the choice of productions. As in the case of George W. Bush and Tony Blair, a 'special relationship' was often deemed to exist between the two. Then Elliman would casually reinvent the relationship, as he did, for example, in the autumn of 1942.

Elliman made it known that year to his amateur clients that he had five dates available between 5 October and 13 December. Some were succulent plums, others were barely serviceable damsons. Rather than, as the R&R would have expected, offering them the juiciest fruit Elliman showed his relative indifference to the feelings of the society by proposing that the dates be put into a hat and lots drawn. The R&R was not keen on programming by lottery. It was particularly disappointed with the arrangement in light of its spring successes of that year and because the society had 'lent' a number of members to the theatre for a production of *The Beggar's Opera* in July 1942.[62] But Elliman was not given to unbusinesslike sentimentality. Ironically, within a few months, when the DGOS and the Belvedere society both cancelled their spring 1943 runs he was forced to go cap in hand to the R&R and ask them to extend their season. The society proved more obliging than the impresario on that occasion and filled three weeks.

At various times in the 1940s the Dublin Grand Opera Society would behave like medieval chieftains and 'raid' into the territory of the R&R. Their object was not to steal cattle but to 'borrow' some of the society's more talented performers, especially those who were, in effect, semi-professional and being compensated by the R&R for loss of earnings elsewhere.

The response of the R&R was to adopt the approach of a lioness defending her cubs from jackals. In 1941 and 1942 Arthur Healy reacted to two such incursions much as Alex Ferguson might have to the news that one of his players was being 'tapped up'. In the first instance the DGOS approached R&R regular Robert McCullagh, a semi-professional performer, enquiring about his availability the following spring. Healy harrumphed that 'a little more courtesy and etiquette could have been displayed'.[63] That was mild in comparison to his reaction the following year when the DGOS came back for more, in the shape of an approach to the equally valued Joseph Flood. He was offered a small part in another spring production. On this occasion Healy positively fumed. He insisted that 'a letter of protest should be forwarded to the Hon Sec of the DGOS'.[64] Whether Healy had any particular right to be so territorial is a moot point. Flood had been remunerated for his services by the R&R for some time and had not been a paid up member of the society since 1939.[65]

At around the same time an invitation had arrived from the DGOS asking the society to participate in a production of Handel's *Messiah*. Healy was instructed to reply that the R&R had too many commitments to enable it to take part.[66] This is not to say that the amateur musical scene in Dublin in the 1940s and 1950s was a nest of vipers. There was co-operation between the R&R and many of its rivals. Costumes and sets were exchanged, many performers divided their loyalties without causing consternation or rancour and, on occasion, theatre dates were exchanged if one or other society found itself in some difficulty.[67]

· ·

COMPENSATING THE WANDERING MINSTREL

Of perhaps greater import to the R&R than the machinations of Churchill, Hitler and Stalin between 1939–45 was its attempt to secure the loyalty of a promising young performer. Robert McCullagh was a rising star on the Dublin music scene. He had been performing with the society spasmodically from 1927, and once spurned an offer from the D'Oyly Carte Company to join Sam Mooney in its ranks. In September 1939 the committee, aware of his capabilities and seeking a male tenor lead for forthcoming productions of *Patience* and *H.M.S. Pinafore* (*Pinafore* would be eventually be replaced by *The Gondoliers*) mooted the casting of McCullagh. In doing so the officers accepted that his status meant he would

Patience, 1948: Eamonn Beale, J. McCutcheon, Ken Smith and George Coleman.

have to be offered compensation for being forced to miss out on other professional engagements. It was agreed to approach him with an offer of six or seven guineas at a time when the payment of principals was becoming a matter of some controversy within the society.[68] McCullagh demurred, on the basis that 'he would feel embarrassed as a result of comments made at a society meeting on recompensing artists'.[69] Assuming that this was simply a ploy to raise his price the committee came back with an enhanced offer of twelve guineas. McCullagh's final word on that occasion was a renewed refusal, this time on the grounds of 'the demands made upon his spare time by his employers the G.M.R.'.

It was May 1940 before McCullagh would make his return to a society he would grace for decades to come. He took the part of John James Cox in *Cox and Box*. He was 'requisitioned' (in the words of the minutes for 4 March 1940) on the basis that he would be paid £10. In addition to his *Cox and Box* role he also played Alexis in *The Sorcerer*. In 1941 he was paid the same amount for appearing as Jack Point in *The Yeomen of the Guard* and Marco in *The Gondoliers* in the spring season at the Gaiety, and for appearing as Cyril in the seldom-produced *Princess Ida* in October. Misgivings about the latter payment were raised in November by comic lead Paddy Henry (Pooh-Bah in the 1941 *Mikado* and Wilfred Shadbolt in the April 1941 *Yeomen*). In response Forde justified the payment, venturing the opinion that the sum involved did not compensate McCullagh for the work he lost by devoting himself exclusively to the R&R. Forde remarked that 'Mr McCullagh was the greatest asset to his fellow artists and supported them beyond measure'. Others concurred. Henry found himself in a minority of one, and there the matter rested, for the time being at least.[70]

But McCullagh was not the only R&R principal who appeared in productions and was compensated for so doing. Staging, by and large, at least two shows a season put considerable pressure on the personnel resources of the R&R. Every spring and winter at least two accomplished tenors, sopranos, basses and baritones had to be found to assume leading parts. Complementing the excellence of McCullagh for many years (and also acquitting himself well as a producer) was Joseph Flood, a quintessential Marco in *The Gondoliers* or Nanki-Poo in *The Mikado*. His first appearance in a leading role had been in *A Waltz Dream* in 1931.

The first official reference to any proposal to pay Flood was not until 1940. It was pointed out at a committee meeting that he had missed an engagement worth two guineas, because of a rehearsal. The feeling of the meeting was that 'it would be a dangerous precedent to recompense all and sundry who lost engagements such as the one mentioned'. However, as Flood was being given a wedding present by the society it was decided simply to add two guineas to the value of the gift.[71]

Both Flood and McCullagh appeared in the elaborately staged *Waltzes from Vienna* in May 1942. At the AGM the following month questions were asked about payments to some of the artists involved in that show. One member outlined to the meeting how he had spent two days auditing the accounts 'and one thing that struck him forcibly was the number of payments made for services rendered. The practice seemed to be on the increase and it was clear to him that the day was coming when a halt would have to be made if the society was to continue on an amateur basis.'[72] In his defence Healy pointed out that, under Rule 12 of the society's regulations, it was permissible to make payments to performers.

In the wake of the row with the DGOS (mentioned earlier) Paddy Henry was asked, in January 1943, to approach Flood and to ascertain whether he wished to be viewed as a professional or as a society member.[73] He reported the following month that 'Mr Flood's position was that he was in the musical market to get what recompense he could and that was his reason for accepting parts from the DGOS.' His services would come on a professional fee-paying basis.[74] Further discussion followed on the casting of *The Student Prince* for the following May. Richard Midgley,[75] who would play Detlef in that production, asked the perennial question, why casting had not taken place from among the society's members. In essence he was enquiring as to why Robert McCullagh had been cast in the lead role of Prince Carl Franz. The response from Healy was that 'it was usual to recompense Mr McCullagh for loss of engagements' and that the casting committee had said he was the only person suitable for the part.

It was at around this time that one of the stalwarts of the society, Mabel Home, who had made her first appearance as The Lady Sophy in *Utopia Limited* in 1918, expressed serious misgivings about the policy of paying performers. Wife of the long-time vice president, Dr George Hewson, Home's appearances had become more episodic since her appearance as Countess Olga Baranskaja in *Waltzes from Vienna*. She had not appeared in the winter Gilbert and Sullivan season, and had only returned in the spring of 1943 to play Augusta in *Wild Violets* after having first threatened to throw in her lot with a Dublin Musical Society production at the Gaiety instead.[76] In November of that year she reprised the role of Katisha in *The Mikado* for the seventh and final time.[77] It was to be her last appearance onstage with the R&R.

After a gap of almost two years a decision was taken, in light of her twenty-five-year career with the society, to admit Home as an honorary member. This was a clear attempt to entice her back. Home's response was far from positive. She spoke to Roderick Tierney and advised him that, as far as she was concerned, her membership of the R&R had lapsed and 'she again said she would refuse to play in any society show in which any payment was made to a playing member'.[78] Further efforts were made to persuade her to take the part of The Lady Jane in the November 1945 production of *Patience*. Initially she agreed to play if no other playing members were paid, but then changed her mind and began to query payments to producers associated with the society: Joseph Flood and Eileen Clancy, both of whom accepted payment, were at the helm of the winter 1945 productions. Hilda White, who had been involved in negotiations with Home, handed the matter over to Tierney who reported, in early October, barely five weeks before production, that 'it was evident that she was not anxious to play for the society'.[79]

Mabel Home's stand had no marked effect on the R&R policy of paying modest sums to performers where it was deemed essential to maintain standards. In 1945 she threw in her lot with Stanley Illsley in the Illsley-McCabe Company, which was based mainly at the Olympia, but also undertook Irish tours of West End plays. It was while involved in one such tour, playing at the time in the Cork Opera House, that Mabel Home, still a young woman in her early fifties, was suddenly taken ill and died of a heart attack on 23 September 1949. Her daughter, Heather, was a teenager at the time.

Two years after the stand taken by Home, Eileen Clancy stood her ground when it came to casting the part of Rosalinda von Eisenstein in the spring 1947 production of *Gay Rosalinda*. The part was to have gone to the recently married Maureen Harold who, somewhat belatedly (late February), indicated her unavailability. In her absence Eileen Clancy had been reading the part at rehearsals. When she heard that the committee was contemplating importing either Kyra Vane or Marion Davies, two West End

Iolanthe cartoons: Robert Midgley, A.E. Glynn and Jack O'Connor, 1947.

performers, at a cost of £20–£25 plus expenses, she issued an ultimatum. Demanding to be considered for the part she also stated that she would contemplate resigning if the part was not cast from within the society. After consulting the producer, Ivor Hughes, the casting committee gave Clancy the part.

Subsequently the device of issuing gift vouchers was used to make the payments appear less blatant. Robert McCullagh and Sam Mooney were, for example, given £10 gift tokens for their work during the autumn seasons of 1946 and 1947 while Joseph Flood was refused compensation for engagements missed in November 1947.[80] The issue of payment never quite went away but it was rarely discussed overtly at committee meetings over the following decade. One exception was a response in December 1959 to a request from Jack O'Connor, who performed with the society from 1940–73, for compensation of £7 due to the loss of professional earnings during the production of *Iolanthe* that autumn. In this instance it was decided that 'to accede to the request would be wrong in principle'.[81]

BREAKING GROUND

As well as keeping the flag flying on board the good ship G&S in Ireland, the society also brought banner musical shows to Dublin at a time when few London companies would undertake such a commercial risk. The 1947 staging of *Gay Rosalinda* was just such a venture. The adaptation of Strauss's *Die Fledermaus* by Max Reinhardt and E.W. Korngold had opened in London in March 1945 at the Palace Theatre. The Gaiety production was the Irish premiere and the first staging anywhere by an amateur company. Despite the feeling that the war had brought about an improvement in local production standards because of the difficulty in importing producers, the R&R imported Ivor Hughes (who had been associated with the Palace Theatre run) from London in order to direct. Terry O'Connor, whose previous experience had been as musical director of the Dublin Musical Society, was recruited to conduct in the absence of Weaving. She began her long association with the R&R by seeking an augmented orchestra. Players were added, some non-union, bringing the numbers up to eighteen. This sparked a row with the unionised Gaiety Orchestra and the threat of industrial action. The situation was smoothed over by Hamlyn Benson and the show went ahead.

The Irish Times described *Gay Rosalinda* as having been 'handled with that polished slickness which one has come to expect from the R&R'. The reviewer was particularly impressed with Eileen Clancy in the title role, describing her as a 'consummate actress'.[82] The total receipts for the week amounted to £1,134, involving a net loss of £4 for the R&R because of the punitive royalty deal insisted on by the publishers. The loss was deemed to have been well worth the kudos the production brought.

But while the small deficit could be written off as a valuable loss leader, it highlighted what would become a growing difficulty in the years ahead: that of covering the cost of increasingly elaborate and expensive musical comedy productions in an age when audience expectations were growing. At a meeting of Irish-based members with the executives of the British and Irish umbrella body for amateur companies, the National Operatic and Dramatic Association (NODA), it had been pointed out that, post-war, Ireland would once again be included on the itineraries of visiting professional companies from the West End. Realistically that was the standard to which Irish companies playing at the Gaiety had to aspire. However, in the 1940s and 1950s that aspiration became much more difficult to achieve. In fact it was only a sharp increase in admission prices imposed by the Gaiety in 1948 that made some of the more adventurous musicals viable. The R&R production that year of *The Student Prince* played to 81 per cent capacity at the Gaiety for a week. In his report to the annual general meeting that year, the honorary secretary A.E. Glynn pointed out that, although the society had made a profit of £34 on the venture, under the old pricing system, it would have lost £133. He welcomed the price increase saying '[it] has come just in time, as with the mounting cost of almost every item of expenditure we were rapidly approaching the time when it would be out of the question to attempt spectacular expensive operas with the faintest hope of paying our way after a week's run'.[83]

. . . .

THE CHANGING OF THE GUARD

Although the world of the amateur stage is more forgiving and less ruthless than its professional counterpart – there is not so much at stake for a start – even amateur companies go through periods of renewal and re-invention. The lyric tenor principal in his twenties or thirties becomes surplus to requirements when he is scraping fifty and is unable to carry off a convincing 'comb-over' or prevent the inevitable paunch from bursting its banks as he woos the soprano heroine. While the vocal chords might be as sweet and efficient as ever, gravity and *anno domini* have exacted a terrible toll which no casting committee or producer can ignore. What goes for tenors is true also for sopranos, and, though perhaps not as starkly, for basses, baritones and contraltos. Alfred, Lord Tennyson had other things on his mind when he wrote that 'the old order changeth, yielding place to new/and God [aka the producer] fulfils himself in many ways'. But he might just as well have been writing about a musical society in transition as the death of King Arthur.

As the grey early 1950s – at least from an Irish point of view – progressed towards the partial eclipse of Frank Sinatra and the big band sound by the raucous emergence of the gyrational pelvis of Elvis Presley, the R&R was doing what all societies of their ilk inevitably do, discovering fresh talent and

Executive committee, Gresham Hotel, 1950: Back: Clem Ryan, Christy Merry, Joan Burke, Ken Smith, Pat Campbell, Eileen Clancy, Chris Bruton, Joe Bowden. *Front:* Kitty Forde, Eileen Furlong, P.L. Forde, Paddy Delany, Mida O'Brien.

discarding 'old reliables'. By the end of the decade the R&R was the only amateur society – other than the DGOS, whose principals by now were largely paid imports – still allocated two seasons at the Gaiety Theatre.[84] Continuation of that arrangement was, however, at the discretion of Louis Elliman and required a disciplined maintenance of standards at all levels. The amateurs of the R&R were required to be thoroughly professional and provide the Gaiety with consistent and satisfactory box-office returns or risk going the way of other, less successful, companies.

The R&R was only as good as its next outing, so standards had to be maintained. In the early 1950s the practice, for example, of availing of the services of 'inhouse' producers for Gilbert and Sullivan seasons (like Joe Flood, Eileen Clancy and Mida O'Brien) was temporarily discontinued in favour of a D'Oyly Carte producer Anna Bethell (see below). The context was the fear that standards were slipping and that some D'Oyly Carte discipline and stagecraft needed to be injected into the troupe.

All of which meant that new faces took over familiar roles. Heather Hewson, daughter of Mabel Home, took over the role of Katisha and other parts in the G&S repertoire from Eileen Furlong. Furlong, who originated the role for the society in 1913, played it for the last time on the occasion of the society's fortieth anniversary in 1952. As she told *The Irish Times*, 'when I first played the part they used to have to pad me with cushions; they don't bother now'.[85]

Louise Studley first appeared in *The Dancing Years* (1951) where she 'scored a big success'[86] according to the *Irish Independent* music critic Joseph O'Neill – a former R&R member – before playing the female lead, Josephine, in *H.M.S. Pinafore*

Heather Hewson.

(1951). There her performance was described as 'polished'[87] by *The Irish Times*. She went on to play the title role in *Princess Ida* (1952). In so doing she placed herself in the line of succession to 'leading ladies' of the past like Eileen Clancy, Maria Viani and Maureen Harold. Studley would become a regular on musical stages all over the country in the years that followed, often being imported to play the lead in productions alongside the likes of Austin Gaffney. She played principal parts for the Dublin Musical Society before it went out of existence.[88] Her value to the R&R was apparent. When, for example, it was clear that she was available to play the part of Anna in the production of *The Merry Widow* in 1959, the committee took the unusual step of immediately casting her in the role. Normally roles were apportioned by the 'caste [*sic*] committee'. The show proved highly successful and relatively lucrative at a time when the society was in financial difficulties.

Eileen Furlong signing the Roll of Honour Life Members with P.A. Delany and C.P. Ryan, 1953.

In its review of her performance the *Irish Independent* described her 'vivid and convincing characterisation'.[89] She reprised the part in 1961. Studley also played a small part in the 1955 Hollywood film *Captain Lightfoot*, shot in Ireland and starring Rock Hudson as an Irish rebel turned highwayman. This did not lead to a burgeoning celluloid career; her only other listed film credit was in *The Real Charlotte*, released in 1990. She resisted the notion of a film career, describing herself as a 'homebird'. She also declined a contract with the D'Oyly Carte in 1952.[90] Studley continued to play lead roles for the R&R into the 1970s, largely because she declined to make singing a full-time career. As she told *The Irish Press* in 1966, she never felt she had the temperament for it: 'I get so worked up and worried about every part I play.'[91]

The Merry Widow: Louise Studley.

Hazel Yeomans, whose day job was with the CIÉ Information Bureau, was slightly later on the scene than Studley, first appearing in *Show Boat* in 1955 as Ellie, an actress on the most famous vessel never to have plied its trade on the Mississippi. Although only 24 years old at the time, she did not lack for experience: she made her first stage appearance at the age of 3 and her first film at the age of 11.[92] In 1956 she was starring in the title role of the crack-shot Annie Oakley in Irving Berlin's *Annie Get Your Gun*. The demands of the part, according to *The Irish Times* at least, led to her taking sharp-shooting lessons with the army.[93]

Her first part in a Savoy production was as Phoebe in *The Yeomen of the Guard* in November 1956. She followed that up with 'excellent work'[94] as the flirtatious Ado Annie in Rodgers and Hammerstein's *Oklahoma!* the following spring. One of her final appearances for the R&R was as Grete in the 1960 production of Ivor Novello's *The Dancing Years*.[95] Yeomans played for a number of societies and also worked with Milo O'Shea in the Gate and in the Gaiety.[96] In 1963 she played alongside O'Shea

Hazel Yeomans.

and Ray McAnally in the Irish-composed musical *Carrie* by Wesley Burrowes and Michael Coffey at the Olympia Theatre. In the mid-1960s Yeomans moved to the UK and performed under the stage name Lisa Shane. In 1966 she was understudying for Barbra Streisand in *Funny Girl* in the Prince of Wales Theatre in London when, on 28 April, the star was stricken with gastric flu. Yeomans was told she would play the part that night and was forced to sit in her dressing room while a noisy 'lynch mob' stormed the box-office and demanded their money back. Her onstage reception was not much better until one of the more gallant male members of the audience – 80 per cent of whom had remained in their seats for the performance – yelled out 'give the girl a chance'. Her rendition of the show-stopper 'People' finally won the crowd around and, at the end of the show, she took five curtain calls. La Streisand sent flowers, and hurried back.

The enduring comic diva of the R&R's 'middle years' was undoubtedly Heather Hewson, an employee of the Guinness brewery and an accomplished pianist. Daughter of Mabel Home and Dr George Hewson (Professor of Music at Trinity College), she was brought into the society by Victor Leeson, himself a virtuoso in the 'Henry Lytton' Savoy parts and founder of the St James's Gate Musical Society. Over more than a quarter of a century she played virtually all the so-called 'Bertha Lewis' or 'female heavy' D'Oyly Carte roles – often opposite Leeson, Alf Branagan or Pat Campbell – in a career that properly began with a small part in Act 2 of Ivor Novello's *Perchance to Dream* in 1954. This show was directed by the Australian producer Freddie Carpenter, and his ever-present dog 'Ruggles of Red Gap'.[97] On that occasion she played alongside Louise Studley, Jack O'Connor and Eileen Clancy. Her first G&S role was as Inez in *The Gondoliers* in 1955. By 1959 she had risen up the ranks of the aristocracy and was playing the Duchess of Plaza-Toro, a market she cornered until 1967. Her

Heather Hewson and Victor Leeson in *The Gondoliers*.

near-monopoly of the role of Katisha for a decade and a half, following in the footsteps of her mother, has already been noted. In an interview with Mary McGoris of *The Irish Times* for the seventy-fifth anniversary publication, she memorably described herself as 'the seventh Katisha of a seventh Katisha'.

In addition to male stalwarts like Chris Bruton,[98] Paddy Henry,[99] Fintan Corish,[100] Jack O'Connor (1940–73), Roderick Tierney (fifty productions), Maurice O'Sullivan (over forty productions), Pat Campbell (over forty years) and Victor Leeson, who between them racked up nearly 500 shows, there were a number of distinguished male leads who, for a variety of reasons, passed through the society rather more rapidly. Liam Devally played Ralph Rackstraw in *H.M.S. Pinafore* in 1957 and speedily migrated to Radio Éireann where he presented music programmes for a number of years (including the Eurovision song contest on radio, 1972–9). His 1963 turn

Kismet, 1963. Fintan Corish and Kay Condron.

as Nanki-Poo in *The Mikado* drew the praise of the often testy *Irish Times* critic Charles Acton. Acton wrote: 'Liam Devally is a much better singer than most Nanki-Poos and a better actor than most tenors.'[101] Later he became a barrister and a Circuit Court judge.

Limerick-born Patrick Ring who went on to a distinguished career as a classical tenor, played Nanki-Poo in the 1957 *Mikado*. *The Irish Press* was highly complimentary about his voice but observed, with a sting in the tail, that 'he should endeavour in his acting to acquire significant gestures and facial expressions'.[102] Many of the regular principals, like McCullagh and Flood in earlier times, did not confine themselves to performing with the R&R. Jack O'Connor, for example, went straight from *Bless the Bride* in 1954 to another Gaiety production of the Dublin Musical Society, *Blossom Time*, where he shared top billing with Louise Studley.[103] Despite the occasional rearguard action of the R&R to hold on to its assets, movement between societies was commonplace and generally accepted.

The cast list for *The Gondoliers* in the autumn of 1953 includes the name of one Ralph McKenna in the part of The Duke of Plaza-Toro. Patrons may have been surprised at the callowness of an actor cast in a part normally allocated to performers no longer in the first flush of youth. He was a mere 24 years of age, while his Duchess, Eileen Clancy, was in her late forties. What might have surprised them even more was that McKenna, from Mullagh in Co. Cavan, was performing under his father's name. His real name was Thomas Patrick McKenna, aka T.P., and he was acting under an alias in an increasingly vain attempt to conceal his extra-curricular activities from the powers-that-be in the Ulster Bank in Camden Street where he was employed at the time.[104] 'Ralph' already had considerable experience in Savoy productions from his student days at St Patrick's College, Cavan, where he first appeared in *The Yeomen of the Guard* in 1944 at the age of 15.

The following year he was cast as Pooh-Bah in a production of *The Mikado*. This much is confirmed by a playbill from 1945 on a website dedicated to his memory (T.P. died at the age of 81 in February 2011).[105] However, so the story goes, the 16-year-old Lord High Everything Else contracted a bad case of laryngitis a day or two before opening night. No understudy had been readied for the part. In an exhibition of startling initiative, someone recalled that St Eunan's College, Letterkenny, had just finished a run of *The Mikado*. The president of St Patrick's contacted the president of St Eunan's with an urgent request to send their Pooh-Bah to rescue the Cavan production. He arrived the following day. His name was Ray McAnally!

Shortly after his Dublin debut as the Duke of P-T, T.P., who had managed to miss out on a number of vital bank exams because of his appearances with the R&R and the Dublin Shakespeare Society, was threatened with a transfer to Killeshandra, Co. Cavan, a town lacking a musical society. He resigned his safe, pensionable job, to the consternation of his family, and shortly thereafter joined the Abbey Theatre Company to begin a long and distinguished professional career.

Terry O'Connor, Roderick Tierney, Vi Barry and Joe Flood.

Replenishment and reinvention did not just occur onstage. By the early 1950s T.H. Weaving had dominated the rostrum for thirty-five years, since taking over the baton from C.P. Fitzgerald in 1917. For decades Weaving was peerless and unchallenged as the R&R musical director and principal conductor. That started to change subtly, and then more markedly, when Terry O'Connor began to conduct some of the non-Savoy productions – in which Weaving had little interest – after her debut in *Gay Rosalinda* in 1947.

Terry O'Connor had begun her professional career as a violinist with a 2RN/Radio Éireann trio that grew into a full orchestra, the Radio Éireann Symphony Orchestra, of which she was leader. She had retired from that position by the time she first wielded the baton for the R&R but, at that time, she was professor of orchestra at the Royal Irish Academy of Music and the first female conductor in Ireland. From 1947 until 1953 O'Connor alternated with Weaving in R&R shows. She conducted the musical comedies (*The Student Prince, Wild Violets, Bless the Bride, The Dancing Years, Bittersweet*) while Weaving stuck to what he was, by then, more comfortable with – the Gilbert and Sullivan operettas.

That arrangement, however, ended in 1953. The three shows chosen for the autumn season of that year were *Patience, The Gondoliers* and *The Yeomen of the Guard*. A terse committee meeting minute indicates that the R&R's own guard was about to change. It merely stated that Terry O'Connor was to be asked to conduct the three autumn shows in the Gaiety.[106] There was no indication or explanation as to why Weaving had fallen out of favour. When O'Connor agreed to accept the position the effective removal of Weaving from his customary position proceeded rapidly. At a subsequent meeting a final decision was taken not to ask T.H. Weaving to conduct the autumn G&S shows. The minutes tell a certain amount of the story.

T.H. Weaving, last night speech with the cast of *H.M.S. Pinafore*, November 1946.

It was decided that a letter should be sent to Mr Weaving explaining that continuing adverse criticism made it essential for the society to make a special effort to improve the standard of its productions; that this would make extra demands on everyone associated with the shows and that the committee therefore felt it would be unfair to ask him to undertake expected special attendances at rehearsals and the subsequent arduous duties of conductor. Mr Weaving would remain as musical director, however, and the committee expressed the hope that he would continue to give the society the benefit of his advice and guidance.[107]

At least some of the 'continuing adverse criticism' would have come from the ever-vigilant committee, where powerful figures like the chairman, Paddy Forde, policed production standards thoroughly, in the knowledge that if they did not maintain values then Louis Elliman would fill the vacuum in his quietly ruthless way.[108] But some of the negative commentary was also coming via adverse reviews of the orchestral standards at R&R shows in the early 1950s. Discussing, for example, the 1952 productions of *Pirates* and *Cox and Box*, *The Irish Times* had written that: 'it was a pity that in both pieces the orchestral work was so faulty. It sounded as if the players had not had enough rehearsal.'[109] 'Orchestral deficiencies' were also highlighted in 'An Irishman's Diary' in the same newspaper by Quidnunc (Seamus Kelly), the newspaper's sometime drama critic.[110]

Weaving failed to respond to the letter. He remained in position as musical director of the R&R but did not conduct any society production thereafter. In 1956 O'Connor was appointed musical director and Weaving was made an honorary life member.[111] According to the society's fiftieth anniversary publication, *Fifty Golden Years*, Weaving sent 'hearty congratulations to his friends in the society' on that occasion. The booklet doesn't elaborate on who those friends were. We may surmise that they did not include the officers of the 1953 committee who had brought down the curtain on his R&R career. Weaving died in 1966 at the age of 84.

· ·

THE R&R AND THE D'OYLY CARTE

But what of the troika whose work was at the core of the R&R repertoire? And a troika it definitely was, as business manager Richard D'Oyly Carte, whose son and granddaughter dealt directly with the Dublin society, was an integral part in the success, the standards and the legacy of Gilbert and Sullivan.[112]

The role of the entrepreneurial D'Oyly Carte, while not as central as that of the composers, was, nonetheless, crucial in bringing the work of the often dysfunctional musical collaboration to a worldwide audience. That exposure was often mediated through the work of companies like the Rathmines and Rathgar, when Carte eventually permitted amateur companies to produce G&S comic operas. Licencing was initially subject to the maintenance of a D'Oyly Carte production template, though this was relaxed over the years.

In addition to pioneering a very English brand of comic opera for Richard D'Oyly Carte, Gilbert, as stage director, and Sullivan, as musical director, introduced more exacting performance standards than had been the case heretofore. Actors were not allowed to improvise, play scenes for cheap laughs, demolish the fourth wall or embellish Sullivan's score with elaborate demonstrations of their own virtuosity. A new regime of directorial discipline (through the uninhibited use of sarcasm) was introduced with the composer's particular scorn reserved for errant thespians incapable of adhering to either script or score. It was obedience to elements of this tradition that prompted the frequent recruitment by the R&R of London producers with experience of working in the D'Oyly Carte environment. In 1940 Rupert D'Oyly Carte personally recommended two members of his company as potential producers of *Ruddigore, The Sorcerer* and *Cox and Box*.[113] The job, however, went to another of his alumni, Sam Mooney. As late as 1949 (at the annual general meeting of that year) a discussion took place on the advisability of engaging only D'Oyly Carte producers for G&S shows. One member observed: 'We are inclined to play these shows in a musical comedy fashion and are losing some of the "quaintness". A D'Oyly Carte producer might greatly improve our presentations of these operas.'[114]

The expansion of the G&S 'franchise' into the world of amateur production had begun in the 1880s and had greatly assisted in the growth in popularity of amateur drama, to a point where, by the outbreak of the Great War, British societies were, 'now accepted as useful training schools for the legitimate stage, and from the volunteer ranks have sprung many present-day favourites'.[115] In the immediate post-war period the same was true of the R&R.

While tremendously supportive of performances by amateur companies the Cartes also insisted on the maintenance of production standards. Amateur companies like the R&R were required to follow the staging instructions originated by Gilbert himself. This requirement post-dated the death of Richard D'Oyly Carte in 1901 and, to some extent, even that of his son Rupert in 1948.[116] Permission was rarely given for the simultaneous production of more than two operas.[117] Such was the level of historic paranoia about production standards, and the possibility of the refusal of a performing licence on that basis, that there would be occasional eruptions of breast-beating at R&R committee level. One of the members, generally but not exclusively of an older vintage, would decry declining standards of staging, diction or chorus work – often quoting an adverse review in support of the diatribe – and recommend radical re-education along quasi-Maoist lines.[118]

Just such an outpouring of self-flagellation occurred in early 1950 when the quality of the 'deportment and diction'[119] of the society members was criticised at a committee meeting. It was suggested that classes in both should be conducted before the next production. But as with many such fulminations the criticisms, while accepted with grunts of approbation, were actually seen as the ranting of the sort of petits-Savonarolas who haunt all societies and who 'harrumph' about how things were 'in my day'. In this instance, discussion of the issue was mysteriously deferred to a future committee meeting. The matter was safely and conveniently long-fingered until after the spring production that year (*Bless the Bride* by A.P. Herbert and Vivian Ellis – set in Victorian England where deportment must have been at a premium). When the committee met on 6 May 1950 consideration of the issue of organising lectures on diction and deportment was again raised but discussion was deferred for further consideration. The same happened at the subsequent committee meeting. Thereafter diction and deportment, presumably still shackled to each other, fell off a cliff and were carried out to sea.

Bless the Bride programme, 1950.

But an obsession with exactitude and the maintenance of Savoy rituals never quite disappeared. Although the society had been managing perfectly well and quite economically with 'inhouse' G&S producers for some time, fears of falling standards finally led to a decision to inject some D'Oyly Carte discipline into the troupe. Given the job of returning the company to the gold standard was the experienced D'Oyly Carte producer Anna Bethell. Bethell was married to the great D'Oyly Carte veteran Sydney Granville who had been with the company since 1907. Despite the fact that she cost 150 guineas plus expenses (to an eventual overall total of £250), Bethell was imported from London for the November 1952 productions of *The Mikado*, *Princess Ida*, *Cox and Box* and *Pirates*, to be assisted by Joe Flood, Eileen Clancy and Mida O'Brien. The policy worked, with the *Irish Independent* noting 'the expert direction of Anna Bethell, a Savoyard of distinction, who took care of every movement and gesture of chorus and principals, to comply with the current D'Oyly Carte standards'.[120]

Bethell returned in 1953 before giving way to Norman Meadmore, a former D'Oyly Carte performer, for much of the late 1950s.

As well as licensing the R&R (and, by and large, none other) to stage Gilbert and Sullivan pieces in Dublin, the D'Oyly Carte Company occasionally offered direct competition itself, as it had done up to the 1920s. In 1953 Paddy Forde was tipped off that the

Colm Geary, Des Bowden and Vi Barry in *Bless the Bride*, 1950.

The Yeomen of the Guard, 1956, a break in rehearsals.

Savoyards might be returning to Dublin (the Olympia) in May 1954. He warned his fellow committee members that 'the information should not be repeated' as it might damage the R&R season in November 1953 if the news got out. In fact the London company played *Mikado, Gondoliers, Iolanthe, Yeomen* and *Patience* in July 1954, causing the R&R to abandon its regular G&S autumn season that year in preference for a revival of A.P. Herbert's *Bless the Bride*. The D'Oyly Carte Company returned in 1956 but their Dublin run did not dissuade the R&R from staging *Yeomen, Patience* and *Iolanthe* in the Gaiety that autumn. All were produced by Norman Meadmore. The staging of *Iolanthe* on 21 November 1956 marked the society's 100th production of a Gilbert and Sullivan opera.

One of the possible reasons for the enthusiastic resumption of the D'Oyly Carte's 'provincial' touring policy was the fast-approaching fiftieth anniversary of the death of W.S. Gilbert. Under the copyright law of the time – subsequently amended with the accession of Ireland and Britain to the European Economic Community in 1973 – that meant the end of the D'Oyly Carte licencing stranglehold over G&S operas was imminent. The R&R would not have to deal with Bridget D'Oyly Carte, Rupert's heir, after 1961. Neither would the society have to pay royalties on its most lucrative source of revenue. A note of alarm appears in the society's minutes in September 1958, however, when it was recorded that a letter had appeared in *The Irish Times* from an *ad hoc* body recently formed in England which was organising a petition to be presented to parliament. This would petition that the Gilbert and Sullivan copyright be maintained and invested in public cultural activities. The initiative, to the undoubted relief of the R&R, came to nothing.

YEOMENGATE

The tenacity of the Joyce estate in policing its copyright is legendary – until, that is, the works of the Irish master entered the public domain in January 2012. Almost as resolute in its preservation of its rights to the legacy of Gilbert and Sullivan was the D'Oyly Carte family.

The Cartes also had an understandable abhorrence of the mechanical recording of amateur productions of licensed operas. In the aftermath of the death of Rupert D'Oyly Carte and the succession of his daughter Bridget to the family birthright, the R&R was responsible for a significant transgression that caused the committee to be seized with a bout of extreme paranoia. This involved the covert audio recording of *The Yeomen of the Guard* in November 1949. The culprit was never identified but someone illegally taped the show and brought the 'bootleg' tape to the post-production party. Recognising that, if word got out that a recording existed, all future licences from Bridget D'Oyly Carte would be in jeopardy, the playback of the tape was quickly stopped. The committee recognised that 'the recording of the *Yeomen* on the last night had created quite a problem and was calculated to land us into trouble… and we were in touch with the people concerned with a view to destroying the recording'.[121]

There then followed a series of cloak and dagger meetings and negotiations in which, at one point, it looked as if the R&R was being blackmailed. A week after the incident had first been brought to the committee's attention the members met again and decided 'they would endeavour to purchase the spool on which it was made and in that way ensure that the recording…would be taken into safe keeping and any harmful results prevented'.[122]

The issue was settled, along the lines of an IRA weapons decommissioning event, in January 1950. The mysterious bootlegger agreed to put the tape beyond use after having been contacted by treasurer Fred Holland, straying far from his profession of chiropody. There was, however, a problem. Tapes and spools were expensive and the culprit wanted both of his returned. Paddy Forde and Fred Holland were required, therefore, to visit the bootlegger's house 'to witness the wiping off of the recording from the spool'.[123] Thus ended Yeomengate and, with it, any possibility of the R&R being denied future lucrative G&S licences for being in breach of mechanical copyright. Sadly, the quasi-clandestine service done for the society by Fred Holland on this occasion was one of his last. He died in January 1951.[124]

Fred Holland, honorary treasurer (1937–1950).

KING LOUIS…EMPEROR ELLIMAN[125]

For thirty years the Rathmines and Rathgar Musical Society was largely dependent on the whim of one man, Louis Elliman. And it was a whim of iron. Elliman, along with Patrick Wall, had bought the Gaiety Theatre in 1936. He sold it in 1965 and Fred O'Donovan and Eamonn Andrews took up the lease from the new owners. In the intervening years he brought the great comedian Jimmy O'Dea to the theatre and forged a relationship that entertained a generation of Dubliners. The Gaiety was only one of Elliman's entertainment interests. He also had an association with the Theatre Royal, produced two films with the Gate Theatre (*Return to Glennascaul* and *From Time to Time*) and later co-founded Ardmore Studios with World War I and Irish Civil War veteran Emmet Dalton in 1958.[126] *Inter alia* he also, in effect, controlled the artistic policy of the R&R while he ran their chosen venue.

The 1950s began with the R&R as one of a number of amateur societies allocated one or two 'seasons' of a week or a fortnight each year. The decade ended with the R&R as the lone amateur survivors, assuming the DGOS is discounted as an amateur company. Much of the credit for this tenacity was down to the shrewd management of officers like Paddy Forde, Arthur Healy and Clem Ryan, and to the public relations talents of Gladys MacNevin (see below). But the principal reason the R&R remained *in situ* was that it carefully toed a line drawn by Elliman.

In a piece written about the 1950 R&R production of *Bless the Bride*, the writer of the weekly *Irish Times* 'In Theatre' column, Ken Gray, identified the dilemma of an amateur company attempting to bring first-rate musical comedy to the Dublin stage.

> It must be discouraging for the hard-working members of a musical society to realise that their principal lack is money, for there is nothing that can be done about it. Obviously one cannot plan the production on a London scale when the run will be measured in weeks instead of years and the receipts in hundreds instead of thousands of pounds.[127]

Dublin box-office receipts were a fraction of those of the West End. And as the decade progressed a box-office 'slump' identified by Elliman in 1949[128] was showing few signs of improvement. The wolf that had been beaten from the door by the R&R in the late 1930s returned with a vengeance a decade later and showed no signs of leaving. Losses, some quite significant, were made on a number of shows in the 1950s, including the normally money-spinning Savoy operas. Production costs, almost always higher in the case of musicals than 'legitimate' theatre, habitually outstripped box-office takings. While the R&R struggled to justify continuing its connection with a venue that insisted on retaining 50–60 per cent of its revenues, Louis Elliman had frequent cause to grumble at the R&R's inability to cover his overheads despite the box-office share for the theatre that he insisted upon. There was parallel grumbling in the R&R ranks with the influential Joe Bowden declaring at a 1951 committee meeting that the society's officers seemed 'far too prone to pay too much attention to the wishes of Louis Elliman'.[129] Bowden was well aware of the number of occasions on which the Gaiety proprietor had vetoed the desire of the R&R to produce certain shows and his particular penchant for insisting on annual productions of the 'old reliables' from the Savoy stable.

The question of whether the R&R, or any amateur company for that matter, should occupy three or four weeks a year at the country's largest and most popular theatrical venue was not just being discussed in the Gaiety boardroom either. In an op-ed piece in *The Times Pictorial*, as the R&R autumn season was in full swing in November 1951, the newspaper's theatrical correspondent fulminated against amateurs being given access to 'professional' venues.

Is Dublin's principal theatre the place for these amateur shows? That the forty or fifty members of the company don't line up on a Friday for their pay-packets is the only reason that such a society can afford to hire the Gaiety. And by occupying the Gaiety they are taking the cake, if not the bread and butter, from the mouths of the professionals. Equity, and the newly-formed Theatre Council, take the reasonable view. Dubliners want musical comedy; economically the amateurs are the only people who can supply it, and if they can afford to hire the Gaiety – more luck to them. Both Equity and Theatre Council, however, would like to see some sort of balance struck in the respective time allotted to musical shows, revue and legitimate drama in each year at the Gaiety.

A sequence of loss-making years from 1952 to 1956[130] in which deficits exceeded £1,000[131] led to the establishment of a plan devised by the resourceful Paddy Forde. After a meeting with Elliman, in which the Gaiety overlord had stated baldly that if the R&R wanted continued access to the Gaiety they 'must produce new shows and present them in a spectacular manner', Forde and fellow committee member Clem Ryan were concerned about the society's future at the venue. Forde calculated that given Elliman's threat/strictures, in the current economic climate, losses of around £400 a year would inevitably result. He proposed a 'guarantor scheme' under which companies or individuals would be asked to indemnify the society against losses over a five-year period up to a maximum of £100 each. Ten contributors were required to make the scheme viable.[132] Within less than a year the required ten benefactors – they included the *Irish Independent*, *Evening Mail*, Guinness, Jacobs, McConnells Advertising and New Ireland Assurance – had come forward and freed the society from the worst of its financial concerns.[133]

But the financial health of the R&R was of marginal concern to Louis Elliman. He required their productions to provide the sort of return that would cover his weekly running costs and provide him with a respectable operating profit. After renovations to his theatre that kept it closed for most of 1955 – the R&R 'toured the provinces', playing in Carlow, Dundalk and Mullingar during the hiatus – that cost base had changed somewhat. The provincial tour was partly prompted by the fact that Elliman had made it clear to the society that transferring to the rival Olympia during the renovations was not an option. A press release was issued to the effect that the R&R would not be playing the Gaiety because of the building work and, rather than settle for a lesser Dublin venue 'was availing of this break to respond to some of the provincial invitations' the society had received.[134]

The refurbishment had meant the installation of extra seating and enhanced revenue potential, but Elliman had also addressed his overheads. The Gaiety orchestra had been disbanded and there would be no scenic artist at the venue to construct elaborate sets. This would add to the costs of companies, like the R&R, wishing to hire the theatre for musical events. Elliman was transferring some of his own costs to his clients.

That the R&R submitted to Elliman's will so often – consulting him about programming choices before making them official – was a function of its own desire to continue to be identified with his theatre. The R&R wanted to remain, as Clem Ryan made clear on one occasion, 'the premier [musical society] in the country' and to be seen to occupy that position it was essential to retain their slots in

Irish Festival Singers tour of the USA, 1954, with Frank Sinatra, Grace Kelly, Celeste Holm and Bing Crosby. R&R members in the group: Kitty Corcoran, Kay Condron, Patrick Ring, Jack O'Connor, Louis Browne, Maureen Concannon and Claire Kelleher.

the Gaiety as assiduously as Aer Lingus has fought to retain theirs in Heathrow Airport. In 1959 the society even acceded to a request from Elliman to move into the Gaiety a week before its planned opening of *Ruddigore*, *Iolanthe* and *The Gondoliers*. The Dublin Globe Theatre and a London production company called Spur had fallen foul of Elliman when they had refused to make cuts in a staging of an adaptation of J.P. Donleavy's controversial novel *The Ginger Man*. The play, due for a two-week run, had been pulled after three nights.[135] According to Donleavy himself, Louis Elliman was visited by Roman Catholic Archbishop John Charles McQuaid's private secretary, a Father Nolan, who requested, or advised, him to close down the show. Elliman, as a Jew, 'was anxious to maintain good relations with the Catholic authorities'[136] and complied. He then asked the R&R to step into the breach, which it duly did, much to the annoyance of a number of committee members who had not been consulted. One of those, Reggie Cleary observed at a meeting that 'taking over theatre a week early was a matter of major policy for the society and if it had been done to suit Louis Elliman he [Cleary] strongly objected'.[137] The move did no favours to the R&R's bottom line, however. The productions lost nearly £450 and the society was forced to seek an overdraft facility from the Munster and Leinster bank to allow it to continue operating in 1960.

With the wolf salivating at the door, the Rathmines and Rathgar Musical Society prepared to enter what nobody suspected would turn out to be the 'Swinging Sixties'.

CHAPTER THREE

The Dancing Years: 1960–1989

CHAPTER THREE

The Dancing Years: 1960–1989

The Rathmines and Rathgar have something timeless and durable about themselves, like the Liffey or the Comédie-Française.

Quidnunc, 'An Irishman's Diary', *The Irish Times*, 5 November 1967.[1]

Of course no one knew much about the 1960s until they'd been and gone. The transition between the 1940s and 1950s hadn't brought any great social, economic or cultural change, so there was little reason to suspect that the new decade, as it dawned on 1 January 1960,[2] would be any different. It turned out to be very different indeed. It was an era of technological change, economic expansion and of generational conflict. In 1959 few knew what a cusp was but, for a variety of reasons, the R&R was approaching one with the insouciance of Captain Edward Smith of the R.M.S. *Titanic* three days into the vessel's maiden voyage.

For some of the younger members of the Rathmines and Rathgar Musical Society, it felt like a good time to kick over the traces. The most up to date show from the R&R 1950s repertoire had been Emile Littler's *Love from Judy*, written in 1952 and performed by the society in 1958. Of the thirty-seven shows staged in the 1950s, twenty-six had been G&S productions. A passionate discussion took place at the 1960 annual general meeting on future artistic policy. The issue was whether 'new or nostalgic' pieces were to be performed. The house was divided. The minutes tell us: 'Some members were of the opinion that the public wanted bright new shows and that we should cater especially for the younger generation. Others felt that Dublin audiences wanted the nostalgia and sentiment which the older shows provided.'[3] The conservatives prevailed on this occasion. The first productions of 1960 were Victor Herbert's *Naughty Marietta* and Ivor Novello's *The Dancing Years*. Neither was exactly cutting edge, although *Naughty Marietta* was an Irish premiere.

A subsequent committee meeting highlighted the arrival of another serious competitor for the time and seriously depleted financial resources of the society's audiences. The R&R acknowledged the incipient arrival of a native television channel with a charmingly naive offer to Radio Éireann. Clem Ryan was to commence talks with Fachtna Ó hAnnracháin of Radio Éireann to see if members of the Radio Éireann choir might be available for stage work in the future. Ryan was to adopt the role of Good Samaritan, a helpful benefactor, as 'it was pointed out that with the advent of television R[adio] É[ireann] might consider it desirable to obtain stage experience for these persons'.[4] Radio Éireann must have found other ways of coaching its choristers in stagecraft as the approach, not the first of its kind, met with a stony silence.

My Fair Lady, 1969. Louise Studley and Roderick Tierney.

Wild Violets, 1962: Roderick Tierney and Ita Little

But there was no doubting the power, and the potential threat, of this relatively new medium, especially with the promise of local interest programmes materialising from 31 December 1961. There was no serious discussion of the possible impact of television on box-office receipts but the allure of what was then known disparagingly as 'the goggle box' would quickly become clear. A fortnight after the establishment of Teilifís Éireann, Joseph Flood, producer of *Wild Violets* in March 1962, agreed in advance to accept a television set *in lieu* of payment.[5] It was hardly akin to the population of the ancient city of Troy accepting the delivery of a large but fascinating wooden horse, but it was, nonetheless, an interesting piece of symbolism.

The R&R quickly adapted to the new medium in one respect at least. While it was a potential rival for the attention of prospective theatre-goers it was also only partially state-funded and it was required to carry advertising to make up the deficit. The R&R was in early to book its 'on air' time. The first show to be advertised was *Wild Violets* in March 1962. Joe Flood would not have seen the ads, at least not on his own TV, as he was not 'paid' until after the run. The experiment was deemed a success and when the autumn G&S season approached 'it was considered desirable to advertise on Teilifís Éireann again this time – stressing the "new look" of the productions.'[6]

Of course while television commercials in particular, and advertising in general, cost money, there were other ways of bringing a product to the attention of an increasingly distracted Dublin public.

As the successful series *Mad Men* suggests, the 1960s also saw major advances in the worlds of advertising and public relations, largely dictated by the infant medium of television. The very phrase 'public relations', or the art of managing the flow of information between corporations (or individuals) and the general public, was relatively unfamiliar until the 1960s. It existed, but it largely operated under the public radar. The practice of managing or manipulating the public perception of a 'brand' or an individual still had something of the feeling of (at best) misdirection or (at worst) propaganda about it

Gladys MacNevin.

in the aftermath of World War II. This dark art was brightening to a lighter shade of grey by the 1950s. It began to enter to public consciousness in the 1960s as it came into its own and the public became more sophisticated at being manipulated.

The R&R's 'white witch' of PR for decades was the indefatigable Gladys MacNevin. An ESB employee she had joined the R&R in the mid-1930s, playing Mabel in *Pirates* in 1937 and Fiametta in *Gondoliers* in 1938. From there she had moved on to the Radio Éireann Choir. But her best work for the society was done far away from the stage. Unlike the publicity drones charged with the task of PR by most amateur societies, MacNevin was literally a professional. She lived, moved and had her being in the world of public relations. In 1955 she became honorary secretary of the Public Relations Institute of Ireland, which had been established just two years previously.[7] She held the post for over thirty years, almost up to her death in 1995.[8]

It was another ESB employee, Paddy Forde, who brought her back into the society in a PR role. In doing so he warned her that her R&R duties should not be allowed to interfere with the all-important 'day job'.[9] In her early years with the society she had just as much of a struggle 'within' as she had 'without'. The more conservative elements on the committee did not always appreciate her artifice. MacNevin was aware that journalists had to be 'sold' a story so that her efforts could be turned into useful column inches. Her preferred method, and that of the preponderance of her profession then and now, was to create 'personalities'. Her raw material was the casts of the shows she was promoting, *gratis*, on behalf of the society. Her approach was no different to the one she would have adopted had she been working on a professional show. But not everybody appreciated the spectacle of 'celebrities' being created from within the ranks of an amateur musical society.

In the early years of her work there was an obvious tension between the committee and the rather free-spirited *modus operandi* of MacNevin. Although she was singled out for much praise for her efforts, there were also voices, implicitly at least, calling for her wings to be clipped. While the disinclination of some committee members might well have been based on what was perceived as being the good of the society, the distinct impression is sometimes created of opposition from members whose noses were seriously out of joint because others were being singled out for newspaper coverage.[10] In March

The Yeomen of the Guard, 1956, press conference: Proinsias O'Sullivan, Terry O'Connor and Fintan Corish.

1960, for example, it was suggested at a committee meeting that 'in future, publicity policy with regard to any show should be discussed by the committee' and that MacNevin 'should bring the committee more into the picture regarding publicity'. MacNevin was obviously not one to consult with amateurs on the most effective method of maximising public attention through the media. Another injunction at the same meeting would also have been anathema to her. It was recommended that 'in all future publicity for the current show no names should be published'.[11] It was the sort of policy that dogged the American film industry during the early part of the silent era before audiences demanded that the stars of the movies they were watching should be identified.[12]

Renowned in her profession for her 'efficiency and courtesy'[13] MacNevin's forte was the 'press conference'. Today, stripped of all pretensions to any real consequence, they would be styled 'press launches'. These would take place, usually in the Gaiety itself, a few weeks before each production. MacNevin, according to the 1988 seventy-fifth anniversary publication, had 'numerous and loyal friends in the media whom she bullied unmercifully in the interests of the R&R'. At press conferences 'she positioned herself at a fireside table in the Gaiety tea rooms and swooped'.

Some of her most egregious *coups* came in the 'Irishman's Diary' column of *The Irish Times*, which she appeared to have virtually 'owned' for a couple of decades. The number of R&R-related pieces carried by the diary increased exponentially in the 1950s and 1960s. Between 1945 and 1955, 'An Irishman's Diary' carried nine pieces about the R&R – an average of less than one a year. From 1956 to 1966 Quidnunc and his accomplices featured the society in sixteen columns. Some of the pieces focused on R&R 'principals', but the variety of London-based producers coming over to direct also offered a useful and steady stream of new 'copy'. In a typical 'Irishman's Diary' column Maxwell Wray, who produced *Naughty Marietta* in March 1960, claimed to have 'discovered' Greer Garson and Vivienne Leigh. That, in itself, was not of much assistance to the humble R&R. But the pound of flesh was skilfully extracted by MacNevin with Quidnunc's reference to the fact that *Naughty Marietta* was an Irish amateur premiere and Wray's published comment that the amateurs with whom he was working made for 'an excellent cast – many of them on a professional level'.[14]

Sometimes MacNevin herself was the 'angle'.[15] Sometimes it was a debutant/e freshening the stock of potential 'celebrities'.[16] Sometimes, bizarrely, Gilbert and Sullivan themselves became the stars worthy of coverage.[17] On one occasion the focus was on R&R marriages, where real-life Frederics had found their Mabels.[18] Whatever the story, the message was always the same and rarely subliminal: the show was going to sell out, so book now to avoid disappointment.

From the mid-1970s the number of substantial pieces on the activities of the R&R began to diminish. This was likely to have been a function of a notable increase in the scale of professional theatre in Ireland as well as competition for space from a more vibrant popular music scene. It didn't help either that Gilbert and Sullivan productions were seen to have passed their sell-by date shortly after coming out of copyright.

However, a Kevin Myers piece in 1982 testifies to the determination of the R&R to continue its relationship with 'An Irishman's Diary'. Myers wrote in a March column that 'the R&R are quite the most persistently thorough professionals ever to besiege this column, and when they have a production in the oven at the Gaiety, waiting for the pastry to rise, a steady and remorseless allowance of literature reminds us of the imminent pie'. He candidly admitted to an element of coercion in that the R&R 'have a mole in this newspaper who surfaces every time the pie is ready for consuming'. The 'mole' in question was the tall and angular chorus member, and *Irish Times* employee, the late Seán Hogan, who sadly passed away in September 2013.[19]

Hogan later became the society's business secretary as well as a regular player in the chorus and minor speaking parts. One wonders if the occasional rapture about his performances, on the part of freelance *Irish Times* theatre reviewers in particular, had as much to do with his status within that organisation as they might have had with his qualities as a thespian. In 1973, for example, he was the solitary male performer in *South Pacific* – he played the barely visible character of Professor – who was singled out for praise by reviewer Kane Archer. Archer otherwise characterised the production itself as having 'all the impact of a poorly-aimed plateful of half-set Jell-O'.[20]

THE 'STURDY THEW': FROM *BITTER SWEET* TO *THE FLORAL DANCE*

One person who didn't garner much publicity via Gladys MacNevin's well-oiled machine was a young Limerick man, Michael Terence Wogan. He was a low-profile member in the late 1950s for about four years. He later made up for his relative invisibility with the R&R in a distinguished career with the BBC, whose airwaves he seemed to dominate for more than thirty years. The citation for the conferral of his University of Limerick honorary doctorate succinctly traces his *curriculum vitae* in this country. 'He showed early promise with the Rathmines and Rathgar Musical Society and, after a brief interlude in banking, he joined RTÉ…'.[21]

His principal role in RTÉ was as a radio announcer. Wogan was part of an influx that included Mike Murphy and Brendan Balfe and preceded by a few years the arrival of a young engineer, Pat Kenny, onto the radio announcing staff. In RTÉ, where Wogan also presented the television game-show *Jackpot*, he was known as a wicked practical joker. He had demonstrated a similar proclivity in the R&R. While never making it above the rank of NCO, artistically at least, he managed to draw quite a lot of attention to himself. His specialty was mischievously attempting to upstage the principals. During rehearsals for *Love from Judy* in 1958, male lead Jack O'Connor was forced to draw the attention of producer Margaret Boyle to one of Wogan's more distracting bits of onstage business. The future radio star and knight was shown a 'yellow card' by Boyle, according to the 1988 seventy-fifth anniversary booklet.

In that same publication the man himself underplayed his musical qualifications. 'Don't ask me how I got in; they must have needed a couple of sturdy thews to fill a gap in the back row of the chorus, but what a time I had – before they found me out!' Not that the Limerick man had it all his own way when it came to practical joking. In the November 1956 production of *Iolanthe* fellow cast member Lucy Lane, then McCarthy, remembers some of the female members of the troupe exacting revenge on a young Wogan in one of the hospital touring productions. As recounted to Tom Glennon in 'An Irishman's Diary', it appears that: 'Wogan was playing a noble peer in court dress with a long ermine-trimmed cloak. The girls in the chorus pinned this long cloak to the stage backcloth.'[22] The habitual jester, hoist with his own petard, was like Ko-Ko in *The Mikado*, later released on his own recognisances.

Wogan participated in other society activities as well. In the 1963 Golden Jubilee publication, there is a photograph on p.51 of the R&R Cricket XI at Clontarf Cricket Club. A smiling Wogan stands

Cricket team at Clontarf, 1961. *Back:* Brian Kelly, Terry Wogan, R.J. Tierney, Ray Joyce, Tom Murtagh. *Middle:* Ken Brayden, Noel Byrne, Eoin O'Brien, Fred Taylor. *Front:* Dodo O'Hagan, Heather Hewson.

in the back row beside Roderick Tierney, appearing to be looking in an entirely different direction to everyone else. His later career certainly suggests that he could see things that were invisible to others.[23]

Wogan, who received a knighthood in 2005, was mentioned in dispatches for his portrayal of the similarly ennobled character of Sir Harry Blake in the 1960 production of Victor Herbert's *Naughty Marietta*. Oddly, it was actually the Dublin premiere of an operetta by an Irish-born composer that had opened in New York in 1910. Blake is described in the script as being 'an Irish adventurer', so credit to the R&R cast committee for its intuitive anticipation. In his critique of the evening, Charles Acton described it as 'the best R&R show I had seen'[24] adding that, 'I wish there was more space to praise' a list of performers that included the future Sir Terry as the adventurous Sir Harry. Likewise *The Irish Press* included Wogan amongst its 'notable performances'.[25] The actual knight of the realm himself remembers feeling significantly challenged in his portrayal of the fictional Irish nobleman. 'Have you ever tried to play a stage-Irish character to an Irish audience? And you think 'live' television is difficult?'[26]

While the R&R (by dint of its part in educating the vocal chords of Sir Terry) must accept at least some responsibility for the release of Wogan's version of *The Floral Dance* in 1978 and its attainment of a heady #21 in the British charts, the society has many more worthy achievements to offer in extenuation.

· ·

FEISEANNA

R&R fundraising concert for Feis Ceoil, 1977.

R&R Cup: presented in 1946, won outright by John Conroy in 1971.

The Feis Ceoil, Ireland's premier competitive music event, dates back to 1897 when there were thirty-two categories, twelve of which were for composition. Since then the emphasis has shifted more to performance. Today's Feis has 176 categories of which only five are for composition.[27] One of the great myths about this national institution is that in the early 1900s the great tenor John McCormack won a gold medal in one of the solo voice categories at the expense of James Joyce. In fact, McCormack triumphed in 1903 while Joyce won the bronze medal in 1904. But it's still a great story.

The competition had already been up and running for sixteen years before the R&R began its life, and it wasn't until 1921 that the society realised the potential for recruitment offered by the Feis. By that time the event was held annually in Dublin after initially having circulated between Dublin, Belfast and Cork. That year the society sponsored a silver cup for 'dramatic solo singing' that quickly became dubbed, the Dramatic Cup. In addition to the silverware, the winner was to gain free membership of the R&R for a year. Most of the contenders for the Dramatic Cup in the early years, however, seemed to be more focused on grand opera than on operetta. In 1924, for example, the nineteen competitors selected works by Verdi, Bizet, Puccini, Leoncavallo and Borodin. The judge that year was unimpressed with the standard of male competitor but still managed to patronise the female contenders, observing that: 'The ladies as a rule knew what to do with their voices better than the men, perhaps because they practiced [*sic*] so much in speaking. (Laughter).'[28]

The first staging of the Dramatic Cup was won by Isidore Myers, who went on to play Sir Roderic Murgatroyd in *Ruddigore* in 1922 and Francois in *The Duchess of Dantzic* in 1924 before disappearing altogether from the annals of the R&R. That was despite winning the cup again, between both appearances, in 1923.[29] Only the 1926 winner, Patrick Kirwan, featured in more than one subsequent R&R show. He played Marco in *The Gondoliers* in 1926 and Leonard Meryll in *The Yeomen of the Guard* in 1927, before he too vanished from view after a final appearance in *Iolanthe* in 1935. Dorothy Griffith was a four-time winner, firstly in 1930 – she later won the trophy outright – but she appears in only a single cast list from the 1930s, *Florodora* in 1934. In 1927 an attempt was made at the R&R annual general meeting to force the Feis Ceoil committee to acknowledge the sponsorship of the R&R by changing the name of the competition to the Rathmines and Rathgar Musical Society Cup. This was, presumably, designed to remind the competitors of who was providing the supper for which they were singing. The motion, however, was ruled out of order by then president, Dr Lombard Murphy, who pointed out that the syllabus of the Feis did, in fact, state that the cup had been presented by the R&R.[30] Such footnoting, however, was not providing the society with new recruits.

After Miss Griffith won the cup for the third year in a row in 1934, and was thus entitled to retain the trophy (she had shared the honours with Patrick Black in 1933 and won outright in 1932) the society decided to abandon the experiment on the basis that most of the winners preferred to pursue options in grand rather than light opera.[31] The society was actually accruing greater benefits from identifying and recruiting the talented winners of competitions other than their own. One of those was Robert McCullagh, winner of a tenor solo award in 1926 and of eleven silver medals between 1928 and 1933.[32]

The relationship was re-established in the 1940s when Eileen Clancy approached the Feis committee with a proposal to promote another R&R competition.[33] This time, however, the rules were formulated so as to discourage operatic vocal chords. Under the regulations proposed by the R&R, competitors would be given a choice of solos from six light operas and musicals. *The Yeomen of the Guard*, *The Gondoliers*, *The Sorcerer*, *Lilac Time*, *Monsieur Beaucaire* and *Merrie England* were chosen for the inaugural running of the competition in 1946. The selection clearly reflected the priorities of the sponsors.[34] Rupert D'Oyly Carte was contacted and gave his permission for songs from the three Savoy operas to be performed in public. The Feis committee was offered a choice of three cups from Wests (the Grafton Street jewellers) and chose one that cost the society £25. Again, a year's free membership was offered to the eventual winner. The committee settled back to await the influx of new talent.

The first winner of the R&R Cup was Mary Todd Johnston. A report to the committee noted that the adjudicator, a Mr Cranmer, was 'a notoriously particular gentleman [who] said the competition gave him genuine pleasure, as compared with the other competition he had judged that week'.[35] However,

Miss Todd Johnston, while gratefully accepting the cup, appears to have decided to give the year's membership a miss. Her name does not appear on the cast list for the autumn G&S productions or for any show thereafter. The following year the programme restrictions were relaxed to allow the competitors to choose from any of the G&S operas or from 'the better class musical comedies from the society's repertoire'.[36]

By 1950 only a single winner, Joan Burleigh (1948), had subsequently appeared in an R&R show (in her case she managed three before vanishing into the ether) and the society ordained that four of the most promising Feis competitors each year – in any category – were to be selected and offered vocal training at the expense of the R&R with a view to 'provide talent for the society's productions'. The proposal, which came from Paddy Forde, himself a non-performing 'associate', met some opposition from active members who felt that already 'there was considerable talent within the ranks of the society'.[37] Clearly some of the established choristers, and perhaps even some of the principals, didn't want talented young whippersnappers coming along and taking their parts.

In 1952 things had gone from bad to worse when only five competitors turned up to perform in the R&R Cup.[38] Eileen Clancy, who was making the most of the thankless running on the Feis Ceoil/R&R relationship, proposed that T.H. Weaving, Terry O'Connor and Eileen Knowles 'should be called upon to draft new rules in connection with the R&R Cup due to the deplorable standard of the competition for the past couple of years'. It was decided that a new test would be set 'that would renew

Michael Forde and Valerie Taylor Fildes with Padraic Rowan, winner of the Forde Taylor prize at Feis Ceoil 2013.

Shay Gibson with Oisín Friel, runner-up in the R&R Cup, 2013

Brian Gilligan, winner of the R&R Cup, 2013, with Pat Campbell.

interest in the competition'.[39] In addition, the cup would be withheld if an acceptable standard was not reached and, once again, set pieces would be chosen by the R&R rather than be left to the discretion of the competitors themselves.[40] That resulted in no cup being awarded in 1953 and the competition being abandoned entirely in 1954.

When normal service resumed in 1955 there were nine entries and the winner came from Newry. Nuala Neary was cited by the adjudicator, Henry Cummings, as having 'the best voice in the class' but, he added, 'the runner-up was the better actress'.[41] The runner-up proved to be of more consequence to the R&R than the winner that year. Second-placed Maureen Concannon went on to play the title role in *Iolanthe* in November 1956 before following that up with the female lead of Laurey in *Oklahoma!*, which she played opposite Fintan Corish's Curly in the Gaiety in 1957. By the mid-1960s the committee felt inclined to add an element of coercion to the rules of the competition, dictating that 'the winner should be tied in some way to appear in the society's productions over a reasonable period'.[42] It is rare that a winner has to be compelled to accept part of his or her prize.

Mary O'Callaghan in *South Pacific*, 1973.

Although the R&R Cup itself was clearly not operating as a well-greased assembly line of talent for the society, the same was not true of the competition in general. In 1963, Clem Ryan, speaking to the Dublin Rotary Club, acknowledged as much when he pointed out that 'the Feis Ceoil shows us the talent and this year we have ten Feis Ceoil winners'.[43] Neither Concannon nor Lucy McCarthy, another emerging talent, were included in that list. Both had been runners-up in the R&R Cup.[44] However, the 'success rate' of the R&R Cup began to improve from the mid-1960s. Most of the winners from 1965–71, when the cup was won outright by John Conroy, featured in society productions. These included Kevin Hough (1965), Elizabeth Smyth (1966), Catherine McAuliffe (1967 and 1968) and Conroy himself (1969, 1970 and 1971). After Conroy won the cup for the third time, a new trophy was presented by the society's vice president E.C. Bewley. It remains the main prize to this day.[45]

In addition to the R&R Cup, in the mid-1960s the society decided to present the Michael Devlin scholarship. Called after its benefactor, and designed to last for ten years, it was established to coincide with the society's golden jubilee. The Devlin scholarship offered a grant of £50 'to be awarded to the person who, in the opinion of the committee, is deserving of help to advance in the study of music or drama'.[46] However, given the experience of the revived R&R Cup, there were certain strings attached to this particular educational instrument. One of the earliest winners was Mary O'Callaghan.[47] It was recommended that her bursary be used to allow her to train with Veronica Dunne for a year. The condition attached to the award was that she offer the R&R her services for a period of two years.[48] This she duly did, appearing as Nellie Forbush in *South Pacific* (1965), Sarah Brown in *Guys and Dolls* in March 1966, and in the title role in *Patience* and as Melissa in *Princess Ida* later that same year. Released from her 'contract' O'Callaghan became a professional cabaret singer in England before returning to the Gaiety stage with the R&R as Nellie Forbush again in the 1973 production of *South Pacific*.[49] A decision taken by the committee in 1966 meant that, in future, the Devlin scholarship would not necessarily be awarded to the candidate with the best voice 'but rather on the basis of general benefit to the society'.[50] The lessons of the R&R Cup had been well learned.

Fred and Cynthia Taylor.

The association of the R&R with the Feis continues to this day. In 1987 in honour of Paddy Forde, his sister Kitty, and Cynthia and Fred Taylor,[51] a further prize was added to the R&R Cup. This was for the best performance of a Gilbert and Sullivan piece. The Forde Taylor Prize started at £25 and rose to €600 in 2013. In 1996, as part of the Feis Ceoil centenary, in honour of Robert McCullagh (a singer and administrator who had graced both organisations), a special bursary was included in the syllabus on a 'once-off' basis.[52] In 2013 the society, and the Forde and Taylor families, augmented the prize fund for both the R&R and Forde Taylor prize. Past winners were invited to a reception in the RDS on the night of the competition – which was also attended by the CEO and Board Members of the Feis Ceoil Association. There were a record twenty-nine entries, and adjudicator Lynne Dawson awarded one 'highly commended' and three 'very highly commended' in addition to the three prizes.

Brian Gilligan took First Prize of the R&R Cup and €700. Oisín Friel took Second Prize of €300. Padraic Rowan was awarded the Forde Taylor Prize. In a piece of centenary serendipity, he also won the Dramatic Cup. Both Brian Gilligan and Padraic Rowan study with erstwhile R&R star, Mary Brennan, at the Royal Irish Academy of Music. Over the years singing teachers like Mary Brennan, Dr Veronica Dunne and Professor Paul Deegan, as well as preparing their pupils for the Feis Ceoil, send their brightest and best to the R&R to get the sort of performance experience that cannot be taught. While the R&R benefits from this talented throughput of performers, the artists themselves have the opportunity to work in prestigious venues like the Gaiety and National Concert Hall, in professionally staged and costumed productions, with a full orchestra of professional musicians.

As in all previous years, the 2013 winners became eligible for membership of the R&R the following year. The long-standing and mutually fruitful relationship between the society and the Feis Ceoil, though not constant, is now as old as the state itself.[53]

· ·

CHARITY WORK

From its inception as a musical society the R&R had offered support to Dublin-based charitable organisations. Even the earliest pre-World War I productions had included a benefit night during the run. This charitable 'outreach' grew to include annual Christmas visits to local hospitals. Generally one of the autumn/winter Gilbert and Sullivan shows would be chosen to tour half a dozen hospitals between Christmas and early New Year. The policy began in the 1940s and continued up to the 1970s, before it lapsed. Much of the impetus for these tours came from long-time member Hilda White.

In 1946, for example, the itinerary was to include the Royal Hospital for Incurables in Donnybrook, Cappagh Children's Hospital, High Park Convent in Drumcondra, the Magdalene Asylum in

My Fair Lady cast at Shaw Bequest: Pat Campbell, Glynis Casson, Louise Studley and Maurice O'Sullivan with curator Adrian Le Harivel, National Gallery, 2006.

Gloucester Street, and, after 5 January, any general hospital that applied for a performance.[54] The engagement in the Magdalene Asylum, institutions latterly dogged by controversy for keeping women in slave-like conditions, did not actually happen in the end. The religious order running the Gloucester Street convent pulled out because they couldn't supply refreshments to the cast and felt it would be unfair to ask for a show in the circumstances.[55] The Gloucester Street convent did not feature on the hospital itinerary again.

Institutions that did feature often over the years included all the main acute hospitals in the city of Dublin as well as smaller specialist venues like St John of God in Stillorgan and the Central Mental Hospital in Dundrum (both in 1951). The tours went ahead whatever the meteorological conditions. The winter of 1962/63 was one of the worst on record, with the country covered in a blanket of snow and ice for weeks. Meeting on 8 January 1963 the committee thanked the cast of *The Mikado* for the five hospital shows that went ahead 'in appalling weather'.[56]

It was, indirectly, the great humanitarian George Bernard Shaw,[57] who played a major part in the end of a long sequence of annual hospital tours. The society was due to bring the first production of Lerner and Loewe's *My Fair Lady*, based on Shaw's *Pygmalion*, to Dublin in March 1969. Because it was an immense undertaking, rehearsals began early and the commitment required for *MFL* from members of the G&S casts of November 1968 meant that 'it was decided with regret not to visit any hospitals this year'.[58] The following year, because of the decision to re-run the phenomenally successful show in November, there were no G&S productions ready to tour the hospital circuit. The practice became more episodic from that point, before finally disappearing altogether as the commitment required for some of the more ambitious spring shows increased.[59] To a limited extent the tours had already been rendered redundant by the increasing importance to the society, and to a number of charities, of a new template: the benefit night.

The idea, originated by Paddy Forde in 1958, was already familiar in England and operating on a small scale in Belfast. Essentially, one or two charities were expected to pay a performing society a sum of money (£300 in the case of the R&R)[60] for the first and/or second night of the run of a show, usually on a Monday or Tuesday. It was then up to that charity to set its own admission prices, publicise its involvement in the presentation and take the receipts on the night. There were clear financial benefits for both parties. The charity stood to profit handsomely, while the society had a guaranteed income (albeit not an especially lucrative return) on one or two early weeknights when box-office receipts were generally poor. In addition, the publicity generated by the charity – this was often handled by professional public relations companies – also accrued to the society.

The first R&R charity benefit night took place on 9 March 1959 when *The Merry Widow* opened in the Gaiety Theatre with Louise Studley and Brian Kissane in the lead roles. The charity to benefit was Jervis Street Hospital Artificial Kidney Unit. The R&R got its £300 and the 'buzz' generated by a press conference in the Gaiety Theatre on 2 March. Jervis Street benefited by the not inconsiderable sum of £800.[61] Forde's brainchild – stolen, as are all good ideas, from the very best sources – was up and running.

In the years that followed, the main beneficiaries were medical establishments such as the Bon Secours Hospital (1964), Sir Patrick Dun's (1965) and Peamount Hospital (1967). The opening night of *My Fair Lady* in 1969 went to the Society of Saint Vincent de Paul. The sixtieth anniversary production in 1973 was allocated to the Royal Hospital, Donnybrook – the rather unfortunate 'Incurables' suffix having been dropped from the name since the days of the hospital tours.[62] However, there were also some more unusual beneficiaries as well. The Save Santry Stadium group was allocated the first night of *The Mikado* in November 1962. As *The Irish Press* noted at the time: 'It is not often that athletics and theatre combine, but when that supreme showman, Billy Morton, is involved one's surprise is lessened.'[63]

Though no discernible attempt was made to match the charity to the show – the RNLI with *The Gondoliers*, for example – there were occasional serendipitous synergies. In spring 1980 The Friends of the Rotunda took the first night of Rodgers and Hammerstein's *The King and I*, prompting the *Irish Independent* to observe that 'even though the King had sixty-seven children – he married late, you see – you might just wonder what the "benefits of tranexamic acid in human pregnancy complicated by placental bleeding" could have to do with *The King and I*'.[64] The proceeds were to go to that worthy, if wilfully obscure, cause.

On the debit side of these events, however, was the fact that the audiences tended to be 'friends' of the particular charity being favoured rather than aficionados or even fans of operetta or musical comedy. *Irish Times* drama critic David Nowlan, reviewing a charity performance of *Cox and Box* and *Pirates* in 1977, expressed sympathy with the performers onstage, whose Gilbertian wordiness was more than matched in the dress circle: 'They had some competition from the first night charity audience which trundled in late at the start and after every interval, which banged around and chattered through both overtures and which showed only a reluctant inclination to cease talking during the action. They applauded, of course, as if this made up for the more fundamental discourtesies shown to players and musicians.'[65]

- -

THE GOLDEN JUBILEE

In January 1961 the committee of the R&R discovered, much to its chagrin, that it would not be fifty years old the following January. Given that the twentieth anniversary celebrations had taken place in 1932, the silver jubilee in 1937, and so on, the committee had come to the, not unreasonable, conclusion that the society should celebrate its golden jubilee in 1962. It was Paddy Forde who was first to rain on that inopportune parade. At a committee meeting on 17 January 1961 he arrived with a copy of the minutes of the first-ever R&R meeting. The surviving account of that 1961 meeting has a surreal and disconnected quality about it. It noted Forde's production of the pre-war minutes 'from which it appeared that the society came into existence in the spring of 1913. As a result it appears that the fiftieth anniversary shd. [sic] take place in the spring of 1963'.[66] Forde, a man relentlessly concerned with the R&R's future, had single-handedly recalibrated the society's past.

So twelve months later than expected, the R&R prepared to celebrate fifty years of existence. This it did with considerable aplomb. One of the first moves in a commemorative direction was the authorising of Gladys MacNevin to produce a fiftieth anniversary booklet. This turned into a glossy and handsome sixty-four page volume, entitled *Fifty Golden Years*, costing two and sixpence. Insofar as it navigated the history of the society, the narrative was largely personality based. It began with a potted two-page history of the R&R by incumbent president Michael Campbell, followed by an image of the programme from the first performance which, presumably to the satisfaction of Gladys MacNevin, included a full cast list as well as the names of the members of the chorus.

Most of the rest of the publication was taken up with pen pictures of honorary secretaries, musical

Golden jubilee banquet and ball, menu.

directors and well-known performers over the years. Of considerable value was a list of all society productions since 1913 and of all active and associate members from the foundation of the society. These were described by Charles Acton as 'a remarkable index of the society's achievements'.[67] Advertisements from the likes of Esso, Guinness, the Shelbourne Hotel and the Munster and Leinster bank defrayed the cost of production, which came to £550 (roughly €12,000 in 2013).[68]

One issue with which the committee had to deal was the delicate one of the potential influx of former members attracted back to the fold by an attack of that celebrated ailment *golden jubilitis*. Chronic sufferers were known to exhibit clear signs of nostalgia for their halcyon days and an acute awareness of the significance of a fiftieth anniversary. This was drolly commented upon in the minutes.

> It was felt that the forthcoming season would be likely to attract many persons back into the company who had not been with us for some years whose voices might no longer possess the nightingale qualities of the past.[69]

The fear that the golden jubilee would visit upon the chorus mistress vocal chords that had been allowed to wither and atrophy was handled diplomatically. It was decided to insert a notice in the circular that was to be sent to members concerning the autumn rehearsal dates. Those who had not been in any show since April 1961 would be asked to get in touch in early August so that the question of their taking part might come before the committee. *The Mikado*, appropriately, was chosen as one of those autumn productions, as was the perennial favourite *The Yeomen of the Guard* and the less frequently performed *Patience*. D'Oyly Carte regular Norman Meadmore (see below) was at the helm, so all three pieces 'stuck close to the famous prompt-book'.[70]

The Yeomen of the Guard, 1963. Eoin O'Brien as Jack Point, with Louise Studley (Elsie Maynard), Fintan Corish (Sergeant Meryll), John Comyn (Colonel Fairfax), Hubert O'Connor (Sir Richard Cholmondeley) and Jacqueline Pomeroy (Dame Carruthers).

The Student Prince, 1963. Brendan Doyle, Paul Deegan and John Comyn, with students – Tony Moore, Noel Byrne, Pat Lawlor, Wallie Feegan and Kevin Hough.

Patience, 1963, The Heavy Dragoons.

Golden jubilee banquet and ball: Mrs Rita Childers, Clem and Eithne Ryan, and Erskine Childers.

The jubilee Gilbert and Sullivan repertoire was well-received by the critics, bar some comments on 'choral raggedness'[71] and 'a certain [choral] limpness'[72] across the three productions. President de Valera attended the opening production, *Patience*. Given the ageing president's republican pedigree it was probably fortunate that the society had not chosen *Iolanthe* to open its golden jubilee celebrations. On more than one occasion during a presentation of that operetta at the Gaiety, elements of the audience had opened up with a shower of missiles (largely rotten fruit) on the unfortunate R&R chorus at the beginning of Act II when they were joined by the Earl of Mountararat for a stirring rendition of 'When Britain Really Ruled the Waves'.[73] The previous month de Valera's former party colleague and future president Erskine Childers, then Minister for Transport and Power, had attended the society's jubilee banquet and ball at the Shelbourne Hotel, along with five hundred guests, and had proposed the formal toast to the R&R.

A fitting postscript to a highly significant year was provided in an *Irish Times* op-ed that noted and celebrated fifty years of the existence of the R&R. The newspaper commented:

> There is an argument against amateur dramatic societies that they amuse those performing in them at the expense (in every sense) of the audience, but when a company maintains the standard of this one, and when it can draw houses to a leading theatre for half a century, it justifies itself on the record.[74]

· ·

COPYRIGHT AND D'OYLY CARTE

Just before the golden jubilee the nature of one of the two central professional relationships of the R&R had changed radically. The society was acknowledged to have maintained the Gilbert and Sullivan tradition in Dublin for many years. In times of political or economic difficulty the D'Oyly Carte Opera Company had abandoned its policy of touring productions to Dublin. The R&R had addressed that deficiency. When there was no gap to be filled, as in the periods when the Savoyards resumed their Irish tours, the R&R stood aside and offered alternative material to the Dublin public.

But in 1962, when copyright ran out on the D'Oyly Carte's golden goose, the situation changed overnight. In 1960 and 1961 the R&R had been forced to abandon Gilbert and Sullivan productions entirely when the D'Oyly Carte Company, in a final attempt at gilded egg-gathering, sought to exploit the last months of copyright by touring extensively. Dublin figured on the itinerary and the R&R was prevented from presenting any of the Savoy operas that year.[75]

But from 1 January 1962 the society no longer had to seek permission from the D'Oyly Carte estate to stage Gilbert and Sullivan shows, nor did it have to pay royalties for the privilege of producing them. However, this was not entirely a 'win-win' situation for the society. Whereas Savoy operas had once been a lucrative source of income for both the copyright holders and amateur and professional companies alike, tastes were changing and the time was fast approaching when a *Mikado* or a *Yeomen* would not necessarily be the 'cash cow' of old. In a reference to the expiration of copyright, *The Irish Times* pointed out in November 1962 that 'G&S are losing some of their hold on the public anyway'.[76] As the sixties progressed much of the Gilbert and Sullivan *oeuvre*, which had become rather anachronistic, failed to find new audiences. It would be some time before its very quaintness would become an attraction to audiences rather than a deterrent. To its credit, and frequently to its financial detriment, the R&R kept the Savoy flag flying – though sometimes it flapped listlessly – through unfashionable times. While G&S shows rarely lost money in the late 1960s and early 1970s, they produced only modest profits. The value, however, of the winter seasons, was that the financial outcome was more predictable than the riskier spring shows.[77]

Unperturbed by its lack of propinquity to the *zeitgeist* – the R&R was never going to bring *Hair* to the Gaiety stage – the society planned for an ambitious G&S season in 1962. The plan was, of course, facilitated by the lack of any necessity to budget for royalties. This meant that the society could seek to engage the services of a 'celebrity' producer. In May 1962 it was decided to approach the most distinguished theatrical professional then resident in the country, Sir William Tyrone Guthrie. Guthrie, a second cousin of Hollywood legend Tyrone Power, had made an early name for himself at the BBC as a twenty-something, producing radio plays. In 1953, after a long and highly successful career, he founded the Stratford Theatre Festival in Canada, an event dedicated to the production of the plays of Shakespeare. Guthrie was knighted for his services to theatre in 1961. What gave the R&R hope that they might be able to engage the services of such an *éminence grise* was the fact that he was a resident of a large house/small mansion – now an artist's retreat – in Annaghmakerrig, near Newbliss in Co. Monaghan. Guthrie had just produced *Pirates* and *Pinafore* in London, in post-copyright versions that would probably have deeply offended W.S. Gilbert's directorial sensibilities but were more in keeping with modern theatrical tastes and practices.

Clem Ryan and Sean Dooney travelled to Monaghan in April 1962 to initiate discussions with Guthrie. Their subsequent report may, as events panned out, have strayed into the realms of over-optimism. They suggested to the committee that the great man 'seemed anxious to produce for us'. He rejected the idea of taking on *The Mikado*, preferring *Gondoliers* and *Pinafore*. He held out the possibility of getting access to the costumes from his own London production of *Pinafore*, but his suggestion for the dressing of *Gondoliers* was an honorary treasurer's nightmare. Ryan and Dooney reported, without comment, that Guthrie had in mind new costumes for the whole company for *Gondoliers* at a potential cost of £1,600 – a decent week's gross for a Gaiety G&S production. Guthrie had offered that he 'could possibly persuade Maurice Angel[78] to make them and we [could] hire'. Angel would send his cutter to Dublin to get cast measurements.

Tyrone Guthrie's proposed costume designs for *The Gondoliers*, 1962. Sadly, they proved too costly for the R&R!

The level of detail of the conversation between the three men suggests that Guthrie was genuinely prepared to give the commission some consideration. Ryan and Dooney recorded their 'distinct impression' that the issue of a fee 'would not present an insuperable obstacle', though the matter was never discussed directly.[79] It was an ambitious scheme, indicative of the capacity of the R&R committee to 'think big' but, ultimately, it came to naught. In mid-June the R&R received a telegram from Guthrie 'regretting his inability to produce for us in the autumn'.[80]

If the attempt to entice Guthrie to Dublin represented an inclination to dispense with the 'Savoy style' when it came to the production of Gilbert and Sullivan, that inclination was not sustained much beyond the engagement to direct the 1962 G&S productions of Douglas Craig. This was done at the suggestion of Guthrie. Craig promised, and delivered, 'a rather more modern style than Irish audiences have been used to'.[81] But it was a false dawn. As already noted, the R&R reverted to the orthodoxy imposed by Norman Meadmore the following year. Meadmore and Beryl Dixon, another D'Oyly Carte alumnus, dominated the ranks of R&R producers for most of the next two decades.

Meadmore was 'a dedicated Savoyard'.[82] An assessment of his impressive contribution to the society in the seventy-fifth anniversary publication described how he 'worked strictly from the book and endeavoured to mould his performers to comply with the traditional style of G&S characters...if he had a fault it was that he was too steeped in the D'Oyly Carte'. Beryl Dixon, according to the same source, was rather more open to alternative ideas. She 'was also ex-D'Oyly Carte and was a bundle of energy who combined traditional D'Oyly Carte methods with modern innovations'.[83]

The Gondoliers, 1970. Fred Graham and Des Marron, with Mary Brennan, Marie Rooney and chorus.

In 1970, in one his first R&R reviews for *The Irish Times* – of a Dixon production of *The Gondoliers* – David Nowlan protested that 'surely to goodness...it is time for someone to break the Savoyard mould and to cast Gilbert and Sullivan in some new style, even if only for one wild experiment... after all these years of relative sameness, perhaps it is becoming predictably dull'.[84] Nowlan was, unknowingly, anticipating the more 'free-form' Olympia Theatre/Noel Pearson G&S productions of the early 1980s,[85] themselves founded on the success of the rollicking Joseph Papp/Kevin Kline 1981 New York collaboration on *Pirates*. *Irish Press* critic Robert Johnston, on the other hand, was an aficionado of G&S and liked his Savoy operas 'straight', or as W.S. Gilbert had intended and ordained. Johnston, approvingly, described Norman Meadmore as 'a traditionalist convinced that the D'Oyly Carte production style cannot be improved upon'.[86]

Douglas Craig, who confessed to having seen very few professional performances of G&S operas, approached the material, as would any tyro, with a fresh perspective. 'An Irishman's Diary' in *The Irish Times* in October 1962 speculated that the R&R might try 'a radical variation [that]...will raise a few eyebrows'. Craig himself acknowledged that, although the cast was doing its best to co-operate, an

Rehearsal rooms in Rathmines.

inherent conservatism was occasionally apparent. 'There are times when I catch a slightly baffled look, as if someone is just about to say: "But we always used to…" but so far they have taken it very well.'[87]

However, there must have been at least some institutional reaction to Craig's approach that forced modifications to his plan. Charles Acton's notice of *The Mikado* in *The Irish Times* bore the headline 'Traditional *Mikado* at the Gaiety Theatre'. While the review itself suggests no slavish adherence to ritual, Acton described Craig's approach as 'a conscious interpretation of the familiar tradition'. He dismissed the innovations as 'unimportant'.[88] Craig had made numerous cuts to the original. In the review of *The Gondoliers* in the *Irish Independent*, Mary McGoris's copy was topped off with a similar headline. It read 'Traditional Note in New Production of *Gondoliers*'. McGoris opined that Craig 'keeps pretty closely to tradition; there is little in it to upset Gilbert and Sullivan diehards'.[89] Somewhere along the line the 'raised eyebrows' appear to have won concessions from the modernisers.

A HOME OF YOUR OWN

One of the undoubted keys to the survival of the R&R for a century is the stability created by ownership of a rehearsal space, a repository, a meeting-place, a home. The 1950s had seen a move from the Ormonde Academy in Rathmines – where the landlord had been the elegantly named Madame O'Rattigan – to the national school building at 67/69 Upper Rathmines Road, owned and run by the Church of Ireland. Unsuccessful attempts had been made to buy premises somewhere – anywhere – in the city of Dublin.[90] After the death of Madame O'Rattigan and a request from the new owners of the property to vacate by March 1953, finding an alternative had become an imperative.[91]

After a period of calm and stability the society faced homelessness again in 1967. The Rathmines national school relocated to the nearby grounds of the Church of Ireland training college. Initially the possibility was mooted of the society moving with them.[92] That came to nothing and in April 1968, in a moment of *déjà vu*, the society received a letter from solicitors for the lessors asking how soon they could vacate.[93] The committee then went into overdrive in an effort to secure a rehearsal and administrative premises by purchasing the old school building. Paddy Forde began negotiations with the Munster and Leinster bank,[94] custodians of the society's overdraft. Somehow he managed to persuade a (then) conservative institution to advance a 'loan' of £10,000 towards the purchase of the premises. This was in the form of an extended overdraft facility.[95] As the loan was not advanced as a mortgage, interest rates were relatively high and it was incumbent on the society to pay off the capital sum as rapidly as possible. Solicitor and baritone Roderick Tierney was authorised to bid up to £11,000 at the auction of the school which was taking place at 2.30 on 25 June.[96] He didn't need to go quite that high. The building, an area of 9,000 square feet in all, was secured with a bid of £8,000.[97]

Now that the R&R actually owned the old school it was rather like a husband or wife studying their new spouse properly for the first time. Upon detailed examination, the flaws seemed to become more apparent. The entire building needed to be repainted inside, some of the flooring had to be replaced, large scale rewiring was essential and new convector heaters were also required. The total cost would come to something over £300.[98] Fire insurance, which was to prove crucial two decades later, was secured for £200.[99]

The first, of many, fundraising measures designed to run down the debt as rapidly as possible was a 'type-in' on 12 August 1969 at which letters were typed, on a personal basis, and sent to associate members seeking donations to defray the cost of the new premises. This resulted in the despatch of 430 letters to members.[100] By 1 September over 10 per cent of the purchase price had been raised from donations and fundraising events. By the end of the month that had risen to 20 per cent.[101] By the end of February 1970 over £3,000 had been collected, largely at the instigation of a fundraising group led by Eithne Ryan, Joe Bevan and Paddy Forde.[102]

The drawing of prizes in 1972: Eithne Ryan, Tom Murtagh, Paddy Forde and Michael Campbell.

No assistance was to be expected from the normal cash flow of the organisation because it was, by and large, a negative factor. In 1971, for example, the society had made a loss of £1,500 on the spring production of *Camelot*. There was to be no relief from the box-office.[103]

In February 1972 Paddy Forde came up with the scheme that, ultimately, eliminated the debt on the premises. This was a lottery with generous cash prizes available to purchasers of a ticket (or share) to the value of £100. A limited number of tickets would be issued, increasing the odds of a dividend for purchasers.[104] It was hoped to raise £10,000, of which half would be clear profit to the society.[105] Forde and Eithne Ryan took responsibility for organising the lottery along with honorary treasurer Tom Murtagh. Murtagh, a dapper Dublin jeweller and antique dealer, would blossom into television stardom late in life with a slot on RTÉ's *Live at Three* during which he, on one occasion, demonstrated his talent for ear-piercing on victim/reporter Kevin O'Connor.[106]

At a meeting on 10 August 1972 Forde was able to announce that they had fifty subscribers already.[107] By mid-September 80 of the 100 tickets had been disposed of.[108] By the time the actual draw took place, on 16 December, the target of £10,000 in sales had been achieved and £4,441 had been raised for the building fund.[109] Miraculously, by the end of January 1973 the society's bank account in the Munster and Leinster bank in Dame Street was £300 in the black.[110]

It was a while before the society was able to afford major, as opposed to cosmetic, improvements to the premises. In 1987, 67/69 Upper Rathmines Road was refurbished and rewired at a cost of £5,000. The work, begun in the autumn, was supervised by committee members Malcolm McCambridge and Dympna Bevan.[111] The ultimate intention was to raise the building to 'small theatre' status when funding – anything from £20,000 to £30,000 – was available. But in the short-term there were more practical considerations, such as ascertaining whether or not wet-rot dogged the rafters and if the electrical wiring posed a threat to human life. The work had just been completed when, on the night of 16/17 December, the society became victims of an egregious display of mindless vandalism that could have resulted in the complete destruction of its premises.

On that night the old national school building was broken into, the society's two pianos were placed back to back and set alight. Except that a passer-by noticed the fire and that Rathmines fire station is a mere two hundred yards away, the building might have been entirely consumed. As it was, the fire gutted the floor and ceiling, most of the windows were blown out, fittings were destroyed, and the

Fire in Rathmines, December 1987.

Refurbished rehearsal rooms – ready for the first celebrity concert in 1989.

water used to douse the conflagration also did enormous damage of its own. Society members, after recovering from the initial shock, adopted the philosophy of a future Chicago Mayor, Rahm Emanuel: 'Never let a good crisis go to waste.' Within less than a year the old Victorian building, dating from 1876, had risen from the ashes.

Subsequent rehearsals for the March production of *The Magic of Lerner and Loewe* at the NCH went ahead thanks to the facilities offered by the Church of Ireland training college. Committee meetings moved *pro tem*, to the Orwell Lodge Hotel. An immediate assessment was made of the damage for insurance purposes. The final insurance payout amounted to £55,000 – which translates to €150,000 today – for damage to the structure and contents. Pat Campbell's architectural firm Campbell, Conroy, Hickey was taken on to supervise restoration and extension work. Ambitious plans were made to install a soundproof partition in the main hall, effectively doubling the available rehearsal space. A new lowered ceiling, new flooring and gas fired central heating were also installed. A scheme to extend upwards over the existing toilet and kitchen area had to be abandoned when it was discovered that the foundations would not take the extra load. The R&R, as it has tended to do when adversity strikes, managed to emerge stronger than ever.[112] A planning application was made in April 1988 and work on restoring the premises began in June. The total cost of restoration more than consumed the insurance payment. The final bill was £80,000 and a new bank overdraft facility of £20,000 was required after contributions from the society's guarantors were taken into account.

Paddy Forde.

Kitty Forde.

It was, of necessity, a 'no frills' operation. The only luxury item purchased was a new grand piano, to be named the Paddy Forde Memorial Piano. Forde had died in 1987, pre-deceased by another great servant of the R&R, his sister Kitty, who died in 1985.[113] The buying of the piano was an entirely appropriate gesture. No one had contributed more to the society's ownership of the premises in the first place.[114]

Few could equal the acumen, expertise, energy and commitment that Forde had brought to the R&R over his sixty-plus years of membership. During that time he appeared onstage only once as a performer (see below).[115] In 1981 he had become president of the society on the death of Michael Campbell. He, in turn, was succeeded by Clem Ryan in 1987.

It was confidently expected that through the annual club draw, which had grossed £20,000 in 1987/88 and netted over £8,000 for the society, the debt would be whittled down relatively quickly.[116] Assuming, that was, a few decent years at the box-office, without the need to subsidise loss-making productions. The premises were ready on 5 September 1988 for rehearsals of *Fiddler on the Roof*, to be presented at the Gaiety in November. The

Stephen Faul (honorary secretary) and Clem Ryan (president) with new chain of office, presented by the executive committee in 1988.

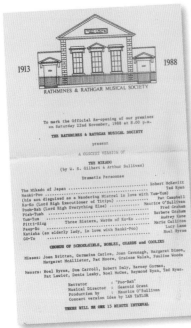

Mikado in Rathmines, 1988.

official reopening, coinciding with the seventy-fifth anniversary celebrations of the society, took place with a concert *Mikado* on 22 October 1988.

A significant and positive by-product of the 'crisis' of the 1987 fire was that 67/69 Upper Rathmines Road, by dint of extensive redevelopment, had finally acquired its 'small theatre' status. It was quickly pressed into service as a suburban arts centre with a moveable stage and a seating capacity of 170.[117] It was opened for this purpose by the Lord Mayor of Dublin, Alderman Sean Haughey, on 27 September 1989. The first recital in the converted schoolhouse, now designated the Rathmines Concert Hall, was given by the great Irish mezzo-soprano Bernadette Greevy on 10 October 1989. It was attended by members of the diplomatic corps from the USA, China, the USSR (soon to be no more), France and Britain.[118] *The Irish Times* critic, Michael Dervan noted in the introduction to his review that 'it can't be often

Recital: Stephen Faul, Fionnuala Hunt, Lord Mayor Sean Haughey, Una Hunt and Wesley Griffiths.

Recital: Soviet ambassador Gennadi Uranov with Clem Ryan (president), Oliver Hill (chairman), Stephen Faul (honorary secretary) and Rita Faul.

Flyer for new Concert Centre.

that Bernadette Greevy gives a concert in Ireland where the venue vies with her performances as a rival for the audience's attention'.[119] Dervan described the seating as 'hard and basic' and the acoustic as being 'on the dry side' but added that 'the feeling of the venue, aided by muted lighting and the *trompe l'oeil* painting of the walls, is pleasingly intimate and only occasionally did the noise of passing traffic obtrude into the music making'.

The nation's outstanding concert performer, who died prematurely in 2008, marked the occasion with a rendition of 'Bless This House' as an encore. Those members of the audience who had worked selflessly to create the space must have exhaled a relieved 'Amen'.

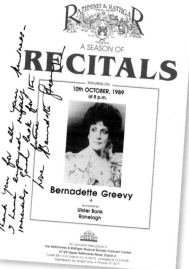

Autographed poster for Bernadette Greevy, 1989.

THE COMPETITION

It is impossible, even in a such a narrowly-defined and insular volume as this, not to place the R&R within a wider artistic context. Previous chapters have referred to the friendly, and sometimes decidedly unfriendly, relationships with other amateur societies. At times there was little love lost between the R&R and the likes of the Dublin Grand Opera Society. However, the latter's expanding budgets, state-subvented status and its essential recourse to the use of paid performers (mostly imported) had moved it well outside the lair of the 'amateur' by the 1960s.

Since the 1970s the R&R's main Dublin 'rival' has probably been the Glasnevin Musical Society. This young upstart, established only in 1958, quickly assumed a significance that belied its youth. It was helped by being able to call on the services of Terry O'Connor as musical director, though the R&R generally remained her priority whenever a conflict of schedules threatened.[120] The Glasnevin society began its life playing in the St Francis Xavier Hall on the north side of the city. But in 1960 it made an early quantum leap by ambitiously and precociously moving to the Olympia Theatre with a production of *Lily of Killarney*, an operetta based on the Dion Boucicault play. In *The Irish Times*, 'An Irishman's Diary' suggested that a hungry young gunfighter had arrived in town ready to take on the jaded sheriff. Quidnunc (Seamus Kelly) wrote that 'the R&R will shortly be challenged on their own ground by a very healthy north-side infant'.[121] Its rude financial health was underscored by the fact that it had engaged the services of soprano Veronica Dunne to play the Colleen Bawn. A number of other (paid) leading performers had Royal Irish Academy of Music backgrounds and/or Glyndebourne experience 'and the up and coming Dublin contralto Bernadette Greevy will be Mrs Cregan'.

Given that the R&R drew its active and performing members from all across the city of Dublin there was no possibility of the two societies establishing lines of recruitment demarcation like civilised New York mafia *capos*. The R&R would never agree to just being the south-side gang. 'An Irishman's Diary' noted on one occasion that 'the Rathgar accent may be as dead as the Harcourt line and the Howth tram, but the R&R lives on – and judging by the accents they're letting in people from far beyond the pale now'.[122] On 11 June 1965, with the north-siders from Glasnevin having gained audiences and enhanced their credibility, the R&R committee prepared to discuss the issue of the alleged poaching of members by other – unnamed – musical societies. That particular agenda item was not reached and debate was instead deferred to the next meeting.[123] The poaching discussion never happened, and so the offending poacher or poachers was never identified.

Two associate members the R&R were very keen not to have poached by other societies were Messrs Gilbert and Sullivan. Despite the perception from the mid-1960s that Savoy operas had had their day, the R&R was determined to retain its status as the leading exponents of 'topsy-turvy' whimsy. In the past they had been abetted in their monopolistic tendencies by the D'Oyly Carte operation. After the ending of copyright in 1962 that was no longer possible. Fortunately few in the city of Dublin were eager to challenge the R&R's hegemony, and certainly not in a venue like the Gaiety Theatre. Typical of the rival productions of G&S was a week of performances by the Clontarf Musical Society of *The Pirates of Penzance*. *The Irish Press* suggested that the run of *Pirates* would 'offer competition'[124] to the second week of the R&R's staging of *Patience* and *The Mikado*. The difference was that the former, no doubt an excellent production and complete with a number of players who had previously performed with the R&R, was staged at the Parish Hall, Clontarf, while the latter was onstage at the Gaiety Theatre. However, the Clontarf society was clearly drawing from the same pool of principals as the R&R. Years before, in August 1966, Clem Ryan had warned the society that the north-siders were proposing to stage *The Mikado*: 'This', he added, 'may exclude a couple of prospective principals from our season.'[125]

In truth the R&R's main 'competition' in the field of Savoy opera came from professional companies, like the D'Oyly Carte itself – no longer touring Ireland in the 1970s – or professional productions, like Noel Pearson's staging of *The Pirates of Penzance* in the winter of 1981/82. The latter provided competition in a number of ways. It offered an opportunity to R&R chorus members, and one or two principals, to realise ambitions to perform on the professional stage. The Joseph Papp production, which diverged markedly from the template of Gilbert himself, had been playing on Broadway for a year when Pearson's version, directed by Patrick Mason with new musical arrangements by Bill Whelan, kicked off in the Olympia. One of those who auditioned was R&R (and Glasnevin) regular Cecil Barror. He was, he confessed to *The Irish Press*, hoping to be cast as Major General Stanley, the very model of a modern Major General.[126] The part, however, went to the experienced professional Niall Buggy. Pearson's 'bright, brash and noisy'[127] romp posed a clear commercial threat to the ascendancy of the R&R in this particular sub-genre of light opera, assuming Pearson decided to duel on an annual basis.[128]

The style of the show, which Pearson touted as being 'totally, totally different' offered additional challenges. Kevin Myers, in 'An Irishman's Diary' underscored this by pointing out that 'the show is an entirely novel form of the Gilbert and Sullivan standard and it might cause many an R&R enthusiast to choke in dismay'.[129] Changes in tempo and arrangement, liberties with the book and lyrics, were all anathema to the D'Oyly Carte style which the R&R had assumed for decades, not slavishly but with a certain degree of loyalty. Were Pearson and Papp bowdlerising or modernising? Would Dublin audiences demand an entirely new style of G&S that the R&R might not be able or even willing to deliver?

Presentation to Terry O'Connor on her retirement at the finale of *Ruddigore* on 27 October 1976. Left: Eva Staveley, presenting a bouquet on behalf of the chorus.

THE BATON PASSES

The relationship between Terry O'Connor and the R&R was never entirely unproblematic. There were periodic eruptions of angst from the committee at the level of her availability for rehearsals and some disquiet over her parallel commitment to the Glasnevin Musical Society. On occasions O'Connor felt undervalued, at other times it was the R&R which hinted that it was being sold short. But the bond between O'Connor and the society was unbreakable and both parties thrived on the relationship. She was 'able to harness the diverse and changing talents of an amateur society and infuse it with dynamic professionalism'.[130]

O'Connor, even in her seventies (she was born in 1897) was a charismatic and ebullient figure on the podium. As she told *The Irish Times* a couple of years before her death in 1983, her tendency to conduct while wearing bracelets, long earrings and a 'slinky evening dress' derived from her passion for clothes. 'I've always loved to show them off.'[131] Her choice of ornamentation was a frequent bane of the irascible Charles Acton. He first drew attention to it in 1962 when he wrote of one R&R production: 'I cannot approve her jangling bracelet as an addition to the percussion section.'[132] He returned to the theme on more than one subsequent occasion. O'Connor ignored him and continued to rattle her jewellery with *élan*. Acton was also critical on more than one occasion of O'Connor's tendency to ignore what was going on onstage: 'She might have found the stage more easily controlled if her eye were there more often than buried in the score.'[133] He launched a personal campaign to get the R&R's musical director to change the habits of a lifetime and offer the players something other than the top of her head.[134]

Gearóid Grant.

In 1976, approaching her eightieth birthday, and after thirty years and over 700 performances, O'Connor decided that it was time to vacate the orchestra pit. She may have been mindful of the circumstances of her own supplanting of her predecessor T.H. Weaving and opted to go before she was pushed. There followed a brief interregnum during which Commandant Fred O'Callaghan of the Army School of Music conducted *The Merry Widow* in spring 1977 and the G&S season that same year. O'Connor was given considerable discretion in the naming of her successor and chose, to the surprise of many and the chagrin of some, a relatively unknown 29-year-old musician, music teacher and conductor. Gearóid Grant, a graduate of the RIAM and University College Dublin, had been examined on piano as a young performer by T.H. Weaving. His name had been advanced and then withdrawn as a possible chorus master in 1974 for the spring 1975 production of *Showboat*.[135] Members of the committee wondered aloud at the wisdom of appointing such a callow youth, a music teacher in FCJ secondary school, Bunclody, Co. Wexford, to such an important position. Grant recalls: 'People were against me getting it. They wanted someone more experienced.'[136] Fortunately, however, Grant had the crucial backing of Paddy Forde.

One of the first changes made by the new musical director was, with the approval of Forde, the augmenting of the orchestra whose numbers had declined. An ever-present in that ensemble has been Grant's wife Sunniva. Grant's children Ronan (trumpet) and Siofra (violin) have also contributed frequently.

In keeping with the familial loyalties inspired by the R&R – others might call it nepotism but that is such an ugly word – Grant was, for many years aided and abetted by the groundwork done by his sister Brid as accompanist. Brid Grant succeeded Carmel Moore in the role.[137] Moore had taken over from Eileen Knowles in 1967. Knowles, appointed accompanist in 1933, and who had played a number of

The Gondoliers, 1982. Dodo O'Hagan (as Inez), Lucy Lane, Pat Campbell, Bob McKevitt and chorus.

leading parts in her early years with the society, died in 1975.[138] Moore, who herself died in 1986, had been resident pianist at the Gaiety Theatre for a number of years.[139]

Grant's debut with the baton was the spring 1978 production of *Gigi*, with Siobhan Scally in the title role, Brendan McShane as Honore Lachailles (the role made famous by Maurice Chevalier) and Jonathan Ryan as Gaston. He faced an early baptism of fire, aggravated by a postal dispute that delayed the arrival of the musical scores from London.[140] Of more significance to Grant, however, was the thriftiness of long-time assistant treasurer Dodo O'Hagan. Opposed by O'Hagan on a number of what he considered to be key expenditures, the new musical director almost became the former musical director: 'I handed in my resignation three times.' Grant, who went on to form a lasting friendship with his adversary, never managed to see eye to eye with the doughty O'Hagan when it came to economies: 'I fought with her for thirty years. She was always on for cost-cutting but I always insisted the standards were kept up.'

Grant was pleased with his debut. 'It was the most spectacular *Gigi* Ireland has ever seen,' David Nowlan of *The Irish Times* agreed. He described the show as 'the best dressed, best set, best moved, best orchestrated show that I can remember in the Rathmines and Rathgar canon…much of the credit must go to Gearóid Grant's musical direction: seldom has an orchestra proved so sensitive to the score and the vocal needs of the R&R performers'.[141]

Having proved himself with musical comedy Grant still had to satisfy the sceptics about his ability to deal with the melodies of Arthur Sullivan. His first opportunity came with *Iolanthe* and *The Yeomen of the Guard* in his first autumn season at the Gaiety. Again he impressed Nowlan who described Norman Meadmore's production as 'satisfactory' before concluding 'most credit for the evening, however, must belong to Gearóid Grant under whose gentle, yet pressing baton, the orchestra and chorus rescued success from uncertainty'.[142] The following year Grant got to grips with his first *Mikado* and drew plaudits from the *Irish Press* critic Robert Johnston, a huge G&S fan. He wrote of the musical direction that 'Gearóid Grant the musical director conducted the orchestra with a steady grip which ensured a musical success especially in the ensembles, and coloured it to the action on the stage.'[143]

Grant was quickly aware of the difference between the R&R and other societies: 'There was a level of intelligence that was of a higher standard. These were people who excelled at things in their professional life, and brought that to the running of the society.' He has also been struck over the years by the level of talent available to the R&R. 'In London the word amateur equals untalented. The R&R elevated the idea of an amateur society. People like Brendan McShane, people like Garry Mountaine, could have been professional; they could have made it anywhere in the world.'

As Ian Fox noted in his profile of Grant in the 1988 seventy-fifth anniversary volume, 'one school, one orchestra and one musical society would never keep the ebullient Mr Grant happy'. Grant would go on to conduct many other

Opening night of *Fiddler on the Roof*, 1988: Heather Hewson, President Hillery and Brendan McShane.

103

orchestras, most notably the two RTÉ ensembles, the Ulster Orchestra, the Irish Chamber Orchestra, and, most prominently, the National Youth Orchestra of Ireland.[144] His increased profile and self-imposed workload has led to some of the inevitable tensions with committees that characterised the tenures of the equally busy Weaving and O'Connor. As he puts it himself, 'the first twenty years were the hardest, but once they started agreeing with me it was fine'. Despite his occasional spats with R&R committees, he acknowledges their central importance in the survival and relative good health of the society. 'A very committed committee makes the R&R what it is. People like Pat Campbell, people like Dodo O'Hagan…on the committee for thirty years. The backroom staff works to raise the standard of every show. It's their society, the people in the background.'

While Grant 'doesn't do committees' he has an innate ability to work with people very different from himself. He was, for example, warned that he would never get on with Heather Hewson, chorus director from the time of his appointment until her retirement in 1993. Hewson had taken over the role in 1975 from Robert Daly. 'It was a south-side Protestant versus a north-side Catholic. I was told there was no way you'll ever get on with Heather.' However he maintains to this day that 'she was the best I've ever worked with'.[145] Since Heather Hewson's retirement in 1993 Grant has worked with Jackie Curran Olohan as chorus director.

Grant views retirement much as he does committees. 'I don't do retirement. I still have the same mentality as the kids. They want it to be the best ever and I'm the same way. I'll go all night until it's right. It has to be right.' Noel McDonough, who has worked with Grant on many occasions as a director since the late 1990s testifies to his continued enthusiasm and expertise, describing him simply as 'the best musical director in the country…he has a unique insight into shows because he's been on stage as well. He always goes with new ideas.'[146]

Fiddler on the Roof programme, 1988.

It is a testament to Grant's enthusiasm, resilience and sheer talent that he has emulated his predecessors in his longevity as musical director of the R&R. In 2013 he overtook Terry O'Connor in terms of the number of shows he had conducted. It is also something of a testament to the R&R that the society has had, once C.P. Fitzgerald's inaugural four-year tenure is subtracted, only three musical directors since 1917.

SEVENTY-FIVE – NOT OUT

In 1988 the R&R celebrated seventy-five years of existence. To some of the society's 'insiders' it must have felt like a landmark achieved against the odds. The R&R seemed to have rolled, with a surprising degree of equanimity, from one financial crisis to another. When insolvency stared the society in the face a lucrative rabbit always seemed to be produced from a previously inconspicuous hat. When businessman

Stephen Faul, a man with no previous R&R history, was recruited – effectively headhunted – from the Investment Bank of Ireland,[147] it was on the back of losses of the order of £15,000 on *Annie Get Your Gun*. Faul, like all his predecessors as R&R treasurer, was required to be eternally optimistic and resourceful.

Unlike the spurious Dublin Millennium year, with which it happened to coincide, the R&R had achieved a genuine benchmark to be celebrated. Another glossy commemorative booklet was produced. This was expected to cost around £6,000 (roughly €16,000 today), a sum to be covered by advertising from the guarantors. The

Ronnie Drew, Ronald Twelvetrees and Pat Campbell, Dublin Millennium Awards, 1988.

volume included a brief history of the society written by Sean Dooney, numerous profiles of members and performers, and an edited version of the text of a lecture 'Seventy-Five Years of the R&R' delivered by Robert McCullagh to the Royal Dublin Society on 28 January 1988. In his address McCullagh described himself as someone who had been accepted for membership despite hailing from 'the frozen wastes of Clontarf'.[148] Crucially, half the publication was taken up with invaluable and comprehensive cast-lists of (almost) every production since 1913.

The anniversary year began with a successful and profitable concert at Mount Argus in January. A full seventy-five-person chorus, with soloists Frank O'Brien, Niamh Murray, Lucy Lane, Ted Ryan and Robert McKevitt, Peter Lewis and Marie Culliton, performed excerpts from some of the 220 shows produced by the society, accompanied by the Army No.1 Band. Pat Campbell, as usual, presided over affairs with his customary lucidity and affability.[149] A somewhat extraneous, but no doubt welcome, addition to the traditional repertoire of the choir was a rendition of the inspiring 'Battle Hymn of the Republic'.[150] The choice was an appropriate one for a society that had withstood considerable civil and internecine strife.

Later in the year the society gained some justified recognition for its contribution to the musical life of the city of Dublin when it was the recipient of a Seal of the City. This was presented to Pat Campbell by Lord Mayor Ben Briscoe on 22 August 1988.[151]

In a celebratory *Irish Times* piece in November, the society's president, Clem Ryan, attempted to shake off its 'middle class reputation' by ascribing that image to a society of previous decades. His case, however, was not enhanced elsewhere in the article by the intelligence that Tony O'Reilly had once been a non-performing member of the R&R. Ryan told the *Irish Times* reporter, Jill Nesbitt, that the future millionaire 'was too big' for the chorus line. However, Ryan informed Nesbitt: 'He did get to play the Mikado at his fiftieth birthday party.' On that occasion the former Irish winger and Heinz CEO, was backed up by the chorus of the R&R who had travelled to his Castlemartin home to provide the entertainment for the evening.[152]

The winter production chosen for such a historic year was *Fiddler on the Roof*. In that show, first performed by the society in 1972, Tevye the poor Russian-Jewish milkman attempts valiantly to protect

R&R at the US embassy, 1980: Clem and Eithne Ryan, US Ambassador William Shannon, Mrs Elizabeth Shannon, and Pat and Joan Campbell.

his family from malign outside influences. At one point he tells Perchik, a young radical student: 'Why should I break my head about the outside world? Let the outside world break its own head.' Perchik warns him: 'Nonsense. You can't close your eyes to what's happening in the world.'[153] It could stand as a metaphor for the R&R. Many of the members, as Gearóid Grant has pointed out, were people with very successful professional careers. Successful but stressful. For them the R&R was a welcome retreat, a parallel universe into which they could escape for a time. But the society itself did not exist within any parallel universe. It had been obliged to cope, over its seventy-five-year history, with an often unsympathetic outside world. That reality did not end in 1988.[154]

In the seventy-fifth anniversary publication, committee chairman Stephen Faul wrote that 'our past is the inspiration for the future'. The R&R was a society with a strong sense of its past and of its own worth. Having survived three quarters of a century, there was an almost axiomatic confidence that the society would manage a fourth. However, the optimism, while not entirely misplaced, would be sorely tested over the twenty-five years that followed.

Ambassador John Moore at the R&R Summer Soirée in 1975, with R&R members Dympna Cummins, Shirley McCambridge, Dodo O'Hagan, Carmel Moore, Eva Staveley, Sally Young, Ena Boylan and Henry Kennedy.

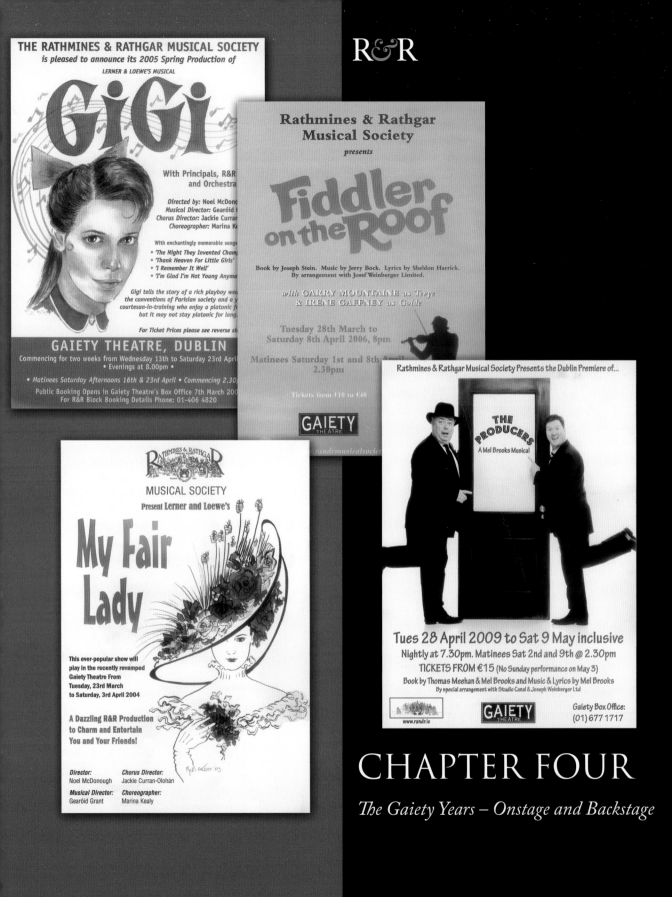

CHAPTER FOUR

The Gaiety Years – Onstage and Backstage

CHAPTER FOUR

The Gaiety Years – Onstage and Backstage

· ·

THE OLD LADY SAYS NO

There never would have been a Gaiety Theatre without the R&R. It is part of the warp and woof of this theatre.

Eamonn Andrews, 1971.

If the link with Savoy opera and D'Oyly Carte was crucial to the development of the R&R the second key relationship of the first half-century of the society's existence involved its status as biannual tenant of the Gaiety Theatre – an association important for the credibility of the society but never unproblematic and often dysfunctional. Tenure at the Gaiety was vitally important to the self-image of the R&R. In the 1960s and 1970s its claim to pre-eminence among the country's amateur societies was largely based on one clearly quantifiable asset, continued access to Ireland's premier commercial theatre. It was an association that came with a large and often painful twice-yearly invoice attached and, as the rental of the theatre became more and more expensive, productions increasingly had to be subsidised with the subscriptions of active and associate members, the contributions of generous guarantors and other fundraising ventures. But it was an unquestioned axiom of the R&R philosophy that a continuing affiliation with the Gaiety was worth the expense and inconvenience.

Perhaps it was a marriage that should have ended in divorce much sooner than it did, given the ill-treatment often meted out by one of the contracting parties. But it continued, monogamously on the part of the R&R, until well into the 1980s when the society found itself drawn to a younger, less high-maintenance, alternative. The R&R then entered into a *menage à trois* which lasts to this day, without even the vaguest whiff of scandal.

The Gaiety Theatre's very existence often seemed in doubt from the mid-1960s to the 1980s. It was too big, and too expensive, to stage anything other than the most financially ambitious domestic commercial theatre. At the same time it was too small, and uneconomic, to allow many of the big West End shows include Dublin on their itinerary. It faced stiff competition, not just from other theatres but from cinema and television. In the final five years of the reign of Louis Elliman only about seven of its own 'inhouse' productions turned a profit for the Gaiety management.[1]

Under the hegemony of Elliman, the Gaiety had moved from being an upmarket variety theatre (upmarket of the Olympia at any rate) to hosting the Edwards–Mac Liammóir company, grand opera

Fiddler on the Roof, 1972: Brendan McShane and Chris Bruton.

and occasional forays into ballet, as well as the R&R and Jimmy O'Dea pantomimes. As early as 1951, when he leased the Queen's Theatre to the Abbey, according to theatre historian Christopher Morash, Elliman 'had sensed that audiences for variety were declining'.[2] That decline was accentuated by the takeover of the Olympia by Stanley Illsley and Leo McCabe, their move into 'legitimate' theatre and the metamorphosis of theatrical 'variety' into television 'light entertainment'. While the R&R survived these changes with its biannual tenure at the Gaiety largely intact, the theatre itself experienced some hard times in the 1960s. In the R&R's 1963 fiftieth anniversary booklet Elliman was allocated a page for a tribute of his own. In it he pointed out that 'the R&R is the only amateur company performing today at the Gaiety'. The continued tenancy was due, as Elliman hinted in his written eulogy, to the capacity and diplomatic skills of officers like Paddy Forde, Pat Campbell and Clem Ryan to bend to the impresario's will, without ever actually breaking.

However, Elliman, in addition to brooking little opposition from the R&R, did play a significant role in the maintenance of standards in the society over the years. The knowledge that his disapproval spelled expulsion from the Gaiety was a powerful motivator, but Elliman also made himself useful in setting up the society with agents and potential producers in London. In 1964 Clem Ryan was despatched on a 'fact-finding' mission with introductions to many key West End players, introductions supplied by Elliman, to the likes of agent Max Kester and publishers Chappell & Company.[3]

This makes the final paragraph of Elliman's tribute in the 1963 golden jubilee publication all the more ironic. He noted that the theatre's own centenary was eight years away, before adding: 'it is my earnest hope that when that time arrives the R&R will be in the forefront of participants in that celebration'. And indeed they were, but Elliman himself was not. Elliman died in November 1965 at the age of 59.[4] The Gaiety, fortunate to survive as a theatre, was sold in 1966 and was, at the time of the centenary, being run by Eamonn Andrews Studios.

Elliman had attempted to sell the theatre to a property development company, BOS Investments – a subsidiary of a London-based company Block Office and Shop Development – for £200,000 a few months before his death. The deal had fallen through after BOS failed to secure planning permission from Dublin Corporation to turn the theatre into a multi-storey office block.[5] News that the theatre was to close – temporarily at least – had been conveyed by the Gaiety management to the R&R committee in June 1965, though the society was assured that it would become available again in the spring of 1966.[6]

There was an element of brinkmanship in the dealings of the Elliman family with the theatrical community. The threat remained that the theatre would be sold for development, despite the Corporation's refusal of the BOS plans. Elliman hoped to activate the theatrical community sufficiently to allow him to divest himself of the building to a buyer intent on retaining the building as a theatre. The concerns of theatre-lovers and practitioners about the venue's future were exemplified within the R&R by the intervention of Heather Hewson. When she became aware of the Gaiety's potential closure she wrote to the R&R committee in June 1965 'strongly urging that we take action in conjunction with the appropriate bodies for the organisation of a campaign to have [the] theatre preserved'. Paddy Forde told the committee that he expected television personality and entertainment impresario Eamonn Andrews to convene a meeting to discuss the status of the venue and the R&R pledged 'to give our entire support to any moves to save [the] theatre'.[7]

In May 1966 the theatre was sold by Bertie Elliman, brother of Louis, to an unknown purchaser. Elliman claimed to have had no knowledge of the identity of the new owners but expressed himself as being 'very glad to get it off my hands'. *The Irish Times* reported it was 'virtually certain that the building will continue to be used as a theatre' and that Bertie Elliman had, rather sanctimoniously, pointed out 'we could have sold it six months ago just as a property'.[8] It later emerged that the theatre had been bought in trust by Daniel F. Stephenson of the auctioneers James H. North for 'an Irishman living in England'.[9] The Irishman in question was, in fact, Joseph Murphy Senior, who achieved a certain notoriety in the twenty-first century thanks to findings of corruption against him and his son, Joseph Murphy Junior by the Flood/Mahon Tribunal.[10] The new owners, who left the previous management in position *pro tem*, proved to be even less accommodating than had Elliman. The R&R discovered a few weeks after the purchase was announced that they were to be charged a fixed rental of £1,200 per week rather than being allowed to continue with the percentage arrangement that had held since 1914.[11]

Gaiety manager Joe Kearns informed them that the theatre had been bought by Murphy and that the old rules and the old dispensation no longer applied. There would be no rental reduction, as had previously been the case, because the R&R was an amateur company. The society would pay the same rate as every other tenant. The new regime would start with the G&S season in November. Forde told

The Gaiety Theatre, drawing from 1965 programme.

111

Kearns that 'our figures for the past six years gave no hope whatsoever that we could meet the new Gaiety rental…we had been lulled by the previous owners into believing that a figure of approximately £800 was adequate to cover theatre expenses and, presumably, a profit for the week'.[12] Ultimately Kearns relented, but only to the tune of £200. The R&R briefly discussed absconding to the Olympia but eventually agreed to stump up the £1,000 per week.[13]

The Mikado, 1966. Men's chorus.

Princess Ida, 1966. Cecil Barror as King Gama.

By September 1967, to the relief of the R&R and the arts community in Dublin, the management of the Gaiety had been taken over by Eamonn Andrews Productions, with Fred O'Donovan at the helm. The relief, however, proved to be short-lived. In taking over the theatre, Andrews had claimed that 'the Gaiety is here to stay' but added the caveat that 'we would not have entered into our present arrangement if we did not see prospects of commercial success'. He warned that ticket prices were likely to rise as the Gaiety's margin of profitability could be wiped out by a bad run of 'inhouse' production of as little as four weeks.[14] The message was clear. Andrews and O'Donovan had a business to run and would be unsentimental when it came to the theatre's bottom line. The new deal offered to the R&R was a weekly rental fee of £1,000, an additional 50 per cent of a box-office 'take' of between £2,000 and £2,600 and 40 per cent of everything over £2,600. A note from Forde to Clem Ryan outlined the stark financial reality for the R&R of this arrangement as a template for future deals between the society and the theatre. He pointed out that the gross take from *Patience*, *The Mikado* and *Princess Ida* in November 1966 had been £5,042. On that figure the R&R had made a profit of £501. Under the new deal, based on similar figures, the society – when its own costs were taken into consideration – would barely have broken even.[15] The new terms were accepted, but 'under protest'.[16] A small measure of grim satisfaction was extracted from this stark situation by the society's decision to decline a request from Eamonn Andrews Studios for the R&R to provide a chorus for a mooted Gaiety production of *My Fair Lady*.[17]

The following year the weekly rental fee had jumped to £1,250 and, as a consequence, the R&R's *Brigadoon* in March 1968 recorded a loss of £1,600. The society faced a 'critical situation' and sought a meeting with O'Donovan and the write-off of almost £700 owed by the R&R to Eamonn Andrews Productions.[18] While the latter objective was ultimately secured, it was at the expense of yet another rental increase. In August 1968 O'Donovan announced that the new weekly rate from November would be £1,420![19]

Brigadoon, 1968.

But the R&R needed the Gaiety (more than the theatre needed the society) so the affiliation continued. In 1971 on the night of the actual 100th anniversary of the Old Lady of South King Street – 27 November – the R&R was onstage with, fittingly, *The Mikado*.[20] As a further part of the theatre's centenary celebrations that year, the society was also asked to stage an October concert in the Gaiety, with Colman Pearse conducting the (then) RTÉ Light Orchestra.[21] Pat Campbell, MC for the night, in what was a musical history of the R&R, tantalised and probably baffled the audience when he led into the intermission by announcing that the second half of the show would include an excerpt from *Hair*.[22] That probably sent some of the older supporters of the society's productions racing to the bar fulminating against modernity and nudity. They need not have been concerned: Campbell was joking. The *Irish Independent* enthused that the show had 'presented a panoramic view of the society's past activities… and will add fresh laurels to the R&R's list of achievements'.[23]

There was (relative) peace in the valley through the rest of the 1970s with the pattern being maintained of two or three G&S productions in the winter followed by a more contemporary musical in the spring. It wasn't until 1983, with the R&R experiencing its own customary financial difficulties, that a new, potentially terminal, crisis coincidentally afflicted the Gaiety. This derived from a dispute between the leaseholders, Eamonn Andrews Productions (EAP) and the Murphy family, owners of the building and landlords of EAP. The Old Lady of South King Street had not had a good 1983. The imposition by the government of VAT of 23 per cent on box-office returns,[24] a 'disastrous summer season'[25] and the loss of a three-week booking for October, forced EAP to issue protective notice to its staff. The lessees had also complained about the state of the building and applied to Dublin Corporation for a grant of £200,000 for essential renovations. The landlords objected, claimed that the lessees had been derelict in the upkeep of the theatre, and demanded the return of the lease. With EAP requiring up to £40,000 to keep the theatre open while it was 'dark' it looked as if EAP would not be in a position to continue as leaseholders. It was announced by the owners, in October 1983, that the theatre was to 'close for repairs'.[26] Many felt this was a euphemism for a renewed attempt to demolish the beautiful old building and erect another essential office block on the site.[27]

Dublin Corporation was urged by some of its members, including Labour councillors Mary Freehill and Brendan Byrne, to acquire the premises in order to ensure its survival as an arts venue. This was opposed by, among others, the infamous Fianna Fáil councillor and practising philistine Ned Brennan, a storied curmudgeon who periodically railed against cultural organisations that staged anything more racy or controversial than *Noddy and Big Ears*.[28] EAP sought Arts Council and/or Dublin Corporation support to keep the theatre open through October to enable the R&R and Maureen Potter to fill their dates in November and December. The alternative was to hand the lease back to Murphy. As far as the official state and local bureaucracy was concerned, the pledge from the owners that the building would be closed, refurbished and reopened as a theatre was a convenient device to refuse to bail out EAP, bailouts being unpopular at the time. The R&R winter season – of *The Sorcerer* and *The Mikado* – appeared to depend on some form of subvention or sponsorship to keep the EAP lease viable.

On 22 October 1983 EAP director Dermod Cafferky, announced that the company would soldier on. EAP would not be handing back the lease, despite the inevitable October closure and the threat of legal proceedings from the owners. EAP was being sued for the completion of 'essential repairs to the building which are now a question of urgency'.[29] The production company intended to keep the theatre

Gaiety Theatre centenary celebrations: R&R 'At Home'.

Gaiety Theatre centenary celebrations:
R&R programme, 27 October 1971.

Gaiety Theatre centenary celebrations: Michael Campbell making a presentation to Eamonn Andrews, with Fred Taylor and Clem Ryan.

115

An Evening with Mr Gilbert and Mr Sullivan, 1984, full cast and production team on stage.

An Evening with Mr Gilbert and Mr Sullivan programme.

open until February at least, at which time it was hoped the lease could be handed over to interested parties committed to retaining the current use of the Gaiety, rather than being returned to its owners. The short-term effect of this move was that the R&R winter season would go ahead in its traditional venue.

But the positive development was short-term only. In 1984 the R&R had chosen to stage Lerner and Loewe's *Gigi* at the Gaiety. Before that date could be honoured Eamonn Andrews Productions had, effectively,[30] gone into receivership and the lease was to be handed back to Gaiety Theatre (Dublin) Ltd. The theatre closed on 21 January 1984 when EAP ceased to operate, and awaited the refurbishment which, according to the owners, would cost in the region of £500,000.[31] The R&R missed the boat that set sail immediately for the Olympia. While the Dublin Grand Opera Society was able to secure its spring season at the Dame Street venue,[32] the R&R was left on the harbour side waving its comely French *ingénue* goodbye.

A plaintive letter to the daily newspapers from Pat Campbell detailed the consequences of the Gaiety closure to the society. Consequences made potentially more severe by a delay in getting work on the theatre underway – the refurbishment had still not begun by the end of March because of a failure to return the lease. Campbell pointed out that the R&R had, in good faith, engaged the services of a production team for *Gigi*. Those individual contracts had had to be cancelled and the National Concert Hall booked for something called *An Evening with Mr Gilbert and Mr Sullivan* from 3–5 April. The letter was half-plaint, half-plug for the NCH show, but Campbell pointed out that as far as the membership of the R&R was concerned 'concert activities, however well presented, are no substitute for the good stage experience which we constantly provide'. He concluded:

Like the Gaiety Theatre itself, the public are 'in the dark' concerning the future of this fine old theatre, which forms such an integral part of Dublin life. We know we speak for all theatrical organisations when we strongly urge that the parties involved would solve their differences with all possible speed and enable the theatre to re-open without further delay.[33]

On 29 January the High Court allowed the liquidator of Eamonn Andrews Productions to surrender the lease to Gaiety Theatre (Dublin) Ltd. Reconstruction work began almost immediately.

The Old Lady of South King Street got quite a facelift, paid for by Joe Murphy in what *The Irish Press* called 'an incredible commercial act of faith'.[34] The final bill was closer to £750,000 than the half a million pounds originally envisaged.[35] The life-threatening 'rake' – which often looked like it was about to pour performers into the orchestra pit – was removed. A new flat sprung-pine stage was installed and the sound system, which over the years had consigned many a good line to a resonant oblivion, was revamped. The seating was totally refurbished, as was the management. Irishman Richard Condon, late of the highly profitable Theatre Royal in Norwich, former manager of the Olympia, was the new major domo.[36]

The Pirates of Penzance, 1984. David Middleton (Frederick), Cathal MacCabe (Pirate King) and Glynis Casson (Ruth) with Pirates' chorus.

The theatre reopened on 26 October with the spectacular 'Night of 100 Stars', produced by Fred O'Donovan. This featured Maureen Potter, Siobhan McKenna, Brendan Grace, Hal Roach, the R&R chorus and the DGOS but is, unfortunately, best remembered for the idiosyncratic rendition of Swift's 'Modest Proposal' by Peter O'Toole. The piece was scheduled to last two minutes but O'Toole, impervious to the *ennui* of a live audience, read the entire twenty-minute-long essay. This led to hisses, catcalls and walkouts from members of the well-heeled audience. They were either offended by the Hollywood star's invocation of eighteenth-century Dublin poverty or bored by the length of time it took him to read the viciously satirical piece, which advocated the fattening and slaughter for profit of babies by impecunious Dubliners as a handy source of revenue. The R&R's renditions of choruses from *The Pirates of Penzance* were far more entertaining than O'Toole's bizarre *faux pas*, but the society's contribution lacked the news value of the meltdown of Lawrence of Arabia.

In 1989 businessman Gerry O'Reilly, owner of a number of Dublin city venues, purchased the Gaiety and added it to his collection. Relations remained on an even keel with the new management until 1992 when the R&R and the DGOS began to experience difficulties with the theatre. The travails of the DGOS are publicly documented, as the opera company took Gaiety Entertainments to court for non-payment of box-office revenue. What was not widely known at the time was that the R&R had been experiencing precisely the same difficulties as the DGOS.

The first hint of any problem came in December 1992. The R&R was still licking its wounds after a loss of £25,000 on the autumn production of Cole Porter's *Anything Goes*. To add insult to injury the treasurer (Ig Lyons) reported that 'a cheque had still to be received from the Gaiety Theatre' for the society's share of the box-office take. 'It was also generally felt that the whole position regarding the Gaiety Theatre would have to be examined in great detail for the future.'[37] The theatre had secured a rental of £17,000 a week for *Anything Goes*, thus adding greatly to the R&R's deficit. By the end of January 1993 there was still no payment forthcoming. In February the R&R despatched a solicitor's letter to the Gaiety demanding its money and threatening legal proceedings if it was not forthcoming.[38] Shortly thereafter, two cheques arrived. One was dated 22 February; the other was for 8 March. The first one had cleared by the time the committee met in early March, though 'it was noted that the cheques were not drawn on the Gaiety Entertainments Co. Ltd'. The consensus at the meeting was that it would not be possible to enter into a contract with the Gaiety in the immediate future without the protection of a bond. This would secure the society's position for payment. In the meantime

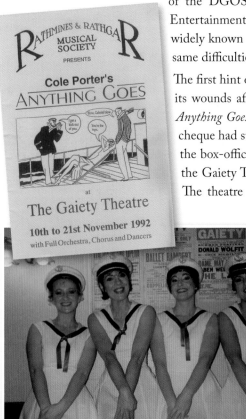

Anything Goes programme.

Anything Goes, 1992. The Angels: Caroline Keane, Pauline Woods, Lynn Branagan and Frances Jones.

other theatre venues were to be investigated as possible locations for future shows.[39] At the 1993 annual general meeting Joe Lane informed the members that there would be no Gaiety production that winter. He was evasive about the reasons for this, referring the members to reports in the daily newspapers concerning the affairs of the theatre.

The wisdom of the March decision was borne out some weeks later when, on 7 May 1993, the High Court granted an order restraining Gaiety Entertainments Ltd, Silverthorn Investments (the entity originally used to buy the theatre) and Gerry O'Reilly from reducing their assets below £50,432. This was the sum the DGOS claimed was owed from the Gaiety box-office for its spring 1993 production. David Collopy, the DGOS chief executive, told the court that the Gaiety had not paid the final instalment of money owed from the DGOS winter 1992 production until 9 March – eighty days late. The £50,432 in dispute had been due on 29 April but, according to Collopy, had not yet been paid. 'He had made repeated telephone calls to the Gaiety in an attempt to secure payment but to no avail.'[40] Five days later the matter was settled when the High Court was told that the money had now been paid over by the Gaiety.[41]

The R&R did not return to the Gaiety until November 1995, two months before O'Reilly sold the theatre to the Break for the Border nightclub and restaurant chain in January 1996 for £2.8 million.[42] The theatre was resold for £4 million three years later to the music promoters MCD.[43] Joe Lane had entered into informal negotiations with the Gaiety in October 1994 but there was still considerable reluctance to return to the venue, based on the economics of hiring the theatre for two weeks. Treasurer Ig Lyons was asked to draw up a report with costings measured against projected income. His research did not make pleasant reading for the committee. Any major production, factoring in rental costs, fees, royalties and sundry other essential items, was likely to lose more than £25,000 based on a seat occupancy of 70 per cent.[44] The risk was clearly too great. Significant losses, on a scale similar to those of *Anything Goes*, were almost guaranteed. The cost of hiring the theatre had risen from £17,000 a week in 1992 to more than £28,000 in 1995. Nonetheless Joe Lane was instructed to sign a contract with the Gaiety Theatre to produce a show, the nature of which was yet to be decided, in the autumn of 1995.[45]

Was it the triumph of optimism over experience, *folie de grandeur* or a sense that while the National Concert Hall was proving to be a profitable venue (see Chapter 5) it still did not feel like a real theatre? The NCH was, by and large, still hosting R&R concerts rather than fully staged musical shows. Up to that point the society had produced only two G&S shows at the Earlsfort Terrace venue. There was a clear desire, whatever the risk, to return to the embrace of the Old Lady of South King Street. In order to hold on to the claim of being the best amateur musical society in the country it was essential to be holding down at least one season a year at the Gaiety. So it was that, in November 1995, *My Fair Lady* was staged at the venue. The sequence that had begun in 1914 and had continued, almost unbroken, until 1993 was resumed.

The link between the R&R and the Gaiety lasts to this day. One of the society's centenary-year productions, *Hello, Dolly!* starring Rebecca Storm in the title role, was staged at the venue. The relationship has survived the stresses of numerous changes of management and ownership of the theatre. However, economic realities and the escalating costs of production, mean that the relationship has stuttered since the 1980s. But it survives. However, the spring of 1984 and the recourse to the National Concert Hall – which had only come into existence in 1981 – established a precedent. The

R&R *could* contemplate life without the Gaiety. It chose not to lead such a life in any meaningful way until 1993 when the first *bona fide* stage show – once again it was the talismanic *Mikado* – was produced at the concert venue. But a bridge was crossed on 3 April 1984 when the R&R took to the NCH stage for its first concert there.

Some of the performers that night, especially MC Pat Campbell, must have been conscious of an ironic twist. In 1980 Fred O'Donovan, who had driven many a hard bargain with the R&R in the 1960s and 1970s, parted company with Eamonn Andrews. O'Donovan ceased to have any connection with the Gaiety Theatre, despite the fact that it may well have been his action in 1977 in having the building 'listed' that saved it from demolition in 1983/84.[46] The following year the veteran impresario took on a new role, as chairman of the National Concert Hall.[47] What goes around comes around.

· ·

'OH HADN'T WE THE GAIETY ...'

Is it possible to choose what was the most successful R&R production during its long association with the Gaiety Theatre? What criteria would be used for making the choice? Consensus? None exists. Everyone has their own particular favourite, and in the case of active members this is inevitably informed and coloured by their own participation, or otherwise, in certain productions. A few lines, a solo, a leading part, and the rose-tinted spectacles are never far from the bridge of the nose.

Box-office takings? While this, at least, has the benefit of offering a more objective test, however, it too

Showboat, 1987. Orchestra call, led by Eddie Guilmartin.

is flawed as a rationale. How do you compare a production from the 1950s, like *Bless the Bride* (1950) with a box-office gross of £3,432,[48] and *Showboat* in 1987, which grossed around £25,000.[49] Granted, you can calculate an inflation-adjusted figure. This would tell us that £3,432 in 1950 equated to £41,808 in 1987, making the box-office take of *Bless the Bride* vastly superior to that of *Showboat*.[50] What it doesn't tell us, of course, is what the production costs were and how much, if any, profit the R&R made from the show after the Gaiety, the rights holders, the costumiers, etc. had taken their cut. In the case of *Bless the Bride*, it was £400. *Showboat* lost over £4,000. So, on that basis *Bless the Bride* was clearly the more successful show. Or was it? How do we account for the prevailing economic circumstances that might have operated as a disincentive to theatre-goers to spend their money? Did the worldwide post-war economic malaise pinch any less relentlessly than our own home-grown variety in Ireland in the mid-1980s?

How do we calculate for cultural differences? In 1950 theatre was one of the very few forms of entertainment available to the (considerably smaller) Dublin population. In 1987 the rival attractions included the ubiquitous television set. How do we factor in other issues like the venerability of the show, the frequency with which it had appeared in the R&R repertoire and the familiarity of the score? *Bless the Bride* was only three years old in 1950, was having its premiere in Ireland, and had at least one saleable hit to its credit already, 'This is My Lovely Day'. By 1987 *Showboat* was sixty years old, it was on its third outing with the R&R (though the first production had been in 1955) but had a slew of familiar songs in its score, including 'Make Believe', 'Can't Help Lovin' Dat Man' and the immortal 'Ol' Man River'.

Best not go there, really.

So what follows is a sample of some of the most lucrative, best-reviewed or most memorable shows staged, mostly in the last half-century, at the Gaiety Theatre. There are, it should be pointed out, a few geese among the swans, notable for reasons other than any well-deserved popularity or artistic merit.

THE ARCADIANS (1931)

By the beginning of the 1930s the R&R had been around for a dozen or so years. No one could have foreseen that it would last for at least a century. The omens were not good. As outlined in Chapter 1, Rupert D'Oyly Carte was being less than co-operative in offering licences to the society to produce the work of Gilbert and Sullivan – and the two 1930 shows, *The Beloved Vagabond* and *A Country Girl*, had performed disappointingly at the box-office. In 1931, at the suggestion of the Gaiety manager Hugh Hyland, the R&R had chosen to present *The Arcadians* by Lionel Monckton and Howard Talbot, as its spring production. It was offered a six-day run at the Gaiety and plunged into rehearsal on a production whose success or failure might well define the society's future relationship with the theatre.

The Arcadians autographed programme, 1931.

121

The Arcadians was a piece of English whimsy dating from the Edwardian era involving the clash of esoteric Arcadians and cynical Londoners. In the R&R production the two key Arcadian parts were taken by Hilda White (Sombra) and Mida O'Brien (Chrysea). By coincidence the two were sisters-in-law and had already claimed a number of leading parts since their mid-twenties.[51] They had made their R&R debuts together in *The Duchess of Dantzic* in 1924 alongside Ria Mooney, May Doyle, Mabel Home and Eileen Knowles. Home and Knowles were also part of the *Arcadians* company.

The show was a welcome success after a couple of lean years. The *Irish Independent*, in its review of the 'lyrical laughing comedy', described how 'the delightful operetta romped its way from scene to scene to the accompaniment of rounds of hearty applause and gales of laughter'.[52] The *Irish Times* concurred, observing that 'the performance went off with a fine swing, the players entering at once into the fun of the piece'.[53] Most of the plaudits were reserved for the comic performances of Billy Harmon, Mabel Home as his long-suffering wife and Alf Gaynor as Peter Doody, a jockey riding in the Askwood Cup. According to *The Irish Times*, 'they brought out cleverly every little turn and trick that the varying situations demanded, and were well supported by the rest of the principals'.

So popular did the show prove during its initial run that the Gaiety brought it back for a second week before the end of May. The total box-office take amounted to an extremely healthy £1,319 and a profit of almost £300 for the R&R. More to the point, the success of the production demonstrated that the society was not entirely reliant on the goodwill of Rupert D'Oyly Carte to make its way in the world and it had the effect of stabilising a relationship with the Gaiety that had just begun to teeter slightly.

. . . .

LILAC TIME (1944)

Such was the nature of the R&R that a production combining most of the society's pre- and post-war principals in a single production was quite a rarity. This makes the 1944 *Lilac Time* an exceptional show. On the female side it was, for example, unusual that Hilda White, Mida O'Brien, Eileen Furlong, Maria Viani, Maureen Harold and Eileen Knowles would all feature in the same production. Running two or three Gilbert and Sullivan operettas in repertory each winter stretched the resources of the company, and it was rare that more than two or three of the recognised female leads would have taken part in the same Savoy production. However, the spring musicals, especially ones with large casts, like *Lilac Time*, offered the possibility of a 'team of all the talents' coming together. While the male cast for the show, produced by Stanley Illsley with the Gaiety's Ernest Broadhurst as musical director, did not feature Joseph Flood or Robert McCullagh, it did include Jack O'Connor, Chris Bruton, Paddy Henry, Roderick Tierney and A.E. Glynn: a stellar collection by R&R standards.

The plot, which centred around the love-life and music of the composer Franz Schubert, is Cyrano de Bergerac gone wrong. Schubert falls in love with Lili but is too shy to make any headway with her. In desperation he persuades his friend Schober to sing a song to her that he has written for the occasion and, you've guessed it, Lili falls for Schober!

In the R&R production Schubert was played by Patrick Kirwan, Schober by Jack O'Connor, and Lili by Maria Viani. Eileen Knowles took the part of Mrs Grimm, a *concierge*/caretaker, Hilda White was Mrs Weber, one of her lodgers, and Mida O'Brien was the flamboyant Signorina Fiammetta Marini, prima ballerina. Glynn played Christian Veit, the court glassmaker and father of three girls: Wili (Kathleen Maher), Tili (Maureen Harold) and Lili (Maria Viani). Eileen Furlong played Glynn's wife, a woman anxious to get the best for her daughters.

The *Irish Independent* described the show as 'a good choice'[54] for the R&R. *The Irish Press* felt the success of the piece lay in the comic playing of Glynn and of P.J. Henry as Novotny, a bumbling detective.[55] Maria Viani as Lili: 'was the best in Saturday's opening performance. There is a great sincerity about her work, and she gave a convincing portrayal of the young girl who mixes human love with love of music.'[56] The *Irish Independent* also observed of Jack O'Connor that 'his singing was sure and of good quality'[57] Mida O'Brien was praised for her 'clever acting' as the ballerina.

Despite the success of the show and although a reprise was suggested on many occasions, the R&R has never returned to *Lilac Time*.

THE VAGABOND KING (1946)

The Rudolf Friml operetta *The Vagabond King*, first produced in 1925, was based on a novel and play: *If I Were King*, by the Irish writer Justin Huntly McCarthy. The author was a former Irish party MP who had joined his father, Justin McCarthy, in opposing the leadership of Charles Stewart Parnell after the 1890 split in the Home Rule party ranks. The story was a fictional episode in the life of fifteenth-century French poet, thief and all-round 'chancer' Francois Villon, and his wooing of Katherine de Vaucelles, a cousin of King Louis XI.

The part of Villon in the R&R production went to gifted baritone Jack O'Connor. Hilda White was cast as Katherine de Vaucelles. A. Davies Adams, producer of *La Vie Parisienne* the previous spring, returned on this occasion as musical director, T.H. Weaving having decided that his baton was only available to be wielded for Gilbert and Sullivan.

The Irish Press described the production as 'lively, light, and humorous and the performance was good musically, dramatically and artistically'.[58] The *Irish Independent* and *The Irish Times* were more enthusiastic, with the latter describing the production as 'one of the most spectacular shows they have staged in their long existence'.[59]

Jack O'Connor as Villon ('poet, pick-pocket and King of the Beggars') was hailed by *The Irish Times* as having 'made this the finest character study he has ever done. He spoke his lines with a rare play of emotion and in singing one heard, as never before, the full weight range and warmth of his baritone voice.'[60] The *Independent* highlighted O'Connor's 'gift of being able to surrender himself completely to the part he is playing. There is a vitality in his movements, and he can assume a fine dignity. He has a sense of poetry and delivers his lines with sincerity and intelligence.'[61]

Hilda White as Katherine de Vaucelles 'was graceful and appealing in the part…her singing was delightful' according to *The Irish Times*, while the *Irish Independent* used the same adjective to describe White's performance: 'Her graceful presence and smooth acting always give pleasure…her singing was artistic and there was warmth and sincerity in the tuneful "Only a Rose".'[62]

The comic turns of A.E. Glynn ('as the foxy old King, Louis XI'), P.J. Henry and Roderick Tierney were also applauded. With Henry, who bore the main comic 'burden' described by *The Irish Times* as having been 'in his gayest and most irrepressible style'. The *Irish Independent* also heaped praise on the hard-working chorus.[63]

> The great asset of the society is its fine chorus. This musical play gives the chorus plenty of work to do and grand tone was given to the full numbers and equal competence was shown in the sectional choruses.

The production performed well at the box-office during its two weeks at the Gaiety, taking in more than £1,400. But there was a price to be paid for the costly 'spectacular' element – the show made a profit of only £30.

. . . .

BITTER SWEET (1952)

Through the 1950s and 1960s many of the R&R shows were built around the talents of Louise Studley. Her debut, in Novello's *The Dancing Years*, in 1951, was in the starring role of Maria Ziegler. She maintained her pre-eminence and helped sustain the popularity of the society for the better part of two decades. A number of talented leading men played opposite Studley, most notably Jack O'Connor, Brendan McShane and Brian Kissane. McShane, one of the most talented and popular male 'principals' in R&R history, began to make an impression in the mid-1960s as Sky Masterson in *Guys and Dolls* (1966). He followed this up as a peerless Henry Higgins in *My Fair Lady* (1969) before underscoring his importance to the society as Tevye in *Fiddler on the Roof* in 1972.

One of the best decisions of the 1950s was to opt for a production of Noel Coward's *Bitter Sweet* in 1952, produced by London-based Bernard Clifton. Studley played debutante Sarah Millick, engaged to be married to the aristocratic Hugh Devon (played by Richard Midgley) but secretly in love with her Austrian music teacher, Carl Linden (Jack O'Connor). The show offered good opportunities for chorus members to shine as there are over forty speaking parts. Songs from the show, such as 'I'll See You Again'[64] (sung by Linden) and the chorus 'Ta-ra-ra Boom De Ay' had become well-established since the premiere of the piece in His Majesty's Theatre in London in 1929.[65] The society had first performed *Bitter Sweet* in the Gaiety in 1944 with Hilda White as Sarah and Robert McCullagh as Carl. On that occasion Jack O'Connor had played one of the minor parts, but otherwise few of the 1944 cast featured in the 1952 production.

The Irish Times review showered praised on the two leads but was just as impressed with the ensemble work.

> Judged even by their own severe standards the performance was on a very high plane…It is a wonderful tribute to this society that, in a work calling for over forty speaking parts, there was not a weak link – each and every one filled the role to exact requirements.[66]

The Irish Press, however, preferred the 1944 Irish premiere of the show, but noted that 'the chorus lives up to its high reputation'.[67] The show went on to play to packed houses, making a tidy surplus for the society of over £300, at a time when it was becoming difficult to make money on spring productions.[68]

. . . .

LOVE FROM JUDY (1958)

Sometimes, if executed with sufficient vivacity, a show, though light on memorable tunes, can impress critics and audiences alike. The 1958 R&R production of *Love from Judy*, based on the Jean Webster play *Daddy Longlegs*, almost qualifies. It was a critical success but audiences stayed away. This was despite the good notices and the fact that Fred Astaire and Leslie Caron had starred in a film version in 1955. The play has something of a *Pygmalion* feel about it. Young girl in orphanage (Judy) impresses mysterious benefactor (Jervis Pendleton) and tries to take the world by storm. Hazel Yeomans took the lead while Jack O'Connor played the guardian she dubbed 'Daddy Longlegs'. Margaret Boyle, who had worked with Yeomans (Ado Annie) on *Oklahoma!* in the Gaiety the year before, produced the show. Boyle was aware that, while *Love from Judy* was long on charm, it was devoid of any killer tunes. In Yeomans, however, she had a leading lady possessed of the almost manic energy required to carry the show. *The Irish Press* noted that the production 'has the maximum of vitality in which principals, chorus and ballet alike keep the show at high pressure from first to last'. The role of Judy was 'well suited to [the] high spirits' of Yeomans.

Love from Judy, 1958, programme.

The Irish Press predicted 'a most successful two weeks season'.[69] *The Irish Times*, while accepting that 'there is no particular merit in the work itself', nonetheless described the production as 'full of colour, laughter and high spirits' that produced 'much fun on both sides of the curtain'.[70]

Despite the energy and exuberance brought to the show by Yeomans and the chorus in particular, and the recommendation of two of the city's daily newspapers, the public response was less than enthusiastic.

125

Love from Judy's box-office gross reflected its limp score rather than the energetic production by Boyle. The show lost almost £500, an outcome that led to a debate in committee on why the society's shows were not bringing in audiences. The question was left hanging because no one could come up with an appropriate or credible answer.

The society had more of its ducks in a row the following year when Studley played Anna opposite Brian Kissane's Danilo in Franz Lehar's sparkling *The Merry Widow*. Gross receipts were twice that of *Love from Judy*.[71] Honorary secretary Clem Ryan deserved some credit for having suggested running the spring production during Lent,[72] but still the show made only just over £400 profit for the society. Musical comedy was becoming more and more expensive to stage and the taste of Dublin audiences was proving hard to predict. In 1960 *Naughty Marietta*, with the same leads – and other excellent performers like Yeomans, Hewson, Lucy McCarthy, Eoin O'Brien (son of Hilda White and nephew of Mida O'Brien) and Paddy Henry, was 'not the hoped-for box-office success and it was hard to know why'.[73]

· ·

THE MERRY WIDOW (1961)

Such had been the success of the Franz Lehar classic in 1959 that two years of financial frustration later, the society went back to the Viennese well – though the action of the piece is set in Paris. Studley reprised the role of Anna and Brian Kissane was to repeat his performance as Danilo. In advance of the show Kissane spoke to *The Irish Press* about his customary 'first night nerves'.[74] His apprehension might have been increased by the knowledge that the President would be in attendance.[75] In the end he was spared any anxiety because he was taken ill a few days before the opening.

Clem Ryan was quick off the mark when it came to finding a late replacement. He immediately contacted Chris Curran, then of the Radio Éireann Repertory Company. Curran had recently played the part of Count Danilo, with his wife Josephine Scanlon as Anna, for the Tipperary Musical Society. Curran, father of future chorus director Jackie Curran Olohan, was tracked down in London and asked to get on a plane and fly to Dublin for the opening that night. Curran's response was: 'Have a car waiting for me at the airport with a script in the back seat.'[76] He fitted in seamlessly. *The Irish Times* reviewer wrote: 'Mr Curran is to be congratulated on his performance, which had not the help of even one rehearsal. He gave a seemingly carefree performance of a gay and very debonair count.'[77] Curran filled the part for the entire two-week run and was paid £120 by a grateful Clem Ryan. He is one of an elite group of performers to have been paid by the R&R since the 1940s.

Just as there is a romantic subplot in the musical itself so was there one in real life. Playing the subaltern lovers Valencienne and Camille were Joe Lane – later famous for his television

The Merry Widow, 1959: Mary McCann, Eva Staveley, Eithne Collins and May Cowle.

ads for the supermarket chain he managed, Londis – and young Cork woman Lucy McCarthy.[78] Lucy had been persuaded to join the society in 1957 for *H.M.S. Pinafore* by her friend, the accomplished dancer and choreographer Dolores Delahunty. Joe Lane joined two years later and played the minor role of Luiz in *The Gondoliers*. In *The Merry Widow* they were cast opposite each other as lovers for the first time. Nature quickly imitated art and they were married in 1963.[79] *The Irish Times* was slightly faint in its praise of their respective performances:

> Lucy McCarthy has a good ringing voice and acts quite well, if addressing too many of her remarks to the audience. Newcomer Joseph Lane could improve his rather pleasant tenor voice by making certain of his time values.[80]

Both would go on to shine in many subsequent productions. Despite the romance and drama onstage and off the 1961 *The Merry Widow* was not as successful as the 1959 show. It lost the society £187 on a box-office gross of £3,822, down 26.5 per cent on its predecessor.

PATIENCE, THE MIKADO, THE YEOMEN OF THE GUARD (1963) — THE JUBILEE GILBERT AND SULLIVAN

There was no particular reason why the three Gilbert and Sullivan operas chosen for the winter of 1963 should have been greatly different from what had gone before. And indeed the productions themselves were rather typical of their kind. The R&R had built up a loyal, though ageing, audience for Savoy opera and it wasn't going to deviate greatly from the template that had proved so successful for the previous fifty years. The engagement of Norman Meadmore as producer was testimony to the intention of the R&R not to rock the boat. Meadmore had first worked with the R&R in 1956 on *Yeomen*, *Patience* and *Iolanthe* as something called 'director of production'. While Eileen Clancy, Joe Flood and Mida O'Brien were the nominal producers, Meadmore had been taken on 'to assist our own producers in the forthcoming G&S season' (see Chapter 2). He had returned the following year to produce *Gondoliers*, *Mikado* and *Pinafore* in his own right.

One thing had changed, of course. As all copyright restrictions had been removed any straitjacket imposed by the D'Oyly Carte 'house style' could safely be untied. But by taking on Meadmore, the R&R

The Mikado, 1963. Geraldine Hannigan, Jane Carty and Carmel Burke as the Three Little Maids.

announced that they were comfortable in the old clothes and intended to keep wearing them. So much at ease were they, in fact, that they intended hiring costumes for the productions from the D'Oyly Carte Company itself.[81]

Meadmore's *Mikado* had a young Jane Carty in the leading soprano role of Yum-Yum. Then a UCD graduate, Carty would go on to become a music producer in RTÉ Radio and the motive force behind the station's Young Musician of the Future strand. *The Irish Times* opined, rather grudgingly, that she 'was an agreeable partner for Nanki-Poo'[82] – played, as mentioned elsewhere, by another future RTÉ Radio star Liam Devally. At the opening night presentation, five surviving members of the original cast and chorus from the Queen's Theatre production of 1913 were honoured guests of the society.

Patience and *Yeomen* ('a lively production – trim and taut – was well served by an excellent cast')[83] both received good notices from the Dublin dailies, with Jack O'Connor and Heather Hewson being particularly praised as Archibald and Lady Jane in the former. The *Irish Independent* observed that 'Heather Hewson was so beguilingly formidable as the Lady Jane that one was pleased when she finally married into the aristocracy'.[84]

People of a certain age, including the present writer, remember where they were in the early evening of 22 November 1963. In the cases of many members of the R&R, they were preparing for that night's presentation of *Patience*. Word filtered through from the outside world of the assassination of President John F. Kennedy in Dallas, Texas. In the seventy-fifth anniversary publication, cast member Noel Magee recalled 'the atmosphere in theatre that night – the small groups whispering in the green room, the palpable tension in theatre and the almost personal sense of loss'.

It was, very suddenly, an inappropriate night for the whimsy of *Patience* and Gilbert's satiric darts aimed at the aesthetic movement of the late nineteenth-century, as represented by the character of Bunthorne. But the show went on.

GUYS AND DOLLS (1966)

Guys and Dolls, 1966: Eddie Guilmartin, Des Bowden and Tony Byrne.

It took the R&R sixteen years to get around to producing *Guys and Dolls*. With music and lyrics by Frank Loesser, based on a number of short stories by Damon Runyon, the show was both of Broadway and about Broadway. It was populated by characters with exotic names like 'Nicely-Nicely Johnson' and 'Harry the Horse' as well as the prim Salvation Army sergeant, Sarah Brown. In 1955 Marlon Brando had stunned the film world by singing – in the lead part of gambler Sky Masterson – in the Hollywood production. Frank Sinatra did a more than somewhat better job as Nathan Detroit.

Could the mean-ish streets of New York translate to the stage of the Gaiety Theatre? The job of conversion was left up to London producer Anthony Cundell and a cast that included Brendan McShane filling the shoes of Brando and Eddie Guilmartin attempting to erase memories of Sinatra. The part of Sarah Brown went to the 1965 Michael Devlin scholarship winner Mary O'Callaghan. Tony Byrne, winner of the scholarship in 1966, played Benny South Street.

If anyone was concerned that the members of the R&R would be unconvincing as Manhattan hookers, crap shooters and good-time girls, and that the production would die a death – and the detractors were lining up as the show opened – they were due for an enormous surprise. Despite the fact that the R&R had been having severe difficulties with the Gaiety Theatre, the show performed so well at the box-office that it was retained for an almost unprecedented third week.

Mary McGoris in the *Irish Independent* praised 'Brendan McShane's fine sense of timing and general ease of style in his finished performance as Sky Masterson, who once refused penicillin for an illness because he had bet that his temperature would go to 104 degrees…equally skilful, indeed almost professional, was Eddie Guilmartin as Nathan…Mary O'Callaghan, a charming heroine, was equally good in prim and lively moods'.[85] Carol Acton in *The Irish Times* was not quite as ecstatic but still hailed the movement, diction and relative simplicity of the production while concluding with the invaluable promotional line: 'The show has vitality and I enjoyed it.'[86]

Both journalists also appreciated the sassy turn of Dolores Delahunty as Miss Adelaide. Delahunty, in addition to her comic acting skills, had brought a welcome element of respectability to the dancing steps of the society.

The Guys in *Guys and Dolls*, 1966.

. . . .

MY FAIR LADY (1969)

There is, as already stated, no consensus as to the 'best' show ever staged by the R&R. But if members over the age of 60 were subjected to exquisite torture, thumbscrews, the rack, waterboarding – that sort of thing – they might well scream '*My Fair Lady*' in answer to the question before passing out. So successful was it in a speculative three-week run in March 1969 that it was reprised in November.

There had been much hand-wringing about the type of shows to be staged at the Gaiety. The autumn/winter season largely looked after itself, with the Gilbert and Sullivan repertoire almost operating as a roster. But the correct choice of the spring show was crucial, especially as the weekly rent began to rise and Dublin audiences became more sophisticated and demanding when it came to production values. The discussion over the wisdom of staging *West Side Story* illustrates the multiplicity of dilemmas faced by the society. In May 1967 it was decided that Leonard Bernstein's re-located *Romeo and Juliet* was, notwithstanding the success of *Guys and Dolls*, 'not an appropriate show for this society'.[87] Then the vacillation began. The high-energy show, set amongst the gangs of the Upper West Side of New York City, was back in the frame a month later and would be played in the Gaiety for three weeks in spring 1968.[88] Less than a week after that, the committee was getting cold feet again and, as with any momentous political decision, it was kicked into a sub-committee 'to examine difficulties, particularly orchestral, which would arise with this new type of show'.[89] From there it was kicked straight into touch, when (rather conveniently) the proposed London producer, William Martin, pulled out of the project.[90] Instead, the safer and simpler *Brigadoon* was staged in March 1968 – and lost £1,600![91] The talk, entirely justified, was of a 'critical situation' and an urgent need for discussions with the Gaiety.

Ironically, it was a decision by the theatre that deposited a very welcome option in the lap of the R&R. Lerner and Loewe's *My Fair Lady*, an inspired – and surprisingly faithful – musical adaptation of George Bernard Shaw's *Pygmalion*, had been an instant and sustained hit on Broadway after its 1956 debut. Its reach and popularity had grown with the 1964 release of the Audrey Hepburn/Rex Harrison film version. By 1969 no staging of the musical had been produced in Ireland. Eamonn Andrews Productions had an option on the piece and, in 1968, seemed set fair to present it at the Gaiety. To the delighted astonishment of the R&R, EAP baulked and the R&R secured the rights to the Irish premiere. It was originally hoped that Hilton Edwards would produce,[92] but when he demurred the society chose instead a veteran West End actor and producer James Belchamber. It proved to be a marriage made in theatre heaven. Belchamber had spent some time living in Ireland as a teenage Blitz evacuee.[93] Through much of the 1960s he had been associated with the Richmond Theatre in Surrey. It was the first of more than a dozen R&R engagements for Belchamber, including the Irish premieres of *Fiddler on the Roof* (1972) and *Gigi* (1978), culminating in his direction of *Hello, Dolly!* at the Gaiety in 1989. All told, Belchamber produced over forty shows in Ireland, north and south.

The, perhaps entirely justified, conservatism in declining to take on *West Side Story* was never in evidence with *My Fair Lady*. If anyone could offer a convincing depiction of Edwardian London it was the R&R. There was an obvious compatibility factor in play. The R&R was more comfortable with Edwardian ladies and gentlemen, Cockney dustmen and Covent Garden florists than with naturalistic New York gang *patois*. There was a palpable sense of excitement leading up to the March premiere, as if the R&R knew that it was on to something. Booking the Gaiety for a three-week run was a gamble, but a finely calculated one. So convinced was the society of the attractiveness of the show that it was decided to charge 'Saturday night' ticket prices for the entire run.[94] Mindful of the exquisite Cecil Beaton 'look' of the 1964 movie, the society engaged Dublin designer Babs de Monte to create the all-important costumes for the show. All were made, as new, at a total cost of £600.[95]

It was either a minor miracle waiting to happen or a potential financial apocalypse. Fortunately, the Four Horsemen gave South King Street a wide berth for the duration. Instead it was theatre-goers of Dublin who flocked, saw and were enchanted.

The society was fortunate in having in its ranks the ideal Eliza Doolittle in Louise Studley and the perfect misanthropic Higgins in Brendan McShane. Maurice O'Sullivan was impeccably cast as the avuncular Colonel Pickering and Bryan Hoey was, if rumour is accurate, put in this world just to sing 'On the Street Where You Live'. But it

Louise Studley and President Éamon de Valera at the premiere of *My Fair Lady*, 1969.

was veteran Roderick Tierney as the rhetorician and dustman Albert Doolittle who, again assuming rumour to be accurate, stole the show from under the elegant noses of the aristocrats, *faux* and genuine.

In the first paragraph of the *Irish Independent* review, Mary McGoris wrote of 'a brilliant performance from the Rathmines and Rathgar Musical Society…produced with great verve and style by James Belchamber'. The show was 'magnificently costumed…the society's chorus was in the best form it has struck for years' and 'the show also had the advantage of an outstanding pair of principals'. Studley was 'looking distinctly beautiful and singing delightfully' and McShane's was a 'polished intelligent performance'. Tierney 'made a joyously undeserving dustman'.[96] In *The Irish Times* Charles Acton admitted having gone to the Gaiety 'in some trepidation'. He was glad, however, to be able to advise his readers that the R&R 'have scored a musical triumph'. Acton praised the sets of Robert Heade, pointed out the applause that greeted the costumes of Babs de Monte when the curtain rose on the Ascot scene, and described Belchamber's production as 'just about ideal'. He acclaimed Studley's performance as 'a portrayal to set beside her Merry Widow' and McShane 'at times reminded me of Sidney Howard – for me the Higgins of all time'. He admitted to having been under the impression that Tierney had 'hung up his boots' but 'it was a joy to see and hear his triumphant Doolittle. If he is still determined to retire, his swansong will have been one of his highest achievements.'[97]

It was so good, they did it twice. *My Fair Lady*, in an unprecedented move for the society, proved so popular that all thoughts of Gilbert and Sullivan were abandoned for the winter and the production returned to the Gaiety intact in November, in what Robert Johnston of *The Irish Press* described as 'a brave decision but a completely justified one'.[98]

My Fair Lady, 1969

My Fair Lady, 1969

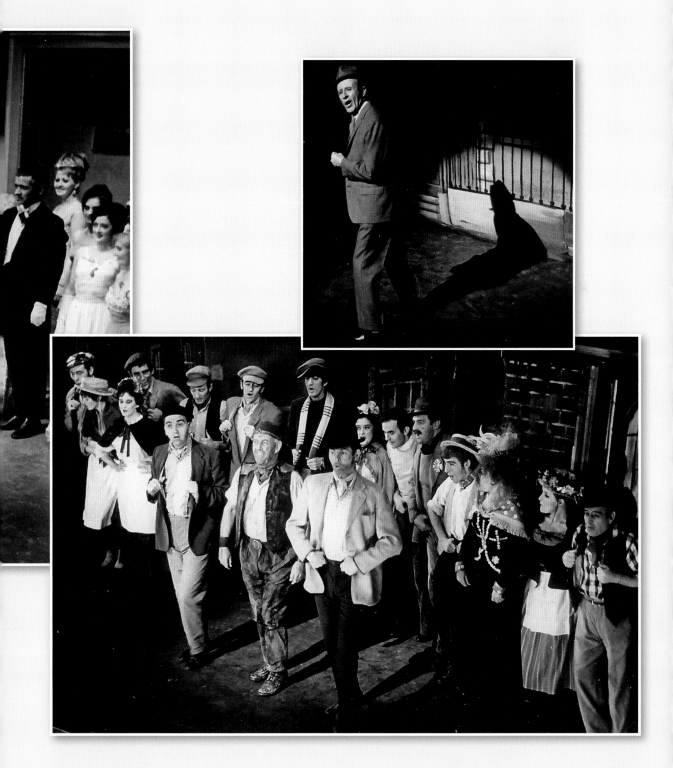

THE YEOMEN OF THE GUARD (1971)

After the success of *My Fair Lady* came the Troubles. This had nothing to do with the perennial economic crises of the R&R but with the IRA campaign in Northern Ireland, occasional retaliatory atrocities south of the border and the kind of fundraising activities on the part of paramilitaries that would have solved the R&R's problems overnight. The introduction of enhanced security protocols meant legal restrictions on the use of firearms onstage. A show like *Annie Get Your Gun* was very likely to bring you to the notice of the authorities. All R&R guns – and we are dealing here with mere replicas – had to be lodged in Kevin Street Garda station. If needed for a production they had to be collected on the night and returned after the show.[99]

Despite their heads being turned, understandably, by the elation of *My Fair Lady* and the success of a show like *Camelot* two years later (in which future producer Cathal MacCabe played King Arthur), the R&R continued, loyally, to 'dance with what brung 'em'. Messrs Gilbert and Sullivan were reinstated in the winter of 1970 (*The Mikado*, and a *Gondoliers* with Kevin Hough of RTÉ as The Duke). They remained a winter staple until 1986 when *Gigi* – with Marion Duane in the title role – was preferred. No Savoy operas were performed again until *Yeomen* and *Gondoliers* in the Gaiety in 1991. Those were the last G&S shows to be staged by the R&R at the theatre. From 1993 the National Concert Hall was the home of Sir Arthur and Mr Gilbert. Such was the standard of Savoy productions in the 1970s that on occasion critics, especially the particularly well-disposed Robert Johnston of *The Irish Press*, compared the work of the R&R favourably with that of the D'Oyly Carte itself.[100]

While it is somewhat disingenuous to select from among the thirty-six G&S productions between 1970 and 1986, the production of *The Yeomen of the Guard* in 1971 has some features worthy of note. It was the companion piece that year to *The Mikado* – with Pat Campbell in his only appearance as Ko-Ko[101] and Heather Hewson at the midpoint of her Katishas – and the R&R season, as mentioned above, coincided with the 100th anniversary of the Gaiety.

Camelot, 1971.

The Yeomen of the Guard, 1971. Derek Chapman as Jack Point and Eileen Donlon as Elsie.

In *Yeomen*, the part of the apparently doomed Colonel Fairfax went to a relative newcomer, future RTÉ presenter Arthur Murphy. The luckless Jack Point was played by another future star, Derek Chapman, soon to grace the stage of the Abbey and other Irish theatres. Eileen Donlon played Elsie Maynard, Lucy Lane was Dame Carruthers and the jailer Wilfred Shadbolt (a character always preceded by his

The Gondoliers, 1970: Kevin Hough, Lucy Lane and Claire Kelleher.

own dark cloud) was played by Billy Blood Smith, who had been an excellent Pooh-Bah in *The Mikado* the previous year. The production also marked the debut, in the role of Leonard Meryll, of Camillus Mountaine. He had 'auditioned on spec and was given the part'.[102] Mountaine, a future honorary secretary (1997–2007) would later have an epiphany in a production of *The Pirates of Penzance*: 'I realised that I was a 42-year-old man playing Frederick, the young romantic lead.' In a previous incarnation in the role in 1977 a much younger Mountaine must have been slightly mortified by David Nowlan's puckish review of his performance. *The Irish Times* critic pointed out that he had been 'asked by a youngster in the interval if he [Mountaine – not Nowlan] was really supposed to be good looking – ah, such a lack of simple faith!'[103]

Much further down the cast-list, in the largely invisible part of Second Citizen was one Niall Dungan. He made a number of brief and undistinguished appearances in R&R shows between 1968 and 1973. Occasionally he emerged from the anonymity of the chorus to be offered a few syllables of dialogue, notably as Chancellor's Attendant in *Iolanthe* in 1968 and the bibulous Bartender in *My Fair Lady* in 1969. No more than crumbs, really. These were delivered with all the presence of a deserted railway siding. All this while his *much* younger brother festered miserably in boarding school. Bitter? Moi?

David Nowlan in *The Irish Times* saw the potential in Derek Chapman, describing his performance as 'the best acting of the night…for this the show is worth seeing'. He was not quite so taken with Chapman's singing. Murphy's was the 'best singing of the night [but] he must drop the speaking style of a sports commentator, with sentences suspended in mid-clause, if he is to convince in Victorian drama'.[104]

Dungan's performance did not merit the attention of the critics.

. . . .

FIDDLER ON THE ROOF (1972)

Was the first staging of *Fiddler on the Roof* in Ireland an R&R production? Or was it actually produced by Eamonn Andrews Productions? While a rose by any other name might well smell as sweetly, there was considerable ambiguity about who precisely was entitled to claim to have premiered the story of Tevye the milkman, his wife Golde and their five daughters. *Fiddler* is set in Tsarist Russia around the time of the 1905 Revolution. The Broadway run of the show, which opened in 1964, ran for more than 3,000 performances, many with Zero Mostel in the lead role. It was so successful that it is reckoned if you had a financial stake in the original production every dollar you invested would have netted you over $1,500.

In 1971 the Israeli actor Chaim Topol, a veteran of the West End production, played the part of Tevye in the movie version of the musical.

It was well flagged at the 1971 annual general meeting that the following year would be a difficult one for the society. *Camelot* had lost over £1,800. The normal spring dates would not be available in 1972 because of a change of schedule for the Dublin Theatre Festival, and it was proving difficult to

Fiddler on the Roof, 1972: Heather Hewson, Brendan McShane and Sean Murphy.

source and select a show.[105] It was mentioned at the meeting that 'there was a possibility of the Gaiety management obtaining *Fiddler on the Roof*' but the precise implications of this were left unclear.

The situation was clarified the following September. Clem Ryan announced that the society would be presenting *Fiddler* for three weeks from 23 April 1972. He suggested that the production would be billed 'Eamonn Andrews Productions in association with the R&R'[106] in the event the name of the R&R never appeared anywhere near any publicity for the show. It had become apparent by December 1971 that the show was to be a Gaiety production with an R&R cast.[107] However, other than driving a hard bargain with the society, the Gaiety appears to have done precious little actual production. Clem Ryan was responsible for most of the arrangements, including engaging the services of Jimmy Belchamber as producer.

The newspaper advertisement for the show was as odd as was the production agreement. It read:

> Brendan McShane, in the first stage presentation in Ireland of the musical *Fiddler on the Roof* with Heather Hewson, *direction reproduced* [my italics] by James Belchamber.[108]

Belchamber had been hired as producer for five weeks, at £100 a week plus expenses. It was, arguably, a waste of his considerable talent and of the society's money. Under the terms of the production licence Belchamber was simply required to reproduce the show staged on Broadway by Jerome Robbins. It was a straitjacketed, cookie cutter production.[109]

Not that the odd provenance of the show had any detrimental impact on the cast. For Camillus Mountaine, playing the part of Fydeka who marries Chava (daughter number three): 'It was probably the highlight of my onstage work in the R&R…it was an Irish premiere of a world famous show and it was a three-week run…The sense of occasion was very much there; it felt prestigious to be doing something like this.'[110]

But who exactly was doing it? David Nowlan in *The Irish Times* claimed to be confused. While accepting that 'it is certainly the best thing I have seen the R&R do in three years', he continued: 'but this production is not billed as an R&R production. Its programme and the bulk of its publicity bills it as a production (professional, by inference) of Eamonn Andrews Studios. As a professional production it leaves a great deal to be desired in terms of both vision and technique…'.[111] On that basis, and predicated on the claim in the programme that what was presented was a reproduction of Hal Prince's Broadway show, Nowlan chose to pan what he saw on stage as 'little short of a travesty'. The show did not 'come within an amateurish asses roar of the original…to suggest otherwise is to debase the imagination and the consummate skill of the people who designed and executed the original'.

Total income over the three-week run came to a highly respectable £9,397. The show was described in committee as 'one of the most successful we had ever performed' but it still made a loss of £2,426. There is no mention of any of that loss having been borne by the production company which claimed to have reproduced a Broadway show on a stage ill-equipped for the scale of such an endeavour and with a cast of gifted and committed but amateur actors.

. . . .

GIGI (1978)

Gigi was another premiere, this time unambiguously presented by the R&R, of Lerner and Loewe's adaptation of the novella by Colette. The original film version, directed by Vincente Minnelli, with Leslie Caron in the title role, was one of the last great musicals produced by MGM. It was released in 1958, so it was no longer in the first flush of youth when the R&R decided to stage it at the Gaiety. Jimmy Belchamber was given free rein – no need to consult Hal Prince or Jerome Robbins on this occasion. Brendan McShane assumed the role made famous by Maurice Chevalier, of the old roué Honore Lachailles, uncle of Gaston (played in the film by Louis Jourdan) who is destined to fall in love with Gigi.

Much of the potential success of the show resided on the slim shoulders of an 18-year-old from Glasnevin, Siobhan Scally, at the time studying for her final qualification exam for the London Guildhall. Despite being domiciled on Glasnevin Musical Society turf, she had been approached to audition for the role.[112] It would also be a crucial production, as already mentioned, for a 29-year-old music teacher: Gearóid Grant was making his debut as musical director.

The part of Gaston Lachailles went to another newcomer with a professional future in prospect, Jonathan Ryan. The production was lavish, the total cost in the region of £24,000. The sets were designed by Bronwen Casson, daughter of Irish actor Christopher and granddaughter of the great British actress Dame Sybil Thorndike. Casson, who was also working in the Peacock Theatre at the time, was the daughter of designer and artist Kay Casson. Her sister Glynis, an R&R regular, was playing the part of Aunt Alicia.[113]

Gigi, 1978: Siobhan Scally, Heather Hewson and Glynis Casson.

Gigi, 1978: Jonathan Ryan, Pat Campbell and Brendan McShane.

The opening night, 6 March, was marred by the death of Micheál Mac Liammóir. News of the passing of one of the country's great stage presences filtered through during the interval. As David Nowlan put it in *The Irish Times*, 'the decision to return after the interval was not an easy one to make…that this flimsiest of shows survived the news at all must be greatly to the credit of what may well be one of the best productions ever staged by the R&R…In fact *Gigi* is the best dressed, best set, best moved, best orchestrated show that I can remember in the Rathmines and Rathgar canon…and it works much better in the Gaiety than it did in the glossy bowdlerised film version…'.[114] *The Irish Press* headline 'Chevalier is Put in the Shade' implicitly heaped praise on the shoulders of Brendan McShane. The *Irish Press* reviewer was almost as pleased with the performance of Jonathan Ryan who 'plays the role with just the right degree of sophistication'.[115]

• •

THE KING AND I (1980)

While the society had, by the dawn of that dysfunctional decade the 1980s, not staged all the major works in the Rodgers and Hammerstein repertoire (*Carousel* was yet to come in 2000, *The Sound of Music* is an itch yet to be scratched) one of the works of the foremost collaborators of the twentieth century that had not yet been attempted was *The King and I*. By 1980 the R&R was ready to grapple with a bevy of small 'Siamese' children and memories of the iconic performance of Yul Brynner in the

The King and I, 1980, curtain call.

1956 film version of the runaway Broadway success. Brynner, described at his audition as 'a bald headed young man who sat cross-legged on the stage and sang a strange Russian gypsy song accompanying himself on the guitar' would be a hard act to follow. Not too surprisingly Brendan McShane was selected by the casting committee as the man to follow him. The hordes of children of the decidedly fecund King, were recruited from the Billie Barry School.

Which left the part of Anna, the governess. The appearances of Louise Studley in R&R productions in the seventies had been few and far between. She had last performed in a revival of *The Merry Widow* in 1977. Before that she had starred in another revival of one of her former successes, the *Dancing Years* in 1974. Studley was prevailed upon to return to the Gaiety with the R&R. She would be onstage with McShane for the first time since *The Desert Song* in 1970. The 'other' love affair in the musical, between the scholar Lun Tha and Tuptim, one of the King's 'junior' wives, was entrusted to Bryan Hoey and Yvonne Brennan.

The result, as far as Robert Johnston of the *Irish Press* was concerned, was, 'the best they have done since *My Fair Lady*.'[116] Mary McGoris in the *Irish Independent*, while not as ecstatic, described it as 'a thoroughly enjoyable performance'[117] Deaglán de Bréadún in *The Irish Times*, in the days before he migrated to political correspondence, observed that 'the Rathmines and Rathgar Musical Society has done itself proud on this occasion'. He also highlighted the omnipresent 'strategically-located bores' who insisted on humming along to the well-travelled tunes.[118]

The show made a tidy profit of £5,230 – a surplus of any kind was welcome in the context of rising rentals in the Gaiety and escalating production costs. Allied to an upsurge in interest in the 1979 G&S season, and profits there of almost £4,000, it was one of the society's better years.

SHOWBOAT (1987)

The rest of the 1980s marked a return to some of the more tried and tested offerings. *My Fair Lady* made its first reappearance in 1981. McShane donned, once again, the comfortable glove that was Henry Higgins. All told, with various societies, he played the part over 100 times, twenty-eight of them with the R&R. His Eliza on this occasion was not Studley but newcomer Anne Grayson. *The Irish Times* was complimentary: 'she hardly put a foot or a note wrong'.[119] Roderick Tierney, supposedly already 'retired' in 1969 returned to bin-collecting duties as Albert Doolittle. Bryan Hoey and Maurice O'Sullivan reprised their performances as Freddie Eynsford-Hill and Colonel Pickering.

With 1982 came a revival of *Oklahoma!*, last performed in 1957 when Hazel Yeomans was in her pomp as Ado Annie. Heather Hewson had graduated from the part of Gertie in the 1950s to Aunt Eller in the 1980s. Philip Byrne and Mary Purcell took the parts of Curly and Laurey and there was at least one debut of major significance to the R&R when Garry Mountaine, son of Camillus, and a future star performer and producer, played Will Parker, the bumbling cowboy smitten by Ado Annie (Frances Campbell).

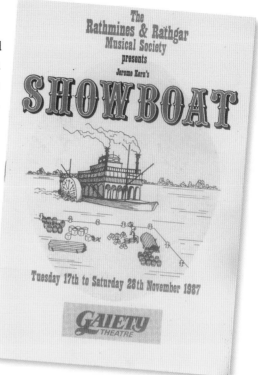

Showboat programme, 1987.

Mountaine (as Tommy Keeler) was back the following year in another revival from the 1950s, *Annie Get Your Gun*, with Anne Shumate taking the part of the female sharpshooter and John Roche as her husband and manager Frank Butler. The Gaiety's own 1984 problems meant an interruption in the spring season but in the title role in *Hans Andersen* in 1985 was one Noel McDonough. He was already an experienced actor and producer with other groups around the city. Although he came to the party with quite a pedigree as a performer, he claims (perhaps slightly tongue in cheek): 'I was discovered by the R&R.'[120] Like Garry Mountaine he would go on to great success with the society as a producer in the nineties and noughties.

Gigi was reprised in 1986, with Marion Duane in the title role and McShane, once again, thanking heaven for 'leetle girls' as Honore Lachailles. His nephew, Gaston, was played on this occasion by Damian Smith.

Jerome Kern's *Showboat* had first been performed by the society in 1955. Sixty years after its Broadway debut, in 1987, it was revived by the R&R in what would be the society's third production of the piece. *Showboat*, in its day, had marked a radical departure from the style and content of the traditional musical. Based on Edna Ferber's somewhat sprawling novel of the same name, which deals with themes of racial prejudice and miscegenation, the show tends towards some sprawl of its own. The ever-reliable James Belchamber was hired to keep it from becoming too diffuse and staggering under its own weight. He had done so very successfully in 1975. The problem was that in the intervening twelve years much of the dramatic content of *Showboat* had dated. While its themes remained current and universal, some of its language and the exigencies of production were apt to offend a modern audience. However much it was used in context, the 'n-word', not to mention blacked-up white actors, made audiences uncomfortable in the late 1980s.[121]

So the show would have to rely on classic songs like 'Ol' Man River', 'Can't Help Lovin' Dat Man' and 'Make Believe' and a talented cast to carry the evening. All the more so, as the investment in the show on the part of the society amounted to a whopping £80,000.[122]

David Nowlan, who had been positive about the 1975 production – 'a good night out'[123] – loathed the 1987 revival: 'It comes across as distinctly antique.' His criticism, however, was more about the vehicle – 'this outdated tale of Edna Ferber' – than the driver. Nonetheless he concluded that '*Showboat* needs a great deal more than has been done here to enable it to excite an audience sixty years on from its origin.'[124]

The production featured Eddie Guilmartin as Captain Andy and some fine young female talent, especially in Anne Maria Smith as the female lead, Julie. The singing of the show-stopping 'Ol' Man River' was entrusted to accomplished bass, Bob McKevitt as Joe.

Despite Nowlan's disparagement, the show appealed to the Dublin public. An unprecedented average 96 per cent attendance – not all paid in, of course – was recorded over the run and the R&R share of the take was £13,392.[125] It was significant that on the basis of that attendance figure the society still lost £4,189 on the show. This, however, 'was regarded as a most successful result'.[126] The Gaiety was becoming something of a 'loss leader' for the R&R. The society's tenure served to attract talented performers and ensured the maintenance of high standards. But it was no longer expected, as of right, that the R&R would come away with a profit from a two-week run there.

THE YEOMEN OF THE GUARD (1991)[127]

After a gap of six years, G&S returned to the stage of the Gaiety with a modern-dress *Gondoliers* and a more traditional *Yeomen*, both directed by RTÉ radio producer Cathal MacCabe, head of music at the station. MacCabe, a native of Derry, had also produced the last Savoy operas staged at the Gaiety: *Iolanthe* and *The Mikado* in 1985.

Yeomen is the darkest of the soufflés concocted by W.S. Gilbert. This may be related to the circumstances of its creation. After Sullivan had sensibly rejected yet another of Gilbert's more fanciful plots – the umpteenth involving the sucking of a lozenge, with magical consequences (a sort of *Deus ex lozenga*) – the irritated lyricist was making his way home via an underground station where he spotted a poster for the Tower of London. The result was a seventeenth-century setting, a planned execution, escape, redemption, love thwarted and triumphant – and melodies closer to the operatic status always craved by the composer.

The doubly-fortunate Colonel Fairfax – he avoided execution *and* got the girl – was played by Paul Kelly, a former 'best male singer' at the Waterford Festival. Noel McDonough played the hapless jester Jack Point, disappointed in love. Phoebe Meryll was played by the experienced and accomplished, though still young, Marion Duane. Duane, as a member of the Duane Sisters, had won *Opportunity Knocks* on ITV in Britain, seven weeks in a row. She and her sisters had considerable commercial success in the UK and Ireland. For the R&R, Duane had played the title role in the 1986 Gaiety production of *Gigi*. By 1991 she was working as a music producer/presenter on RTÉ Radio.

The part of the morose jailer, the exquisitely named Wilfred Shadbolt, was played by Garry Mountaine. Mountaine, by now a well-established baritone on the amateur musical circuit, would parlay his performance into a contract to play the part (along with Pooh-Bah in *The Mikado*) for the D'Oyly Carte Company in London. Lucy Lane played Dame Carruthers and Bob McKevitt played Sergeant Meryll.

Irish Independent critic Mary McGoris hailed the traditionalism of the production, describing it as 'well cast, well sung, colourful and well acted'. Although she was not enamoured of Mountaine's cockney accent, she described his performance as 'quite brilliant'. Gerry Colgan in *The Irish Times* insisted that Mountaine had stolen the show as an actor and that 'his singing is a decided plus'.[128] Duane's Phoebe Meryll was praised as 'delightful'.[129] The one low note in McGoris's review was her evaluation of the 'disappointment' of Noel McDonough's performance as Jack Point 'made so mournful from the start that his final woe, never mind his jesting, hardly registered'. Colgan disagreed: 'Noel McDonough's jester is a significant contribution' in 'an evening of small treats'.

. . . .

SOUTH PACIFIC (1996)

In his final secretary's report to the society, at the annual general meeting in May 1997, Joe Lane described the 1996 Gaiety production of Rodgers and Hammerstein's *South Pacific* as 'arguably, one of the best shows the society has ever done'.[130] While there may be an element of Olympian hyperbole (how often have we heard the IOC president proclaim 'these have been the greatest Olympic games'?) and of personal pride that this success happened on his watch, there is no doubt that this particular *South Pacific* was an excellent show that extended a very positive run of success for the R&R since the financial meltdown of *Anything Goes* at the Gaiety in 1992 (see below). Part of the fallout of the huge loss on that show had been an absence of three years from the Gaiety stage.

South Pacific programme, 1996.

145

South Pacific was produced by Londoner Andrew Wickes, who had been in charge of an equally successful *My Fair Lady* – with Mountaine as Higgins, Eileen O'Sullivan as Eliza, Bob McKevitt as Albert Doolittle and the evergreen Pat Campbell as Pickering – the previous year. Wickes was a producer, writer and West End performer of some note who had worked on many occasions with the D'Oyly Carte.[131]

His cast was led, once again, by Garry Mountaine in one of the two male romantic lead parts of French planter Emile de Becque. The feisty Nellie Forbush was played by Brenda Brooks, an Association of Irish Musical Societies (AIMS) award-winning actress with experience of playing roles such as Maria in *The Sound of Music*, Nancy in *Oliver* and Sally Bowles in *Cabaret*. The part of Lieutenant Cable went to Aidan Conway, who earlier that year had played the outrageously camp Frank N'Furter in the Michael Scott production of *The Rocky Horror Show* in the Tivoli Theatre in Dublin. The part of Cable was, to say the least, slightly more buttoned down.

The object of Cable's affections, Liat, daughter of Bloody Mary (Evelyn Doyle), was the first 'featured' role of Marina Kealy, daughter of Rita Kealy, the R&R's principal choreographer, who had danced onstage at the Gaiety with the R&R for a number of years. Rita Kealy, trained by former R&R choreographer Alice Dalgarno, and herself a previous winner of the AIMS Best Choreographer award, took charge of the dance routines in her seventh season with the R&R.

Derek West of *The Irish Times* was pleased with the Wickes production, Rita Kealy's dancers and Jackie Curran Olohan's GI and nurses choruses. But he was obviously not as happy with certain members of the audience. The charity sponsoring the opening night was the Dublin Eye and Ear Hospital.

> The R&R brings new life to old numbers in an often-sparkling production of the Rodgers and Hammerstein stalwart at the Gaiety. Once the chattering classes finally take to their seats, stop rattling their jewellery and notice the orchestra has started the overture (under the pepped-up direction of Gearóid Grant), they are treated to a feast of fine singing.

Brooks and Mountaine, West noted, 'give particularly strong performances and hold the central story line firmly in place' while Conway 'provides the male cheesecake and is personable, melodic and emotional'.[132] A far cry indeed from tights, suspenders and Transylvanian transvestites for Conway.

The show also made a surplus of almost £9,000 (€11,000), a slight dip on the performance of *My Fair Lady* (£13,000–€16,500) the year before but significant for the restoration of morale and the confidence that the society could still stage profitable shows at the Gaiety, despite escalating rental and production costs.

Fiddler on the Roof, 1998: final rehearsal, Rathmines.

Fiddler on the Roof, 1998: President Mary McAleese with Gay Byrne and Kathleen Watkins, the Israeli Ambassador,
Zvi Gabay, Pat and Joan Campbell, and Mrs Gabay.

FIDDLER ON THE ROOF (1998)

The most notable entry in the printed programme for *Fiddler on the Roof* at the Gaiety in 1998 had nothing whatever to do with the production. It was a fulsome tribute to the late Clem Ryan, long-time secretary and then president of the R&R, who had died earlier that year. He had been succeeded by one of the other great servants of the society, Pat Campbell, himself the son of a former president, Michael Campbell.

It was the first of many outings of Noel McDonough as producer. He had graduated from the Drama Studies programme at Trinity College, although it was his long experience in charge of musicals and successful Tops of the Town shows, rather than his academic prowess, that prompted the R&R to eschew the delights of the West End and begin an extended sequence of employing Irish-born producers. From 1998 until the present day McDonough has shared production duties with Garry Mountaine. The former D'Oyly Carte principal has been charged with continuing the society's G&S tradition, while McDonough has been responsible for the Gaiety and NCH musicals.[133]

McDonough was far from overawed by the responsibility entrusted to him by the R&R. 'I had done six shows at the Gaiety before so I knew what to expect.' Garry Mountaine was McDonough's Tevye. Siobhán Fawsitt, who had played Queenie in *Showboat* the previous year, was his wife Golde. One of the five daughters was played by Lisa Kelly, later to become one of the Celtic Women. Thanks to some excellent marketing, the show was almost sold out before it opened.

John Allen in his *Irish Times* review described the production as 'heart-warming'. This is often a euphemism for 'a decent effort – for a bunch of amateurs', but not in this instance. Allen did not detect a single 'weak link in the big cast'.

Noel McDonough's tautly-directed staging, abetted by Rita Kealy's rumbustious dance movement, is a perfect example of how a well-executed traditional approach can make even a 34-year-old show sparkle anew.

Fiddler on the Roof programme, 1998.

Allen singled out Mountaine and Fawsitt for special attention.

> Gary Montaine [*sic*] bestrides the production as Tevye, the milkman who converses, Don Camillo-like, with his God. His range of dynamics in both speaking and singing is impressive and his timing is splendid. He is ideally partnered by Siobhán Fawsitt as his wife, Golde. Her sympathetic playing and warm singing voice enhance the stature of this role enormously.[134]

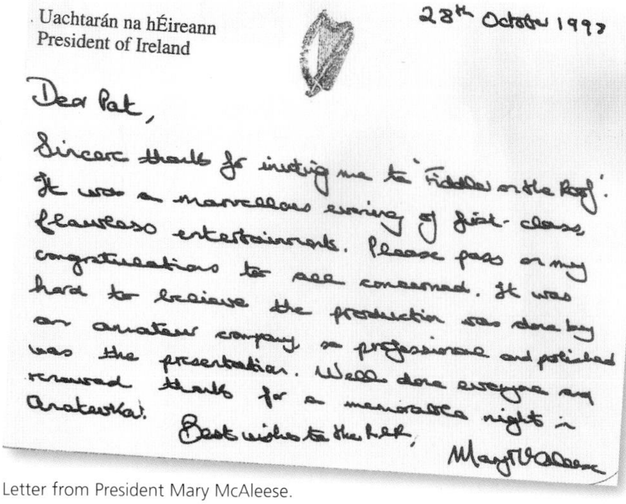

Uachtarán na hÉireann
President of Ireland

28th October 1997

Dear Pat,

[handwritten letter]

Letter from President Mary McAleese.

Of less interest to the critics, but of huge sentimental importance to the society, was the appearance of Chris Bruton in the role of the Rabbi. Both the R&R and its long-time stage manager were 85 years old at the time – although Bruton, who had originated the role in 1972, was probably wearing his age better than the society to which he had devoted much of his spare time since the 1940s.[135] Bruton, an optician by profession, was something of a technophile and an 'early adopter' of technology. He was the owner, in the 1960s, of a cine camera and often recorded shows in the 1960s and 1970s. The recordings have been presented to the society by his family. His final appearance onstage for the R&R, also as the Rabbi, was in the ninetieth anniversary concert at the NCH, in the *Fiddler on the Roof* segment of that show. The stage manager for that performance, as for so many others, was Nora O'Rourke. Each night, before he would step onto the stage, the impeccably dressed and coiffed 90-year-old, would ruffle his immaculate hair. When she finally challenged him on this, Bruton explained that he did it 'to make me look old'.[136]

. . . .

GUYS AND DOLLS (2001)

If this volume establishes anything, it is the almost hermetically sealed world of the R&R. Although buffeted by wars and economic crises the R&R, as a society, generally tried to ignore what was going on around it in the outside world. While the individual members could not avoid the Great War, the Second World War, the Cold War, the Gulf War and the Cod War (though probably of concern to Icelandic associate members only) the 'collective unconscious' of the society tried, sometimes unavailingly, to shut reality out.

But even the R&R was unable to blot out the 2001 Al-Qaeda attacks on the Twin Towers in New York, the Pentagon in Washington, and the planned attack on the White House that ended in a fatal air crash in a field in Pennsylvania. The Gaiety had been booked in 2000 for an October 2001 run

149

John Hurley in *Guys and Dolls*, 2001.

of *Guys and Dolls*. Then Osama bin Laden and his trainee pilot/suicide bombers intervened on 11 September. When it came to creating the sets of a musical that takes place entirely in New York, the set-painters demurred at the requirement to paint the New York skyline. Not that it included the Twin Towers: those iconic skyscrapers were built in the 1970s, long after Sky Masterson first succumbed to the unattainable charms of Salvation Army sergeant Sarah Brown in Damon Runyon's story. But there was an understandable reluctance to create any representation of a defiled skyline so soon after such a traumatic event.

It was marketing secretary Peter Nolan who came up with a solution to the problem. It was agreed that the following note would be inserted in the programme.

Guys and Dolls is set, in the majority, in New York City. The Society's Executive Committee's decision to stage this production was made during the year 2000, long before the recent sad events in New York, Washington DC and Pittsburgh. The society extends its sympathy to all our friends throughout the United States of America.[137]

The R&R hadn't attempted the show since 1976, when Eoin O'Brien took on Nathan Detroit and Brendan McShane reprised his 1966 Sky Masterson. The part of Adelaide was played on that occasion by a rising star whose life had been tragically cut short, Loreto O'Connor. O'Connor had gone on to play one of the leads in the highly successful Gaiety production of *Side by Side by Sondheim*, narrated by Gay Byrne in 1977.[138]

In Noel McDonough's 2001 show, the part of Sky Masterson was taken by John Hurley. An actor who had played a lot of non-musical roles, Hurley (who was acclaimed for his performance as the boy prince Chulalongkorn in the 1980 *The King and I*) had lived for a while in California and had made appearances in television shows such as *Ally McBeal* and *Melrose Place*. The Sarah Brown part went to Sandra Kelly, who studied with former R&R star Mary Brennan at the DIT Conservatory. Kelly, a Feis Ceoil gold medallist, had already played Tessa in *Gondoliers* and Magnolia in *Showboat* for the R&R. Garry Mountaine was Nathan Detroit, a part played in the movie version of the musical by Frank Sinatra. Nicky Drew, who played Peep-Bo in the 2001 *Mikado*, was Miss Adelaide.

Reading between the lines, the *Irish Times* critic, a young Peter Crawley, was starting out on his trade and was not overly fond of musical comedy[139] – 'Musicals may not be to everybody's taste,' he wrote. But he found *Guys and Dolls* to be 'a safe bet', offering 'enthusiastic chorus lines, copious dance sequences and a galloping pace'. Crawley praised two performances in particular.

It isn't until Nicky Drew's marvellously adenoidal performance of *Adelaide's Lament* that we get our first real surprise. Drew is an excellent performer, well paired with Garry Mountaine's Detroit, and their duelling duet *Sue Me* provides comic relief from an unsatisfying central couple.[140]

MY FAIR LADY (2004)

The escalating costs of staging musical theatre will be dealt with elsewhere (see Chapter 5) but in 1995 the price tag for *My Fair Lady* in the Gaiety in November of that year was a stark indicator of the nature of 'production inflation'. Already, in the 1990s, the rental on the Gaiety had increased by over 70 per cent. The 1995 annual general meeting was advised that the cost of staging *My Fair Lady* would be of the order of £130,000.

By 2004, barely a decade later, the Gaiety rental had increased by a further 40 per cent. The total cost of staging the Lerner and Loewe musical had more than doubled, to £271,000. The Celtic Tiger did not just wreak havoc on property prices.

Noel McDonough took charge of the production, Garry Mountaine took the role of the irascible, misanthropic and misogynistic professor of phonetics, Henry Higgins. Roisin Sullivan, a graduate of two complementary institutions, the Billie Barry School and University College Dublin (her degree was in Business Studies) played Eliza. Sullivan had appeared on the amateur stage with the Glasnevin Musical Society and with Lyric Opera. Another rising star, young tenor Paul Byrom, played Freddie Eynsford Hill. Byrom, who recorded his first album at the age of 14 as a boy soprano,[141] had appeared in the society's 2001 *Mikado* as Nanki-Poo and as Frederic in *Pirates* the following year. Glynis Casson, who made her debut in *Pinafore* in 1975, was Mrs Higgins. She had first played the part in the 1981 production.

Reviewing for *The Irish Times*, Gerry Colgan suggested that although the vehicle itself was largely 'critic-proof' nonetheless 'there may always be something in the production to facilitate the waspish comment'. He admitted he could find nothing 'because this Rathmines and Rathgar Musical Society outing is so in tune with the material that one can only acknowledge the fusion of diverse talents that underpins a memorable evening's entertainment'.

> Garry Mountaine is a brilliant Henry Higgins, carrying the character, songs and monologues with élan… Eliza Doolittle, as played persuasively by Roisin Sullivan, sings beautifully.

Colgan 'awarded the top laurels' to Noel McDonough and 'the energetic Gearóid Grant' and concluded: 'It is a long evening, about three hours, but I wouldn't shorten it by a note. It was really lovely.'[142]

Despite being an excellent show, well attended by the public, *My Fair Lady* cost €20,000 more to produce than was taken in at the box-office. Furthermore, the cost of hiring the Gaiety for that season was the last five-figure fee agreed between the R&R and the theatre until April 2013 (*Hello, Dolly!*) by which time the Celtic Tiger had given way to the Dead Cat Bounce. Over the next decade, the R&R would stage seventeen shows and concerts; only four – *Gigi* (2005), *Fiddler on the Roof* (2006), *The Merry Widow* (2008) and *The Producers* (2009) – were Gaiety productions. The traumatic financial repercussions of the latter show (see Chapter 5) will haunt the society for many years to come.

The society had never had an entirely unproblematic relationship with the Gaiety Theatre. The likes of Louis Elliman and Fred O'Donovan had always driven hard bargains and looked after the interests of their venue. But both had been prepared to take some of the risk associated with R&R shows. The modern Gaiety Theatre, like the other major venues in the city, generally adopts a 'four wall' approach. The venue is for hire and if you are not prepared to pay the price, then someone else will. It's part of the harsh and undifferentiated economics of modern commercial theatre. That the R&R, an internally funded, amateur musical society, has been able to operate in such a cut-throat environment is testimony to the excellence of its productions and the astuteness and dedication of its administrators.

. . . .

MISHAPS AND MISADVENTURE

Of course it wasn't all guts and glory. Although the dedication was seldom in doubt – except during occasional tremors when the performers would be accused of lassitude or dereliction by the committee[143] – sometimes the excellence and astuteness was replaced by haplessness and injudiciousness. It might be an inadvisable choice of vehicle – a rear-wheel drive when something of a more off-road nature was required. Occasionally it was an off-key (literally and metaphorically) performance. On at least one infamous occasion it was dodgy scenery. But the R&R's tenure at the Gaiety, like the course of true love, was never entirely smooth.

La Vie Parisienne flyer, 1945.

The 1953 staging of *La Vie Parisienne*, with settings by Victor Herbert and A. Davies Adams of the music of Offenbach, was a financial disappointment. But it had none of the fireworks of the April 1945 production. The society, despite the persistence of World War II, had managed to secure the services of London producer Charles Ross. Ross, however, had advised against staging *La Vie Parisienne* and preferred *The Vagabond King*. Although Louis Elliman sided with Ross, the committee stuck to its guns and insisted on the Parisian rather than the Vagabond life.

Elliman's problem was not so much with the material as with the duration of same. The show was 'only' two hours long. Those were the days when no one left a theatre until their posteriors were entirely numb. To extend the running time, Ross chose to make some interpolations. The two pieces he selected were, sensibly, by Offenbach. However, he also wrote two additional scenes and changed the finale. T.H. Weaving was unavailable to conduct the show, so someone had the bright idea of engaging A. Davies Adams himself as musical director. What followed has been adequately dealt with in the Melanie tune from the 1960s: '*What Have They Done to My Song, Ma?*' Adams was incensed at the liberties Ross

The Desert Song, 1970, finale.

had taken with *La Vie Parisienne*. A new front was immediately opened in the global war that was otherwise drawing to a conclusion in the outside world. Adams made his displeasure apparent and Ross responded in kind. Hilda White was delegated by a traumatised committee to act as peacemaker. Eventually *La Vie Parisienne* went on, realising a profit of £27.3s.11d – a surplus which, according to the committee, 'fully justified' their choice of show.[144] When the show was restaged in 1953 it was left intact and Terry O'Connor conducted. With no 'creative tension' in evidence, it lost money. In retrospect the committee decided that it had been a bad choice 'due to its music not being well known'.[145]

From the 1960s onwards the society tended to attract more rigorous reviews from certain critics. Many of the notices in the first fifty years of the society's existence read like they had been written by fans, rather than dispassionate critics. In an otherwise positive review of the March 1970 production of *The Desert Song*, Robert Johnston of *The Irish Press* referred to the mid-1960s as a 'valley period' for the society. '[They] have been giving us twice a year shows such as *Rose Marie*, *Show Boat* and *Oklahoma!* and other poor and dated pieces.'[146] He suggested *My Fair Lady* (1969) and *The Desert Song* (1970) signalled that the R&R was out of a serious slump.

Even some G&S shows – which still greatly outnumbered musicals in the 1960s – did not go down well, especially with the more exacting reviewers of *The Irish Times*. Sometimes the music critic would attend; at other times it would be the drama critic. Charles Acton, the musical sentinel, always teetered on the edge of censure. In the society's 1963 fiftieth anniversary publication, Acton wrote that 'one goes to every event hoping to enjoy oneself, hoping to be able to praise, but knowing that undeserved or insincere praise does far more lasting harm than any amount of deserved blame'. Doubtless a generation of R&R principals would have been perfectly happy to have drawn some 'insincere praise' from Acton.[147] When his mantle passed to drama critic David Nowlan in the early 1970s the latter's standards were, if anything, even more exacting than those of the terrifying Acton. Nowlan seemed to harbour some resentment at being required to review the work of an amateur company merely because said company inhabited the Gaiety Theatre from time to time. He took a mallet, for example, to the sixtieth anniversary production of *The Mikado*, carping at the diction of the chorus and principals, the 'general blurriness' of the costumes, the 'sloppy' make up and wigs, and missing 'the required hard edge in Beryl Dixon's production'.[148] The following year he advised that 'the company could benefit from using more economy in grimace, more discipline in move and gesture and more thrust and certainty in singing'.[149] In 1975 he issued a blanket warning to the leads in *Trial by Jury* and *H.M.S. Pinafore*: 'Professionals on musical stages cast unobtrusive looks at the conductor to save their dramatic lives and reputations. Last night there were too many amateurs ignoring the conductor at their peril and the reputation of their musical society suffered accordingly.'[150]

The Dancing Years, 1974, curtain call.

Sweet Charity, 1979, curtain call.

Having regular recourse to the production of some fatigued old chestnuts well past their 'best before' dates also drew the ire of some critics. The normally well-disposed Mary McGoris took issue with the 1974 choice of Novello's *The Dancing Years*, last produced with Louise Studley in the part of Maria Ziegler in 1960. That McGoris felt the vehicle was beginning to creak is clear from her introduction. There she exonerated the principals – Studley was, once again, playing Maria – and lacerated the piece itself 'with its mawkish plot and hollow imitative music [it] never had any real substance and certainly hasn't worn well'. She was also unhappy with production values that required but did not display 'considerable opulence of staging to cover its basic poverty of original invention'.[151] David Nowlan for *The Irish Times* was *ad idem* with his Abbey Street contemporary. He began his review with this scathing comment: 'It is possibly a good thing that someone should, from time to time, trot out *The Dancing Years* and allow it to stagger around for a while – just to remind everyone of how far the musical theatre has progressed since Ivor Novello concocted his frightfully awful schmaltz. On Tuesday night, in a three-and-a-half-hour fit of either bravery or foolhardiness the Rathmines and Rathgar Musical Society did just that with predictable results.' Nowlan refined the plot of the musical to the withering nostrum 'making people dance is so much better than being a Nazi'.[152] In the face of such negativity all the R&R could do was remind anyone who was still listening that *The Dancing Years* was the society's 200th production, more than 190 of which had been presented at the city's premier commercial theatre.

Choice of material for production over the years has been based on availability and suitability. The R&R has always been conscious of its audience and the capabilities of its company. But every now and again the comfort zone would be abandoned and the society would threaten the zeitgeist with something a little more edgy than *The Yeomen of the Guard* or *The Merry Widow*. This could, of course, easily backfire and result in the R&R, metaphorically, driving around Irish country roads with the GPS on the blink. The decision, for example, to stage *Sweet Charity* in 1979 was an adventurous one. Based on a Federico Fellini film *Nights of Cabiria*, about the life of a prostitute, the Broadway stage version (which opened in 1966) was more circumspect than the original. With music by Cy Coleman, lyrics by Dorothy Fields and a book by a young Neil Simon, the heroine of the stage show was a dancer-for-hire at a hall in Times Square in New York, rather than a practising member of the oldest profession. Bob Fosse, who choreographed the Broadway production, later directed the film version in 1969 with Shirley MacLaine in the lead.

It was a brave choice for an amateur company to stage the show in the Gaiety, and an egregious deviation from the ten G&S and three musicals (*Guys and Dolls*, *Gigi* and *The Merry Widow*) that had preceded it. Unfortunately it didn't work at the box-office. As Noel McDonough sees it, the artistic policy of a company doing what the R&R does needs to be firmly based on probable success rather than hazard: 'They need to do potboilers. *Sweet Charity* was a show about a ticket dancer, and as a result no one turned up. They got burnt by it.'[153]

The critics didn't help either. In *The Irish Press* Robert Johnston, while admiring the zest and élan of the two principals (Helen Jordan and Jonathan Ryan), was critical of Mavis Ascott's production.

No matter how sweetly charitable one might be, it is impossible to return a verdict other than that this is a *Sweet Charity* which in presentation is far too slow, so lacking in pace, however, that on the opening night it frequently seemed the midnight hour might come before the fall of the final curtain.[154]

Hans Andersen programme, 1985.

Sometimes lack of commercial success was less explicable. The musical version of the life of Hans Christian Andersen, imaginatively titled *Hans Andersen*, was hardly an edgy, 'alternative' offering. It was based on the 1952 film, equally imaginatively titled *Hans Christian Andersen*, starring a peppy, over-active Danny Kaye. It had a number of hit songs, most notably 'Wonderful Copenhagen', 'The Ugly Duckling' and 'Thumbelina'. It was a heart-warming family show staged in the spring of 1985. However, an inadequate number of hearts, and seats, were warmed. The show bombed and lost the R&R £30,000.[155] No expense had been spared, as Pat Campbell told Elgy Gillespie of *The Irish Times*: 'We felt we had to pull all the stops out – special costumes, new sets by a West End designer – because we have a tradition of premiering new shows.' It was of no consolation whatever to the R&R that they were not alone.

Hans Andersen: Heather Hewson and Noel McDonough, 1985.

The DGOS played to 25 per cent houses that season. Campbell blamed the fact that the R&R had followed 'several other family-type shows like Paul Daniels and Val Doonican' into the Gaiety: 'We think there simply wasn't the money for yet another show.' It was, after all, the mid-eighties, when the Irish economy was, to use a twenty-first-century euphemism, 'significantly challenged'.

And then there was the dodgy scenery!

In 1981 the society staged for the seventh time – the first since 1973 – the G&S show *Princess Ida*. Gilbert's haughty satire on the education of women and the theory of evolution, had a cast that included Brendan McShane as King Hildebrand, Barbara Graham as Princess Ida, with Camillus Mountaine, Pat Campbell, Arthur McGauran, Ted Ryan, Heather Hewson and Fred Graham in support. Gearóid Grant was guiding proceedings from the orchestra pit.

Princess Ida, 1981: including John Coulter, Arthur MacGauran, Henry Kennedy, Ted Ryan, Pat Campbell, Camillus Mountaine and Fred Graham.

It was a humdrum Tuesday night. Camillus Mountaine remembers an audience that was failing to get to grips with the show. Mountaine, Ted Ryan (Prince Hilarion) and Fred Graham (Florian) were on stage waiting behind a tree trunk (artificial) for their entrance. They were about to storm the walls of Castle Adamant 'when all of a sudden the set just collapsed around us. We stood there in shock as the scenery fell down, and then we were just silent. I think one of us went to speak and that's when the curtains closed.'[156]

The unruly wall was hovering dangerously over the pit as the action was unavoidably suspended. Despite the imminent threat of losing his strings Gearóid Grant sprang quickly into action.

> There was no overture to the show, so without any real communication between myself and the orchestra we began playing the overture to *The Mikado*, which was thankfully seven minutes long. The piece finished, the audience applauded and the curtain reopened.[157]

As with all good disaster movies, there was a sequel. The audience had just got settled when Ted Ryan uttered the next available line. It just happened to be: 'They must be lovely ladies indeed, if it takes walls such as these to keep intruders off.' It was a show-stopper. Camillus Mountaine, however, believes that all the extra-curricular activity was good for the soul of the audience. '[They] were really amazing after that. It got them right into the play.'

The relationship between the Gaiety Theatre and the Rathmines and Rathgar Musical Society has lasted almost a hundred years – with a hiatus or two thrown in to keep it interesting. It was always chequered and never based on sentiment. Today it seems to be not dissimilar to the working relationship between Gilbert and Sullivan themselves. It endures as long as the economics of the arrangement warrants its continuation. The utterly businesslike nature of the connection, however, doesn't detract from the memories of a century of achievement, of accomplishment, of occasional pratfalls, and of the camaraderie and excellence that have marked more than two hundred shows staged by the R&R under the proscenium arch of the Old Lady of South King Street.

CHAPTER FIVE

Patience

THE RATHMINES AND RATHGAR
MUSICAL SOCIETY

*Souvenir of
Twentieth
Anniversary
Performances*

THEATRE

*Commencing:
...ber, 1932*

THE
RATHMINES
AND
RATHGAR
MUSICAL SOCIETY

A CELEBRATION OF SEVENTY-FIVE YEARS
1913 — 1988

*Souvenir
Programme*

*Rathmines and Rathgar
Musical Society*

THIRTY YEARS RECORD

OF THE

*Rathmines and Rathgar
Musical Society*

1913–1942

RATHMINES AND RATHGAR
Musical Society

Fifty Golden Years

1913-1963

Price 2/6

Sixty Diamond Years

1913-1973

Rathmines
and Rathgar
Musical Society

SOUVENIR PROGRAMME
PRICE 50p.

CHAPTER FIVE

Patience

The 'or and or' – or the 'are n' are' – depending on which end of the fifteen tram line you used to live...

David Nowlan, *The Irish Times*, 29 October 1971.

· ·

FIN DE SIÈCLE: THE 1990S

While the 1980s had been, commercially at least, a mixed period for the R&R, as the final decade of the second millennium dawned there was some cause for optimism. A series of concerts at the National Concert Hall from the mid-1980s, though not primarily what the society was about, had been financially successful, and *Fiddler on the Roof* (1988) and *Hello, Dolly!* (1989), both Gaiety productions, had been profitable. Enough had been made to cover the bill for the extensive refurbishment of the Rathmines premises.

However, general secretary Stephen Faul, a highly successful businessman in his own right, counselled both caution and hazard. His concern was that this favourable trend might not continue. His suggestion was that the society come up 'with a source of income…other than its main productions'. His suggestion was that the R&R become promoters, much as the DGOS was about to do with their sponsorship of a recital by Luciano Pavarotti. He believed they should try and entice Kiri Te Kanawa, then charging a recital fee of £10,000 a night, to perform in Dublin, in the hope of making a profit of £30,000 on the venture.[1] While that proposal hung fire – it was accepted in principle – another venturesome idea was broached. It was time the R&R made a record!

In late 1989 the members had been circulated by questionnaire, and in January 1990 the committee made a decision to invest £15,000 in 'cutting a disc'.[2] It turned into a three-way partnership between the R&R, RTÉ and Lunar Records/Westland Studios. The society was to provide the arrangements, performers, orchestra and musical director, while the record company and studio would offer recording facilities and would produce the tapes and CDs. RTÉ agreed to promote the recording on its airwaves. Tapes would retail at £6.99; CDs for £10.99. When production and promotion costs were taken into account it was clear that the R&R was not going to make much of a killing unless sales went

An Evening with Mr Gilbert and Mr Sullivan, 1984: Pat Campbell and Maurice O'Sullivan.

Curtain Call CD cover.

stratospheric. Lunar Records and the R&R would split a royalty of 40p on each tape and £1.50 on each CD.[3]

The fourteen-track recording was entitled *Curtain Call* – the original suggestion was *Centrestage*[4]– and included show songs like 'Rose Marie' (sung by Peter Lewis and the R&R chorus), 'Almost Like Being in Love' from *Brigadoon* (Paul Monaghan and chorus), 'Deep in My Heart' from the *Student Prince* with Niamh Murray taking the lead, and Anne Maria Smith doing the honours on 'Love Will Find a Way' from *Maid of the Mountains*.[5] The recording, though not expected to lose large sums of money, was primarily intended to be a promotional tool or 'loss leader'. The idea was to add to the lustre of the society and, in the process, lure more talent into the ranks and more theatre-goers through the front doors of the Gaiety.[6]

The record was launched in early November 1990 in the boardroom of the National Concert Hall. It was, to say the least, not an unqualified success. *Curtain Call* never exactly threatened the summit of the Irish album charts. The issue of how much the whole venture cost was raised at the 1991 annual general meeting by, among others, Maurice O'Sullivan. It transpired that almost £7,500 had been written off in the accounts against the outlay on the recording and that £11,000 worth of tapes and CDs remained in stock. When O'Sullivan pressed the matter, Dodo O'Hagan rose to the defence of *Curtain Call*. The long-time assistant treasurer declared the many surviving tapes and CDs to be 'a continuing asset'.[7] Warming to her theme, she pointed out that the society had gone into the venture with its eyes open and 'the publicity gained could not be paid for…this was one of the reasons why the National Concert Hall was booked out'. She finessed the fact that the Concert Hall had always managed to sell out long before *Curtain Call* was ever committed to tape and CD. In a final defence of the decision to

Sherrill Milnes concert, 1990. Rita and Stephen Faul, Sherrill Milnes, Clem Ryan, President Paddy Hillery, Mrs Maeve Hillery, Seán Hogan, Jon Spong, [unknown] and Mrs Eithne Ryan.

make a record, the society's then PR secretary Mary Neville took a cut, probably well-deserved, at the membership when she tartly pointed out that 'if the active members had sold more tapes we would have made more money'.[8]

Meanwhile progress had been made on Stephen Faul's proposal for a concert promotion, but the performer was to be an American baritone rather than an Antipodean soprano. Kiri Te Kanawa was thrown over in favour of the slightly more accessible Sherrill Milnes, best known for his work with 'the Met' in New York and especially for his performances in Verdi operas. Milnes, the son of a dairy farmer, was also a major recording artist, having collaborated with Plácido Domingo and Luciano Pavarotti. In an NCH concert on 15 September 1990, attended by President Hillery and the US Ambassador Richard Moore, Milnes (accompanied by pianist Jon Spong) sang a programme that included a selection of operatic arias, lieder and, in deference to his hosts, excerpts from Broadway musicals.[9]

Forward progress was being made. Momentum was building again. Both came grinding to a halt in the Gaiety Theatre in November 1992. While the R&R could never be described as the *Titanic*, the society's first production of the Cole Porter vehicle *Anything Goes* hit an Atlantic iceberg. The show itself was well within its hefty budget of around £95,000 but took just over £60,000 at the box office. The idea of premiering the frothy Porter musical, from a book by long-time collaborators Guy Bolton and the inimitable P.G. Wodehouse, was first mooted in January 1992. It must have seemed like an excellent idea at the time. The 1934 show, set on board the fictional ocean liner the *S.S. American*, included hits like the title song, 'You're the Top' and 'I Get a Kick Out of You'. It couldn't really go wrong – but it did. The show was directed by London-based Peter Frazer-Jones, a veteran of British and American television 'turning back to his first love, musical theatre', according to the programme notes.[10] The cast included accomplished performers like Marion Duane, Heather Hewson, Ray Barror and a highly talented newcomer in Anna Jennings, who earlier that year had won the R&R performing scholarship named in honour of Robert McCullagh.

In 1991 the society had abandoned its plans for a spring season in the Gaiety because of escalating costs. Eighteen months later the rent had increased by a further 13 per cent to £17,000 a week.[11] A putative budget for the twelve-night run of *Anything Goes* suggested that there would be a loss of between £6,000 and £10,000, based on a 65 per cent attendance. The final loss would be more than double that optimistic projection. The first indication that there was trouble on board the good ship *America* came in early November when it was reported that booking for the show was poor.[12]

The box-office activity continued to be sluggish up to and including opening night. The critical reception was mixed as well. In the *Irish Independent* Mary McGoris was unenthusiastic about any of the performers other than Duane ('the only one with the zip and pertinacity that the show demands') and Jennings ('the agreeable soprano') and criticised the 'distraction of some uninspired dancing'.[13] In *The Irish Press* John Brophy disagreed, calling the company's effort 'a sparkling and convincing performance'.[14] Despite the onstage sparkle, the show's box-office performance was as flat as Manhattan. It showed a crippling loss of £25,557.[15]

The disappointment led to much heart-searching. After the usual suspects were blamed (inadequate marketing and PR, indolent members not selling enough tickets) a debate opened within the society about the Gaiety as a venue. It was agreed that a real Gaiety 'full house' was closer to 750 than 1,100 patrons. The upper and grand circles, remote from the stage but comprising fully 25 per cent of the available seating, were deemed to be virtually 'unsaleable' unless the show was a runaway hit.[16] However, another more worrying reality was also beginning to impinge. The society was entering a new era, one in which rival attractions threatened to swamp R&R productions at the Gaiety. It was almost axiomatic in the world of musical theatre in Dublin up to the 1980s that if you booked the Gaiety Theatre for two weeks you were, in effect, shutting down the competition. There was virtually nowhere else for any potential rival to go. But since the opening by Harry Crosbie of the Point Theatre (now the O2) and the staging of major musical and concert productions at the venue, that was no longer the case. At the 1993 annual general meeting, the new general secretary Joe Lane laid much of the blame for the financial debacle that was *Anything Goes* at the feet of the *arriviste* upstart in the Dublin docks area.[17] It was probably nothing personal, but Kiri Te Kanawa happened to be one of several major artists playing the Point during the run of *Anything Goes*. With a *daily* capacity equivalent to a week at the Gaiety, the venue (even on a mediocre night) was capable of drawing a huge percentage of available patrons away from South King Street.

An element of financial discretion and an imperative to retrench, in part, dictated the end of an enduring tradition. While the R&R and the Gaiety did not necessarily go together like a horse and carriage, the love and marriage between the two bodies had lasted, almost continuously – bar the flight into Egypt (the Olympia) in 1937 – since 1914. With a serious effort being required to fix the balance sheet after 1992, the society would probably have found that it could no longer afford the rental being demanded by Gaiety proprietor Gerry O'Reilly. But financial rectitude was accompanied by the disillusionment described in Chapter 4 when the theatre was slow to pay over the society's share of the box-office takings for *Anything Goes*. The resulting breakdown in trust meant the R&R absented itself from its traditional home for three years. It returned in 1995 with *My Fair Lady*.

Hear Our Songs flyer, 1994.

In the interim the National Concert Hall – where four concerts and two G&S shows[18] had already been staged – had shown its financial worth to the society. A reserve fund was painstakingly built up that was designed to indemnify the society against another commercial disaster like *Anything Goes*. Between 1992 and 1996 the fund grew from £44,000 to £95,000. It was the growth of this provision that gave the society the confidence to return to the Gaiety. Indeed there was some resistance to the idea of returning to the venue in 1995. Budgetary projections suggested a possible deficit on *My Fair Lady* of up to £25,000 based on 70 per cent occupancy. In late December 1994 there were those suggesting that taking such a risk was premature and that the balance sheet was not sufficiently repaired. In a further example of a classic R&R personality trait, the triumph of optimism over experience, *My Fair Lady* went ahead, as originally proposed, in November 1995.

While the relationship with the NCH was advantageous there were doubts about its efficacy as a 'show' venue. Concerts and G&S

Hear Our Songs chorus, 1994.

were all very fine but there was always a hankering after the relatively claustrophobic but strangely alluring Old Lady of South King Street when it came to the production of musicals. An April 1993 committee discussion sounded a warning:

> All concerned believed that [the] theatrical aspect of the society must never be forgotten and that it was incumbent on it to present a major musical in the future in the professional theatre.[19]

The R&R is rather like a shark: it must keep moving to stay alive. Concert performances, while potentially lucrative and artistically satisfying, were not the life-blood of the society. Live musical theatre was the *sine qua non*.

Andrew Wickes, who had directed *My Fair Lady* on the society's return to the Gaiety in 1995, was back the following year for *South Pacific* (see Chapter 4) and again in 1997 for *Showboat*. The former made a profit of nearly £9,000; the latter showed a loss of £13,000. *Fiddler on the Roof* in 1998, as already noted, was Noel McDonough's first production. He followed that up with *Oklahoma!* in 1999. As the decade drew to a close the combination of concerts and G&S at the National Concert Hall, and a series of largely profitable shows at the potential quicksand that was the Gaiety, saw the R&R finish the millennium in a far healthier state than it had begun the 1990s. Reserves totalled over £200,000

– of which almost £110,000 was a provision against the potential for the biggest financial flop in the society's history.[20] The R&R was armed against the vicissitudes of the new millennium, whatever they might be.

It took a while for those slings and arrows to appear, but when they did, while the missiles didn't blacken the sky, they did find their target.

. . . .

'...AND DANCE LIKE NO ONE IS WATCHING'

It should be stated at the outset of this section that members are admitted to the R&R based on a *musical* audition. They are not required to dance for the chorus director; they are merely asked to sing. From then on the function of chorus directors, like Heather Hewson and Jackie Curran Olohan, is akin to that of a highwayman, they oblige the chorus members to stand and deliver.

Nowadays, however, something a little more energetic is required by an audience in terms on onstage motion. That obligation has often been the Achilles heel of the R&R. In the past, the chorus members and many of the principals tended to hoard their dancing skills for the post-production party or the annual dinner dance. Often the dancing was outsourced. In the 1940s the Abbey School of Ballet supplied a choreographer, in the shape of Muriel Kelly. Kelly had taken over direction of the Abbey School from Ireland's best-known ballerina, Dame Ninette de Valois, founder of the Royal Ballet in London.[21] In the 1950s, under Joy Harvey, the Abbey School often provided the dancers as well. *The Irish Times* noted for *The Dancing Years* (1951) that, with Joy Harvey as dance mistress[22] 'the Abbey ballet helped in the success of the show'.[23]

First Dancing Members: Clodagh Foley, Jan Murnaghan, Jill Margey, Dolores Delahunty, Mimi Eccleston and Cynthia Gaffney (*The Merry Widow*, 1959).

By the mid-1950s more shows were being produced that required dancers. Partly at the instigation of Clem Ryan, who felt a dancing group should be formed within the society, the choreography came back 'inhouse'.[24] In *Oklahoma!* (1957) Dolores Delahunty designed and performed in the 'dream ballet' for the show. *The Irish Press* hailed her work as 'outstanding'.[25] The following year she also choreographed *Love from Judy*.

Marina and Rita Kealy.

For the next decade, Delahunty took charge of the movement and dance elements of most R&R productions. As both a choreographer and a dancer she drew plaudits from the critics. Reviewing *The Gondoliers* (1965) Robert Johnston in *The Irish Press* offered 'a special word of praise for the ensembles – the gavotte was particularly effective'.[26] In her piece on *Brigadoon* (1968) Carol Acton noted that 'Dolores Delahunty's solo at the funeral was moving'.[27] But Delahunty's own onstage excellence, and that of a few other accomplished (usually imported) dancers, could not disguise the fact that the society was not overly endowed with nimble-footed nymphs – male or female. In 1966 Mary McGoris had acidly observed in her review of *Guys and Dolls* 'wisely, the dancing was kept to a minimum…'.[28]

With Delahunty beginning to impress as an actor and to make appearances in more prominent roles in R&R productions, the great Gaiety pantomime choreographer Alice Dalgarno took over the job of persuading cast members that each of them had both a right *and* a left foot. Dalgarno, a former Tiller girl and leader and director of the famous Dublin dance troupe The Royalettes, was paid the princely sum of £30 in 1967 for putting the troupe through its paces in *Bitter Sweet*. Dalgarno was also responsible for the critically lauded *My Fair Lady* in 1969. One of her finest achievements with the society was undoubtedly her management of the Royal Princesses and Princes from the Billie Barry School – not to mention the somewhat less accomplished R&R regulars – in the 1980 production of *The King and I* directed by James N. Healy.

Dolores Delahunty.

Dalgarno's other legacy was Rita Kealy. Kealy, a former Royalette largely trained and nurtured by Dalgarno, came to the society in 1991 to direct the faltering steps of the cast of *The Yeomen of the Guard* and *The Gondoliers* in Gaiety productions directed by Cathal MacCabe. She succeeded Dex McGloughlin as R&R choreographer. McGloughlin had worked on shows in the Gaiety like *Showboat* (1987), *Fiddler on the Roof* (1989) and *Hello, Dolly!* (1989). Her swansong was *Kiss Me Kate* (1990). Kealy had first appeared on stage at the age of 4, in the Theatre Royal's

Romberg to Rodgers, 2005.

167

pantomime production of *Robinson Crusoe* with Noel Purcell. She had choreographed for a host of top amateur companies before coming to the R&R, having won the Best Choreography award four times at the Waterford International Light Opera Festival.

Kealy remained with the R&R for the next decade, choreographing all the big Gaiety shows during that period, as well as many of the G&S productions at the NCH. Her last show, Garry Mountaine's first as director, was *The Mikado* at the NCH (2001). Appearing in a number of R&R shows as one of Kealy's dancers – as well as playing Liat in *South Pacific* in 1996 – was her daughter Marina. In 2002, after Siobhan McQuillan had taken over the role for *Guys and Dolls* at the Gaiety in 2001, Marina Kealy took up her mother's discarded shield.[29] Many things are done in the R&R on the basis of apostolic succession. As well as coming from highly evolved choreographic genetic material, Marina Kealy had assembled an impressive CV before taking over as R&R movement director, a role she has occupied, almost uninterrupted, since 2002. In that time she has missed out on only one Gaiety show, *Me and My Girl* (2002) – Joe Conlon choreographed on that occasion. Both the Kealys have worked with a number of prominent R&R producers, principally Noel McDonough, on more than a dozen occasions. He lauds them for their ability to 'capture the mood and style of whatever musical genre you're putting on'.

Both of the Kealys have also been responsible for producing many of the extremely lucrative NCH 'concert' performances, beginning with *One Enchanted Evening* (1995 – Rita Kealy). Both have separately produced *From Romberg to Rodgers*, Rita in 1999 and her daughter in 2005. Noel McDonough puts the principal attribute of the Kealys very simply: 'They can make ordinary people look like dancers.' Which is, perhaps, just as well!

· ·

BACKSTAGE[30]

George McFall: backstage supremo at the Gaiety from 1947 to 1994.

In its early years the society was fortunate in having the technical and artistic services of the Gaiety Theatre at its disposal; sets were built, painted and stored in the theatre; full wardrobe facilities were available; props were made by George McFall or sourced from the Aladdin's Cave that was his domain. Stage management was provided either by the Gaiety staff or members of the society, especially Chris Bruton who stage-managed many of the big musicals in the 1950s.

In December 1960 the R&R received an application for associate membership from one Seamus O'Neill, described as 'an engineer in the ESB'. He also offered to help out 'in any backstage capacity'.[31] He was pressed into service almost immediately. O'Neill rapidly became indispensable. He was, in effect, the first dedicated stage manager the society had seen, in that he was neither a performer nor a member of the committee. He recruited dedicated ASMs of like mind, replacing the type who habitually hovered in the wings contemptuously regarding performances upon which they felt they could easily improve.

Seamus O'Neill had no desire whatever to step in front of the lights, except when they were being focused. He was renowned in Dublin amateur dramatic circles in the 1960s and 1970s as a stage manager with little regard for the egos of actors. In addition to his work with the R&R he was also principal stage manager of the Dublin Shakespeare Society, where his disdain for thespians who ruined the effect of his lights by stepping onto the stage, was legendary. Notwithstanding his (frequently justified) low opinion of performers, O'Neill was dedicated to his craft and thorough in its execution. He kept a careful watch from 'the corner' and if he had to leave his post made sure that one of his minions was there to 'watch the book'.

This professionalism saved the show on the first night of *My Fair Lady* in 1969 when a piece of scenery fouled a cloth (see Preface). O'Neill quickly called an unscheduled blackout by banging on the lighting platform. Sean Burke, on the board that night, responded quickly and Paddy Jones and George McFall rapidly cleared the obstruction. It was all over in five seconds and the show went on.

In 1972 Seamus wrote to the committee seeking professional technical help for the very complicated *Camelot*. Betty Long was duly recruited from the Eamonn Andrews Studios. Long was a fund of theatrical lore and anecdote and for many years she, Clodagh Foley, Daphne Millar, Nora O'Rourke and Paula Ryan made up the backstage crew. Daphne Millar specialised in the G&S productions, which she oversaw with great good humour, while Betty Long took control of the musicals. Nora O'Rourke took over as stage manager in 1986, joined over the years by Gerry McKnight, Fiona Hurley, Ciarán McDonough, Derek Bunyan and a host of willing volunteers, depending on the complexity and technical demands of the different shows.

Nora O'Rourke at work, Gaiety Theatre, 1992.

As the Gaiety evolved into a 'receiving house' – a 'four-wall' operation largely devoid of inhouse technical staff – the R&R found itself dealing directly with set designers and builders, scenic artists, lighting and sound specialists. Everything relating to the show had to be transported to the theatre on the 'get-in' day and 'got out' after the last performance – an operation made more difficult after Grafton Street was pedestrianised in 1979.

From its early days the R&R had a reputation for good sets and costumes and the modern society has sometimes struggled to maintain that standard as production costs have risen exponentially. The move to the National Concert Hall was a huge additional challenge. But thanks to imaginative productions, and John O'Donoghue's well-adapted sets which magically overcome the technical difficulties of staging a show in the NCH (no proscenium arch, no flies, no wings, no cyclorama and only three entrances), the R&R has managed to make the improbable actually happen.

Of course what most people prefer to remember is when things go wrong backstage. So R&R veterans love to reminisce about the night the set fell down in *Princess Ida*; the night the flying pieces got entangled during *Hans Andersen* and Noel McDonough, in character, entertained the audience until the curtain rose again; the night in *My Fair Lady* when the leg of the sofa collapsed under Louise Studley, Brendan McShane and Maurice O'Sullivan at the end of 'The Rain in Spain'; the night an

Hello Dolly! backstage crew, 2013.

inattentive Gaiety stage hand inadvertently pulled the wrong lever and activated the sprinkler system instead of taking out the safety curtain – as the harassed Nora O'Rourke mopped up the pit before the orchestra came in, a wit in the audience leaned over the rail and said 'I didn't realise you were doing *Singin' in the Rain*'; or when the fire alarm sounded during *Me and My Girl* because one of the cast had put a potato in the green room microwave and then forgotten all about it.

Somehow, however, the shows went on, thanks to the people who are never seen but who command the utmost respect of everyone who is.

. . . .

TWO-THIRDS OF A CENTURY

If the R&R was P.G. Wodehouse's Bertie Wooster, then Pat Campbell would be Jeeves. Loyal and hardworking, but also inclined to occasional scepticism about the activities of the 'young master' and not afraid to raise an eyebrow, clear his throat meaningfully and make his feelings plain.

A year before the R&R arrived at its centenary, Pat Campbell reached yet another milestone of his own. In 2012 he racked up two-thirds of a century with the society. He made his debut in the chorus line of *The Vagabond King* in 1946 and in the chorus he stubbornly remained – bar a line or two in small parts – for a quarter of a century, a remarkable flower 'born to blush unseen'. It wasn't until the 1970s that he began to emerge centre-stage. In *Camelot* (1971) he played Pellinore but his real performing breakthrough came in *The Mikado* the following year, when he was cast as the hapless Lord High Executioner himself. That led to a *tour de force* in the sodden streets of Venice in 1972 as the Duke of Plaza-Toro in *The Gondoliers*. From there he proceeded to pick off virtually every comic lead role in the G&S repertoire. It was a meteoric rise, an unexpected turn of events, the very stuff of the musical itself. In addition

The Gondoliers: Pat Campbell.

to Ko-Ko and the 'limited' Duke he has also played King Gama in *Princess Ida*, the Lord Chancellor in *Iolanthe*, Bunthorne in *Patience*, Sir Despard in *Ruddigore*, Sir Joseph Porter in *Pinafore*, John Wellington Wells in *The Sorcerer*, and the model Major General in *Pirates*. So far, Jack Point in *Yeomen*

has eluded him; and *Utopia Limited*, as well as *The Grand Duke* both eluded the R&R during his reign. So, while he has not assembled a complete 'set' of comic leads, he has still created a record comparable to that of A.E. (Mack) Glynn which is unlikely to be surpassed by any future R&R performer.[32]

Campbell has also appeared in character roles in numerous musicals and has served as the suave master of ceremonies/ narrator/Jeeves in the many concert performances of the R&R in the NCH, beginning with his turn as Mr Gilbert in *An Evening with Mr Gilbert and Mr Sullivan* in 1984.[33]

But Campbell's importance to the R&R has not just been in his abilities as a comic performer. He has also served the society in both functional and ceremonial roles. From 1975 to 1986 he was one of the most resourceful and tenacious secretaries in the society's history. His immense contribution has already been noted in other sections of this narrative. Since 1988 he has occupied the more ceremonial role of president, one previously held by his father, Michael. Although Campbell, as president, does not attend committee meetings and has no formal executive function, he still exerts a significant influence and

Showboat: Pat Campbell and Dolores Delahunty, 1975.

171

Councillor Mary Freehill, Pat Campbell and Nora O'Rourke at the reopening of Rathmines Library, 12 October 2011. The library – like the R&R – dates from 1913.

is seen by many as the 'conscience' of the society. After more than two-thirds of a century of service – comparable to another great P.G. Wodehouse character, The Oldest Member – he is more than entitled to the status of R&R *éminence grise*.

Though, sadly, it is unlikely that a casting committee would be prepared to unleash him as Jack Point at this stage.

A SECOND HOME: THE R&R AT THE NATIONAL CONCERT HALL

For years it was the Aula Max of University College, Dublin, when that august institution was based at Earlsfort Terrace, Dublin 2. Generations of UCD students were familiar with it as an elaborately appointed barn with exquisite ceilings largely wasted on the adolescent participants in annual examinations, conferring ceremonies or more mundane weekly badminton fixtures. In 1981 it finally became the National Concert Hall after having spent a decade in relative limbo after UCD migrated to Belfield in the outer reaches of Dublin 4. In 1984 with the staging of *An Evening With Mr Gilbert and Mr Sullivan*, it became a welcome second home for the R&R. The impetus for the move originally came from Stephen Faul who had been drawn into the society's activities as treasurer in 1983. Looking at the accounts from the perspective of a complete outsider (one with exceptional financial expertise; he was an executive in Bank of Ireland) he came to the conclusion that continuing to perform in the Gaiety on a biannual basis was economic *harakiri*. He invited the committee to a meeting in the Bank of Ireland boardroom: 'And after presenting them with the figures I suggested the only course of action open was to start doing shows in the National Concert Hall. They thankfully agreed with me.'[34]

Faul's idea was that the profits from the NCH concerts would fund the Gaiety shows. The committee was either swayed by Faul's rhetoric or intimidated by their daunting surroundings. The ordinary membership

The Mikado flyer, 1993.

was less convinced. According to Faul 'there was outright war'. While regular concerts, in places like the SFX Hall or the RDS, often with the RTÉ orchestras,[35] had always been a feature of the R&R's activities, there was resistance to the institutionalising of the practice to the detriment of stage shows. If the active members had wanted to sing in a choir they would have joined Our Lady's Choral Society. They wanted to strut their stuff, not hide in the choir gallery of the NCH behind sheet music.

However, when the profits began to accrue, Faul's idea turned into one of those strokes of genius that everyone remembers having supported at the time. The concerts played to packed houses with most of the tickets being sold in advance of the run. As well as a superior chorus, the society had excellent soloists in the 1980s in Alf Branagan, Fred Graham, Eddie Guilmartin, Bryan Hoey, Lucy Lane, Barbara Graham and Heather Hewson. A template was quickly established that was simple and effective. Shows were, by and large, devised and compered 'inhouse'. They were, in the words of *Irish Times* reviewer George D. Hodnett, 'cleverly packaged'[36] with costumes and 'dressing' being used to create an atmosphere. In some cases, where, for example, the repertoire was from Gilbert and Sullivan operas, there were no royalties to be paid either.

The National Concert Hall had two huge advantages as an appropriate venue. Like the Gaiety it was a home for professional shows, performers and production companies. Unlike the Gaiety its rents were comparatively modest, as the NCH did not have to repay large rolls of cash to impatient investors. It had one forbearing shareholder, Ireland Inc. Also, from an artistic point of view, the sustained use of the chorus, essential for the early NCH shows, was bound to improve choral standards.

The Carnation Boys – Brendan Galvin, Tony Sweeney, Henry Kennedy and Bob McKevitt, NCH 1989.

Its major disadvantage, however, was the belief (mistaken) that its design – a thrust stage with no proscenium arch, flies or significant backstage environment – meant that it was only conducive to the staging of concerts and recitals. Even in this limited context, however, the R&R visits there were particularly lucrative. Follow-up concerts in 1986 (*Rodgers & Hart and Rodgers & Hammerstein*), 1987 (*Romberg and Romance*) and 1988 (*The Magic of Lerner and Loewe*) were all highly profitable. In March 1989 the Noel Coward vehicle *I'll See You Again* netted almost £18,000 in just over a week. Compare that with a profit of just over £5,000 from the two-week run of *Fiddler on the Roof* in the Gaiety the previous November. Given that the NCH capacity was virtually the same as that of the Gaiety, that ticket prices could be pegged at a similar rate, and that production costs for a concert were minimal in comparison with a fully-staged show, the R&R could hardly fail. In 1999, for example, the *Romberg to Rodgers* recital made a profit for the society of £21,788. The following year *A Century of Song* topped that with a surplus of £29,516.

The pattern of annual winter Gaiety shows and NCH spring concerts continued until the financial debacle of *Anything Goes* in 1992. For pressing financial reasons, as well as the governance issues already outlined, the R&R absented itself from the Gaiety for three years. In order that the society would not become merely a glorified choral group, the R&R decided to bite the bullet in 1993 and celebrate its eightieth anniversary with a fully staged Gilbert and Sullivan production at the NCH in October. The choice for this experiment, appropriately, was *The Mikado*. Given the strictures imposed

The Mikado finale, 2010.

by the geography of the NCH there was 'a suggestion of scenery' rather than a full set. That remained the practice until 2001 when another *Mikado* was staged with a box set rather than an impressionistic 'virtual' construct.[37] That particular production had sold out before it even opened.[38] Actually the decision in principle to do G&S at the NCH had been taken as early as 1989, but was not finally realised until 1993.[39] From that point on the Concert Hall became the home of Gilbert and Sullivan and remains so to this day. The R&R has not produced a Savoy opera at the Gaiety since 1991.

One of the most interesting and innovative G&S productions at the Concert Hall was undoubtedly the 2010 *Mikado*, directed by Garry Mountaine. Here the title role, of the Emperor of Japan, was taken by a striking 3.6 metre tall model. This was built by Buí Bolg (Yellow Belly – a hurling reference for the sportingly challenged) in Wexford. It sat onstage, Buddha-like, for the entire first act, looking,

The Mikado comes to Rathmines – with Jackie Curran Olohan as Katisha – in 2010.

quite literally, like part of the scenery. However, during the interval a young performer Ciaran Bonner was loaded inside the model, so that when the time arrived for the entrance of the Mikado and his 'daughter-in-law elect' Katisha (Jackie Curran Olohan) the statue suddenly came alive in a marvellous *coup de théâtre*. Backstage Ciaran Olohan, watching on a monitor and listening via earphones, spoke the Mikado's lines and sang into a microphone while a device in the model's head lip-synched the words. Fitzgerald and Weaving might not have entirely approved but the NCH audience lapped it up.

Just as the society 'retreated' to the NCH after the financial misfortune that was *Anything Goes* in 1992, it retrenched to the same venue after the excellent but ill-fated *Producers* in 2009, which lost the society a small fortune. Between November 2009 and April 2013 the R&R once again rebuilt its balance sheet by performing exclusively at the NCH with a combination of concerts, G&S and, finally in 2012, a stage musical in *Oklahoma!*

Given the constraints imposed by the venue, the latter venture could have been a financial and artistic disaster. It was neither. The show sold out a week-long run and was judged to have worked extremely well as a fully-realised piece of musical theatre.[40] While a highly successful revival of *Anything Goes* (the triumph of optimism over experience yet again) had been staged in the NCH in 2007, it required only a single static set. *Oklahoma!* was much more ambitious and points the way for future, economically viable, musical theatre productions at the venue. While rentals at the NCH have not remained static, neither have they advanced over the years at the rate of medical inflation.

In addition, the NCH has been far less problematic than the Gaiety in terms of the service provided in return for the money expended.[41] There is a long history of disputes between the R&R and the Gaiety, exacerbated since the theatre became, in effect, a 'four-wall' operation. The Gaiety now comes at a high price with no frills attached. This was emphatically demonstrated, for example, in the early years of the millennium when the 'get-in' for *Carousel* in 2000 was marred by the failure of the theatre to employ a chief electrician. This resulted in blown fuses and the 'hot-focusing' of the stage lights only a few hours before the show opened.[42] The situation had hardly improved the following year as the R&R prepared to stage *Guys and Dolls*. Camillus Mountaine and Ig Lyons (general secretary and treasurer) had met the theatre's general manager John Costigan about the *Carousel* debacle in January 2001. According to their report 'he had no defence and admitted things were not satisfactory due to staff shortage'.[43] Yet the following November it was reported that there was still 'general dissatisfaction with Gaiety'.[44]

Ig Lyons, honorary treasurer (1992–2006).

Laurey (Anna Brady) and Curley (Brian Gilligan) with wedding guests. *Oklahoma!*, NCH, 2012.

175

The R&R manages each year to attract 6,000 patrons to the National Concert Hall. For some it's the production that draws them in. For others it's brand loyalty. Either way the venue has played a significant role in the survival of the R&R beyond its seventy-fifth birthday. When there was a hole in the balance sheet the right show at the NCH could be relied upon to save the day. The society's great Gilbert and Sullivan tradition – and the society has become, *ipso facto*, an informal Irish guarantor of the Savoy repertoire – is now safely ensconced at the NCH with no real need to stray from Earlsfort Terrace. The reluctance to stage full-scale credible musical theatre at the venue has also been overcome. The kind of risk and reinvention seen in the technically innovative staging of *Oklahoma!* in 2012 marked a significant development in the society's use of the venue and a pointer towards a possible future.

The Gaiety may still have the opulent glamour, it may be the charismatic leading man as against the reliable character actor. It may be the handsome lyric tenor to the less prestigious NCH bass/baritone. But since 1984 the National Concert Hall has kept the music playing.

. . . .

MISE-EN-SCÈNE: HOW A MODERN PRODUCTION IS PUT TOGETHER

HELLO, DOLLY! (2013)

> *The work ethic has been passed on from generation to generation…The challenges of tomorrow will be overcome by the rehearsals of today.*[45]
>
> Stephen Faul, chairman, 1988.

In April 2013 the R&R returned to the Gaiety Theatre for the first time in four years. Sentiment and symbolism have probably been more important to the society than is good for it at times. The experience of the last show at the venue, *The Producers* in 2009, was still an acrid smell in the nostrils rising from severely burned fingers. But there was a tradition to be maintained – going back to 1914 – and this was, after all, centenary year. Wiser counsels kept their counsel and it was full steam ahead for a rollicking 'loss leader' which had the potential, given only a few missteps, to make the years after the hundredth anniversary as lean and hungry as the look of 'yond Cassius'.

The business philosophy of the R&R is 'a show in production, a show in planning'. The choice of what to bring to the Gaiety in centenary year was made months in advance. The original selection was *My Fair Lady*. The society had, after all, premiered the show in Ireland. Unfortunately the rights were discovered to be unavailable for spring 2013. The backup plan was for *Hello, Dolly!* with music by Jerry Herman, book by Michael Stewart, based on the play *The Matchmaker* written by the great American dramatist Thornton Wilder. The title role of matchmaker Dolly Levi in the 1964 Broadway stage production was played by Carol Channing. Later Ethel Merman and Mary Martin (both of whom had originally turned the role down) would star in the musical. Despite the paucity of hit songs from the show – the title number 'Hello, Dolly!' itself became an unlikely chart hit for Louis Armstrong in 1964 – it won ten Tony awards that year. The 1969 film version (which won three Academy Awards) starred Barbra Streisand as Dolly and Walter Matthau as her matrimonial quarry Horace Vandergelder.

The R&R were no strangers to the piece. It had first been produced at the Gaiety in 1989 with Hazel Yeomans in the title role and Cathal MacCabe as Vandergelder. The production was, even by the standards of the R&R, lavish and expensive. It was also a close-run thing. The race to the finish line was between Yeomans and laryngitis. At a committee meeting in September a decision was taken, crucial in retrospect, not to rehearse an understudy for Yeomans.[46] The run was from 14–25 November and Yeomans started to succumb to an increasingly bothersome throat midway through the second week. She managed to stagger to Friday 24th but was doubtful for the final Saturday matinee or evening performance. Stephen Faul, then chairman, who conveniently comes from a family of doctors, summoned all the medical expertise he could. Yeomans was admitted to the Eye and Ear Hospital but the emergency treatment she received was only partially effective. 'Dolly' would be ready for the final Saturday evening performance but could not combine it with the afternoon matinée.

The solution was straight out of the film *Singin' in the Rain*, where, in the final scene, Debbie Reynolds sings behind a curtain while Jean Hagen (the tone-deaf silent movie star who is 'richer than Calvin

The R&R Production Team, 2013.

Coolidge…put together') lip-syncs out front. Choreographer Dex McGloughlin took to the stage in place of Yeomans and spoke her lines, but when she sang, the voice the audience heard was actually coming from the orchestra pit. It was that of Lua McIlrath.[47] Despite the expenditure involved in the production it made a profit of £6,275 for the society.[48]

In preliminary negotiations with the Gaiety for the centenary production, general secretary Shay Gibson sought to minimise the financial risk to the R&R by coming to a profit-sharing arrangement with the theatre. Nothing like this had been seen since the days of Louis Elliman. Gaiety management was prepared to consider the idea but expressed doubts that the society would be able to 'fill' ten days (twelve shows) at the 1,100-seater venue. The Gaiety felt that the pulling power of a well-known name was needed to ensure that *Hello, Dolly!* did not become an even bigger financial misfortune than *The Producers*. Although society policy for most of the second half-century of its existence has been not to pay performers, the popular singer and actress Rebecca Storm – probably best known in Ireland as 'Mrs Johnstone' in many productions of Willy Russell's *Blood Brothers* – was brought in as 'very special guest' in the pivotal role of Dolly Levi. Gibson acknowledges that there was considerable opposition to the end of the shibboleth that had been the basis of society policy for more than fifty years. 'Some of the members were up in arms, but the committee felt that on a once-off basis it was the right thing to do in centenary year.'[49] One of those resolutely opposed to the move was the society's own president Pat Campbell, who feared that this *demarche* was the thin end of the wedge.[50]

Like many older members with long memories, Campbell felt it might lead to the creeping professionalisation of the principals. As the society was increasingly reliant on aspirant professional singers to play the principal parts in musicals, where would it end? Ironically, a short time later, with Storm already on board, the Gaiety pulled out of negotiations on a profit/loss sharing arrangement, though the normal rental was significantly reduced (by 25 per cent) from Celtic Tiger levels. Gibson argues that the negotiated reduction in the rent more than covered the fee paid to Storm. Before auditions began Garry Mountaine, who has worked with Storm on the professional stage, was cast opposite her as Vandergelder.

Chorus and minor principals auditions began in early December and the full cast was chosen in early February. Time was when the R&R had an established 'repertory' company on which it would call to fill the parts of Ermengrade, Ambrose Kemper, Cornelius Hackl and Barnaby Tucker. But notions of a 'company' have eroded over the years. While many chorus members have performed with the R&R for longer than most care to remember, the same is not as true of principals. Prior to casting, production manager Nora O'Rourke wondered exactly how many of the leads in *Hello, Dolly!* would even have appeared at the Gaiety before, such has been the turnover in personnel since *The Producers* in 2009. 'Nowadays performers are attracted by the production, where in the past it was the society.'[51] Many of the stars of today's shows are just as likely to turn up in a Glasnevin Musical Society or Lyric Opera/ Festival Productions cast at the National Concert Hall as they are to return to the R&R.

Shows are not, of course, simply chosen on the basis of availability. The list of musicals appropriate to the R&R is not infinite. Such is the importance of the society's chorus that musicals by composers like Stephen Sondheim, which tend not to feature this type of ensemble work, are never considered. One of the first questions asked before a decision is reached is 'What's in it for the chorus?' This is one of the primary reasons for the continuing popularity of Gilbert and Sullivan in the R&R repertoire. It's more than just an adherence to tradition that keeps the society loyal to Savoy operetta. Gilbert and Sullivan light operas include as much elaborate four-part harmony chorus work as any chorister's little heart could possibly desire. *Hello, Dolly!* features an abundance of strong ensemble numbers, including the title tune, 'Put on Your Sunday Clothes', 'Before the Parade Passes By' and 'It Only Takes a Moment'. So *Hello, Dolly!* passed the fundamental test: there was plenty in it for the chorus.

The gift of parts in an R&R show has always been the responsibility of the casting committee. In December 2012 this fearsome and august group included convenor Dympna Egar,[52] Barney Gorman, Shay Gibson as well as Gearóid Grant, Noel McDonough and Jackie Curran Olohan. Wide-ranging auditions saw the subaltern roles in the show being taken by MacKenzy Cade (Ambrose

Dympna Egar and Dympna Bevan.

Kemper), Marie Kelly (Ernestina), Alison Vard Miller (Ermengrade), Michael Evans (Cornelius Hackl) and Stuart Pollock (Barnaby Tucker). MacKenzy Cade and Stuart Pollock have previously appeared in *Oklahoma!*, Michael Evans has starred in *The Producers*, while Alison Vard Miller was making her R&R debut.

Chorus rehearsals began in early February. Typically, Jackie Curran Olohan, the chorus director, begins to work with the male and female chorus members eleven weeks before opening night. The score is drummed into them twice a week, generally on Tuesdays and Thursdays, at the R&R hall in Rathmines. At around the same time dance rehearsals for the big numbers began under long-time choreographer Marina Kealy. On Monday 4 March the company came together for a 'read and sing through' and from that point onwards the really serious work began.

By late March, when your chronicler attended a rehearsal, principals Rebecca Storm and Garry Mountaine were already word-perfect. The dancing was nimble and confident, the chorus work already sounded polished. Producer Noel McDonough presides over rehearsals like a kindly, indulgent but firm and precise patriarch. Sometimes his job probably feels as much like crowd control as it does direction. A lesser mortal would get lost in the detail. The 'business' of the chorus, for example, is complex but clearly graded and delineated. Nothing can be allowed to happen in a big chorus that will upstage the main action. Activity goes from 'level zero' – subtle dumbshow – to 'level four' – animated boisterousness.[53] McDonough generally allows the action to flow without interruption. A gesture, a look, a wave of his right hand and *voilà*, the stationary chorus moves, as a single organism, two feet stage left. The song continues without interruption, *répétiteur* Niamh McDonough establishing the tempo on the magnificent grand piano offstage left. Niamh and Noel, a husband and wife team, communicate in a sort of clipped code, like a Wimbledon mixed doubles who've been playing together for years.

McDonough puts Garry Mountaine, Michael Evans, Stuart Pollock and the men's chorus through their paces in a scene from Act I. The setting is Vandergelder's hay and feed store in Yonkers. The timid Hackl and Tucker, Vandergelder's employees, are preparing for a romantic flit to New York. Mountaine, as Vandergelder, fills us in on his backstory when suddenly, thanks to the wonders of the musical comedy script, two lingering customers become 'an instant glee club', the stage is full of male singers and dancers, disbelief is suspended – even in the austere surroundings of the R&R rehearsal hall – and we are in the middle of the chorus number 'It Takes a Woman'. Black masking tape outlines the precise dimensions of the Gaiety stage and 'offstage' Rebecca Storm and the female chorus look on. After a near perfect 'take', they applaud. It is hard not to see the Gaiety audience doing likewise three weeks on, after the piece has been honed and repeated until each move and every note has become instinctive.

In bygone days the 'run through' was as much a social outlet for cast and chorus as it was a vital opportunity for a director to shape and hone a production. Everybody was expected and encouraged to turn up in the final weeks of rehearsal. This could often lead to unwieldy and somewhat raucous sessions. In recent times rehearsals have become more focused. A schedule is drawn up and supernumeraries, however sociable, are not required. The pieces are put together in greater isolation and sessions are less likely to resemble Ballinasloe Horse Fair. What is lost in conviviality is, however, gained in efficiency.

Back in late 2012, when asked to produce a tentative budget for the entire production, it became clear to Nora O'Rourke that building a set was not a viable option. Designing and constructing a set for the Gaiety from scratch would be far too expensive. The structure would also have to be consigned to a skip after two weeks in the theatre. 'Even that is more expensive now,' says O'Rourke, 'because it has to be

Hello Dolly!, 2013: Garret Reynolds proposes to Megan McGrath.

environmentally disposed of.'[54] Instead the set was hired from a company called Scenic Projects, based in Brampton in Suffolk.[55] Scenic Projects provided a set designed for a 'medium-sized stage', delivered and later collected it, and sent over its own technical staff to ensure that it was properly erected. All for the relatively modest cost of £8,880 (€11,000).

The R&R has not retained its own costume wardrobe for a number of years now. Pressure on space in the Rathmines premises means that only a small number of costumes are stored there. Even Gilbert and Sullivan attire is hired. The days of renting costumes from Gings or Derry O'Donovan in Dublin are also long gone. A limited supply can still be sourced in Ireland from Pat McGann Productions in Limerick and Theatrical Costume Hire in Newry. The costumes for *Hello, Dolly!* were actually obtained from Utopia Costumes in Forfar in Scotland. Wardrobe masters Edward O'Grady Walshe and Patricia Hough diligently measured the cast and chorus and despatched the details to northern Scotland where Utopia's stock of *Hello, Dolly!* costumes[56] were taken in or expanded as required. The big ensemble numbers like 'Put on Your Sunday Clothes' mean that the show, with its nineteenth-century origins, is a difficult and costly one to dress, as complex and expensive as, for example, *My Fair Lady*.

The work of musical director Gearóid Grant began with the ordering of orchestral scores for the ensemble led by his wife Sunniva. Rights to *Hello, Dolly!* are held by Josef Weinberger in London, so the scores came from there accompanied by injunctions to the players against marking the material with anything other than a 2B pencil. The accompanying documentation carried the dire warning 'defacing the material equates to vandalism'. Before the scores were returned to Weinberger's – 'within FOURTEEN days'[57] – a night was spent erasing the 2B-pencilled notes made by the orchestra. Hamlet would have been impressed.

Grant and his musicians rehearsed separately from the cast and chorus. The two only came together at the dress rehearsal. Up to that point Niamh McDonough kept the musical side of the show on the road from her piano stool.

With about two weeks remaining before opening night the separate elements of the show were locked in place and rehearsed in sequence. At this point Gearóid Grant made his first formal appearance in the rehearsal room in order to dictate the musical pace of the show. Nora O'Rourke always senses a change in the atmosphere when Grant arrives for the first time. Perhaps it's the awareness that opening night is drawing closer, perhaps it's the presence of a new galvanising element, perhaps it's related to Grant's own ebullient personality. But 'the minute Gearóid appears, quite literally, the tempo goes up, and the concentration goes up. He has a wonderful,

Gearóid Grant, 2006.

powerful effect on everybody.' In performance, Grant is totally attuned to what is happening onstage. It is something of an education to watch him in action as he commands his musicians and cajoles his cast and chorus. His energy is intense, his concentration total and his encouragement of the performers is of an order not always associated with the modern MD. If Charles Acton were still working at his trade he would have no adverse criticism to offer on the level of communication between the orchestra pit and the stage with Gearóid Grant wielding the baton.

As with all productions, either in the Gaiety or the National Concert Hall, the logistics of the 'get in' are faintly terrifying. Entry to the theatre's scenery dock must come via a pedestrianised Grafton Street. A short 'window' is available on the morning of Monday 15 April for the large articulated Scenic Projects truck to deliver the set, unload and be on its way back to East Anglia. In 1985 the society was staging *Hans Andersen*. The set was constructed in Ardmore Studios and delivered, by truck, via a largely deserted Grafton Street, early on the Monday before the show opened. The trailer was duly deposited *in situ* and the cab headed back for Wicklow. Then the movable container was opened and found wanting. It was completely empty. The cab had managed to hitch onto the wrong trailer. While the correct one was, at least, only a few miles down the road in Bray, permission had to be obtained from the Gardaí to close off Grafton Street in order to allow the set to be delivered.

Before the Scenic Projects set was installed, the R&R's own wooden flooring was placed over the Gaiety stage. This more pliable structure makes life easier for the dancers. As the scenery was being put in place the lighting designer Denis Twomey worked with production electrician Eamon Fox to mount the dozens of lights required to illuminate the show. The experience with *Carousel* in 2000 means the R&R always brings along its own electrician.

The following day the cast 'walked' through the production in the afternoon for the benefit of the technical staff. Dress rehearsal that night began at 7.30. This is the only real opportunity the cast and chorus get to try out for real what has been practised for weeks within the thin black lines in Rathmines. Noel McDonough watched and made notes as Gearóid Grant took the cast and orchestra through the show. As always he was forced to quell any instinct he might have had to intervene and call an abrupt halt to proceedings. Convention and common sense dictates that only the musical director can stop a dress rehearsal in full flight to make some essential change. The stage director must wait until the afternoon of the show's opening to deliver his final notes. Then there are a few hours left to iron out any serious kinks before curtain rises on the premiere.

Even with a 'name' star like Rebecca Storm and the background presence of a loyal R&R audience, there were no guarantees that a show like *Hello, Dolly!* would attract an audience sufficient to ensure that the R&R didn't suffer a serious financial loss on the entire transaction. Almost as important as the quality of the production itself is the marketing and public relations effort that goes into 'selling' the show. The R&R 'brand' alone is probably worth about 50 per cent of the Gaiety's capacity. Between 5,000 and 6,000 people attend the NCH productions each year, drawn by the standard of excellence established by the R&R as much as by the 'product'. That leaves roughly the same number again who must be enticed into the theatre on some other basis. The presence of another popular 'brand', that of Rebecca Storm, was a distinct bonus for the society's PR and advertising campaign.

Getting out the good news about the R&R is currently down to a small and highly efficient committee led by John McCall. For the centenary year, a decision was taken to bring in professional assistance in the shape of O'Herlihy Communications, a company founded back in the Jurassic era of public relations in Ireland by the avuncular Bill 'we'll leave it there so' O'Herlihy, best known as the voice and face of sanity on RTÉ soccer programmes. The company still has Bill O'Herlihy at the helm but he shares the burdens of management with his daughter Jill. In a moment of inspiration, a combination of John McCall and Jill O'Herlihy managed to secure an ad in *The Irish Times* for *Hello, Dolly!* on the day the paper announced the election of Pope Francis I – himself a keen tango *aficionado*. In musical comedy, timing is everything. The Pope, incidentally, was above the fold.

Hello, Dolly! opened on Wednesday 17 April. It earned four stars from Michael Moffatt in *The Irish Mail on Sunday*, who noted that it was the major production for the centenary year of the society and that it was 'the perfect show for a celebration'. While the gamble did not pay off financially, the show was a great success and has led to a renewal of the relationship with the Gaiety, which, it is hoped will blossom to mutual advantage in the years to come.

The social highlight of the run came when nature imitated art on the penultimate night, Friday 26 April. Dolly presided over a genuine match when chorus member Garret Reynolds got down on one knee, in traditional style, and proposed to fellow chorister Megan McGrath after the final curtain. This was all done under the benign gaze of Rebecca Storm (in character). Megan accepted, thus avoiding a plot complication that would have required an entirely new act in order to be rectified. At the time of writing, almost 30,000 people have witnessed the betrothal on YouTube. And you can watch it all here: http://www.youtube.com/watch?v=GM3XDBV-34M.

CHERNOBYL

Brendan Galvin was introduced to the R&R by his uncle, also Brendan Galvin, the society's long-time production secretary. He describes his uncle as a peacekeeper within the group 'the Kofi Annan of the R&R'.[58] But it was a blatant act of subterfuge on behalf of the elder Brendan that was used to inveigle his nephew into a performing role. Although he'd been going to R&R shows since the age of 4, and was completely comfortable backstage he claims he was bamboozled into joining the chorus. Convinced he was being recruited by his uncle, like a Cambridge graduate innocently entering the service of the KGB, 'just to help him move the set around', Brendan Junior found himself 'thrust into this rehearsal':

> I had no idea what I was doing at all. It was frightening. Then at the interval Heather Hewson called me over and made me sing scales. She then said 'right, you're a baritone' and that was pretty much it.

The profoundly intimidating Ms Hewson kept Brendan Junior on a tight leash and, for fear of offending her as well as disappointing his uncle, he remained loyal to the R&R despite having been, effectively, abducted into a bizarre cult.

Galvin's most significant contribution to the society, with due deference to both his abilities and his feelings, was probably not on the stage. He was primary mover in a 2011 venture that recalled the heady days of the hospital tours. Except this was a charity event with an international dimension.

The idea for the R&R Chernobyl concert emerged from a conversation in 2010 between Galvin and Marie Cox, head of the medical staff at the charity founded in 1991 by Adi Roche – Chernobyl Children International. Roche had famously responded, five years after the catastrophic explosion at the Chernobyl nuclear reactor, to an appeal from Belarusian and Ukrainian doctors to remove young children from the area surrounding the original blast to give their bodies time to recover from radiation exposure.[59] The initial conversation between Galvin and Cox envisaged an R&R benefit concert designed to raise funds for CCI. It quickly metamorphosed into something rather more ambitious after Galvin watched an episode of the RTÉ TV series *Do the Right Thing* that included a performance for the children of the stricken region. The conversation with Cox and the television show changed Galvin's life.

> For the show they built a small stage in the centre of Chernobyl, and through that I got the idea to put our concert on over there instead.

Galvin and a group of R&R members raised enough money to pay for their own flights and bring an additional €17,000 to Chernobyl. This was done euro by euro in late 2010 with the usual round of table quizzes and race nights as well as a Christmas concert in Rathmines. The travelling party was also hired by restaurants to sing Christmas carols to their customers, all proceeds going to the CCI venture.

It was never intended to be a pleasure trip but Galvin and the other eleven members of the R&R group were not prepared to face an intimidating atmosphere when they arrived at the nearest airport to Chernobyl, at Minsk in the Ukraine.

R&R group in Chernobyl, 2011.

It was like going into a different world. The airport at Minsk was very oppressive and when we saw that Marie Cox, who was with us, was intimidated, it only made us feel more insecure. They look for any excuse to turn you away… It was dark when we arrived [at the orphanage] it's a two-hour drive from Minsk so everybody was already asleep. But you're nervously excited… All of us tore into the duty-free vodka just to calm the nerves a little that night.

They were not sure what they were going to witness. They had prepared themselves for the worst.

You could hear the voices of the kids, crying, screaming and talking. Before we went over there we tried to mentally prepare ourselves for what we were going to see, by looking at different pictures and videos. But then they brought us around to the wards and the second you saw them they all had smiles on their faces, and all they want is to be hugged. It really helped us hugely.

For the show the R&R used the stage built for the RTÉ television programme. The children themselves were first to perform – 'I think they were almost more excited about that' – then it was time for only the second R&R concert to be staged outside of Ireland.[60]

We made absolutely loads of mistakes. But it was amazing just seeing their faces because they'd never seen anything like it before. It was probably 1 out of 10 for our performance but 10 out of 10 for our audience. Afterwards they wanted us to go around to some of the kids who weren't able to make it to the concert, the kids in the high dependency wards. Some of them had never even heard music before, and as we sang you could see them reacting. It was hard to concentrate.

Galvin is anything but starry-eyed about the impact of the gesture of the R&R members.

The longer you spent there, the loneliness of the kids becomes a lot clearer. When there isn't a big crowd like us over, they really have nothing. That's the reality they're facing. And seeing the graveyard that really hits home again… Leaving was the hardest part, because we were leaving them behind with nothing. We knew they would have nothing in their days until another group visited them. Some people found it very hard to adjust once we got back.

In 2012, while rehearsals were underway for *Oklahoma!* in the National Concert Hall, the R&R duly returned to Chernobyl. While Brendan Galvin's efforts are part of an enduring R&R tradition, the relationship being built with the children of the stricken Chernobyl region arguably ranks as the most selfless act in a century of zealous charitable work.

PAYING THE PIPER: PRODUCTION COSTS AND THE MODERN MUSICAL

It came crashing home to R&R production manager Nora O'Rourke that theatre production costs were getting out of hand when she accepted a quote to build a set for *Oklahoma!* in 1999. O'Rourke had only recently taken over from the late Brendan Galvin as production secretary, so she was not entirely *au fait* with the actual cost of sets, costumes and even props up to that point. At a modest £20,531,[61] the set, she realised, was going to cost more than her first house! And to think that back in 1913 some of the earliest members of the infant society had been concerned at the deficit for the inaugural year… of £9.

As the recent travails of *Spiderman* on Broadway have borne out, musical theatre costs run into millions of dollars. A show, like Bono and the Edge's tyro effort, that costs $75 million to stage, and requires a run of at least five years to break even, is exceptional. But the public appetite for spectacle is just one element that has fuelled musical inflation over the last half-century. A more banal example than *Spiderman* is the hugely successful *Wicked*. Involving an initial outlay of $14 million, it opened on Broadway in 2003 and took only fourteen months to make back its investment and start paying dividends to its financiers.[62] It costs about $800,000 a week to maintain and usually grosses between $1.2–$1.3 million a week. It could run for fifteen to twenty years. Touring productions (one visited Ireland in 2013) add to Broadway and West End profits.

Irish fans of musical theatre in the 2000s have had relatively untrammelled access to Broadway and West End shows on visits to New York and London. The touring versions of those same shows, only slightly scaled-down, now play in venues like the O2 (Point) and Bord Gáis Energy (Grand Canal) theatres on a regular basis. So how are you going to keep them down on the farm after they've seen Paree? Irish audiences have become accustomed to superior production standards. Cheap sets and shoddy costumes are anathema to the modern Irish theatre-goer. However, elaborate sets and dazzling costumes come with a startling price-tag. But the piper has to be paid.

Playing in a professional venue like the Gaiety, it has long been incumbent on the R&R to put far more money up on the stage than it can comfortably afford. The alternative is redundancy and oblivion. Shay Gibson, far from a senior citizen himself, remembers a time – as recently as the 1980s – when there were more than sixty musical societies in Dublin alone. Today there are barely twenty.[63] Most of the rest have succumbed to the reality of escalating costs and the fear of communal financial liability. It is virtually axiomatic today that only musical groups based securely in a community of a certain size (Wexford, Carrick-on-Suir, Kells) can hope to survive. Idiosyncratic or adventurous programming, which would occasionally produce a surprise 'hit', is also much rarer in the twenty-first century than in the past.

Whether driven by fear of disappointing an audience or the search for redemption through perfection, or a combination of both, the R&R has always invested heavily in its productions. But even in the world of amateur musical theatre the handmaiden of rigour is risk.

The R&R does not have an opportunity to reduce unit costs per production by running a successful show for weeks on end. Pressure on dates is too great and the available Dublin audience is too small to sustain a long run, anyway. Unless you expend very little money, it is asking a lot to make that money back over twelve to fourteen performances. Unfortunately minimal expenditure – an honorary treasurer's dream – is counter-productive when it comes to winning and retaining audiences. An amateur company like the R&R has only two obvious advantages when it comes to staging a colourful and expensive production. It does not have to pay its performers; neither does it have to repay investors. Without those crucial factors in its favour, the R&R would no longer exist. As Heather Hewson pointed out in an *Irish Times* interview in 1969, probably only an amateur company could have produced some of the shows it has staged over the last century.[64]

On the occasion of the sixtieth anniversary of the society in 1973 *The Irish Times* took up this particular theme. In an opinion piece, the newspaper declared: 'Nowadays any group which decides to organise any artistic activity begins by writing to the Arts Council for assistance. There is an ever-increasing tendency to seek help and cushioning against loss. There was not always an Arts Council, nor was it easy in Dublin to get financial support; the people who launched the R&R were pioneers.'[65] This was borne out six years later when the society made a pioneering production choice and staged *Sweet Charity*. It was a commercial flop, and put the society in a grim financial position. Seamus Kelly reported in 'An Irishman's Diary' in November 1979 that 'the society has suffered losses which would have pained a professional company, and which nearly crippled this amateur society…so the usual arms of the usual friends were twisted even more strongly this time, to extract the £30,000 they need to present *The Mikado* and *Patience*'.[66]

The spectacular set for Act 2 of *The Gondoliers* in the NCH, 2006.

Recent Shows

The Pirates of Penzance, 1994:
Ladies' chorus in dresses and
bonnets by Synan O'Mahony.

Rehearsals for the first Pirates of Penzance in the NCH, 1994.

RTÉ Concert Orchestra with
the R&R in the Rodgers &
Hammerstein Concert, NCH, 2010.

Sergeant (Michael Clark) and Police:
The Pirates of Penzance, 2011.

Sarah Guilmartin and Garry Mountaine:
'A Highly Respectable Wife', *The Merry Widow*, 2008.

Ladies' chorus, *The Pirates of Penzance*, 2011.

WESTERN TRAMWAYS

With increasing numbers of people accessing big shows in the West End and on Broadway the problem of odious comparisons became acute. This was articulated with some asperity by David Nowlan in his review of *My Fair Lady* in March 1981. Much had changed in Ireland in the twelve years since the 1969 premiere. 'It would, of course', Nowlan began, 'be grossly unfair to compare a Dublin amateur society with its professional New York equivalent.' He then proceeded to do just that. 'But after spending a week on Broadway I must record how dispiriting it is to come back to see the Rathmines and Rathgar Musical Society in *My Fair Lady* and to note how great is the gap between the two.'[67] Nowlan concluded by getting on 'the appropriate wavelength' as he put it, and enjoying the show, but his attitude explains why the R&R had to put so much money into (a) maintaining a presence in the Gaiety and (b) ensuring that production values did not suffer. Their efforts could more easily be compared with the very best, a situation that would be exacerbated in the 1990s with the arrival of some of the big West End shows at the Point Theatre.

A huge contributory factor to the disinclination towards an annual rental of the Gaiety has been the escalating tariff there. Between 1989 and 2009 the cost of using the Gaiety Theatre for two weeks a year almost quadrupled. The rent charged by the theatre for the 1989 *Hello, Dolly!* was the Irish pound equivalent of €33,000. The theatre cost €122,000 to hire for the run of *The Producers* two decades later. If you choose to go back a further twenty years, to the highly successful three-week run of *My Fair Lady*, costs have increased by a factor of thirty! In 1969 the Gaiety cost the equivalent of €4,000. As a result the society's relationship with the Old Lady of South King Street has had to change radically in recent years. The wrong show at the wrong time in such an expensive venue would see the R&R staging its own dramatised version of the meltdown of Lehman brothers. Antiquity and tradition provide no protection against rapidly rising input costs.

The 1969 production of *My Fair Lady* is a cautionary tale. It was, arguably, the most lauded R&R production in one hundred years of existence. It was an Irish premiere. Both the Gaiety and the R&R were in their pomp. It boasted perhaps the two finest non-professional singers in the country at the time, Brendan McShane and Louise Studley, in the two lead roles. It proved so popular in March that it was retained by the Gaiety for an extra week. As it was about to close, bookings were still so heavy that the decision was made to abandon plans for the customary G&S productions in the autumn in favour of reviving *My Fair Lady* instead. Yet in the spring of 1969, on an income of £18,700 – more than six times the rental – the show made a profit of only £370.[68] Based on a two-week run in November, with more modest box-office returns of £6,347 (despite the benefit of non-recurring expenses for sets and costumes), the show made a profit of £40.[69] Charles Acton had written of *My Fair Lady* in *The Irish Times* that 'a great deal of real trouble has been taken by everybody (and probably a great deal of money spent) to see that everything is good'.[70] He had no idea just how right he was.

It is informative to examine the rise in production costs from the 1970s onwards. In 1975 *Showboat*, it was estimated, would cost £12,000–£13,000 to produce. An attendance of just over 60 per cent (increasingly the norm for the R&R in the 1970s) meant that losses could be contained to about £2,000–£3,000.[71] A deficit of that level could be mitigated by active and associate membership fees. Anything more than that and the society would be forced to have recourse to their guarantors. Up to the early 1980s, guarantors – whose liability was normally capped at around £300 per production – had actually been required to contribute only about 20 per cent of the amount pledged.[72]

But only three years later the outlay on the society's part had almost doubled. *Gigi* required more than £24,000 to mount in 1978.[73] Staging costs had risen geometrically. Admission charges had, in the meantime, increased arithmetically.

The period 1970 to 1990 is not renowned as an era of egregious prosperity in Ireland. They were decades of emigration, rampant inflation (in the 1970s), massive government deficits (in the 1980s), and high unemployment in both decades. Even a musical society with an economically sheltered middle-class membership, that has always prided itself on investing heavily in its productions, had to indulge in some belt-tightening. Occasionally that was reflected in the 'look' of a show. In November 1981, writing in *The Irish Times*, Deaglán de Bréadún in his review of *Princess Ida* suggested that 'neither sets nor costumes are exactly dazzling, which may indicate that the society like the rest of us, is feeling the pinch'.[74] However, despite the recessionary times, expenses still kept rising. In 1982 *Oklahoma!* cost £40,000–£50,000 to stage. That year the society expected to turn over £100,000 in a twelve-month period for the first time.[75] Towards the end of the decade production expenditure had almost doubled again, with *Showboat* (1987) and *Fiddler in the Roof* (1988) both costing £80,000 to put on the stage.

Although rental charges were the most expensive item in any budget, other costs were escalating too. The putative budget, assembled in March 1990, for the proposed November 1991 run of *Yeomen* and *Gondoliers* in the Gaiety Theatre is typical of its time and offers an insight into where the money was being spent.

	£
Rent	15,000
Scenery and backstage	5,000
Costumes	3,000
Orchestra	5,000
Royalties	Nil
Rehearsal expenses	3,000
Marketing, printing, advertising	3,000
Total	34,000[76]

The figure for rent covered a run of only one week. Costumes were hired, sets would still have been built for each production. The figure for royalties would obviously be much higher for staging a piece of musical theatre, amounting to between 10 and 15 per cent[77] of box-office receipts. Income, with good promotion and an enthusiastic audience response, could be expected to be in the region of £30,000–£35,000. The weekly rental of £15,000 being sought by the theatre led the committee to make the decision not to occupy the Gaiety in March 1991. Its next spring show was the ill-fated *Anything Goes*; its huge losses of £27,000 set the society back further than ever and, for a short time, threatened its very existence. That dire financial situation had no sooner been clawed back when the 1997 production of *Showboat*, which cost £153,000 to stage (£55,000 of which went to the Gaiety), showed a hefty deficit of £13,000.

Losses incurred from the mid-1980s meant that the society's guarantors, around sixty in all, had been required to contribute £35,000 (c.€45,000) to sustain the R&R. But by 1990 even the guarantee fund

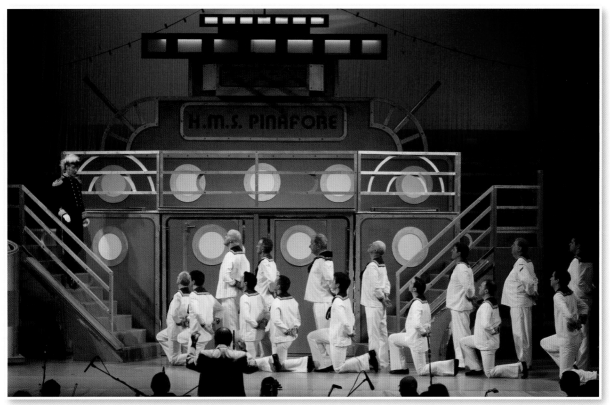

Captain Corcoran (Paul Kelly) greets his gallant crew in the 2009 production of *H.M.S. Pinafore*.

covered barely 20 per cent of the total outlay on Gaiety productions which, in turn, amounted to 80 per cent of the society's expenditure.[78] Biannual shows at the Gaiety were fast becoming unfeasible. Applications to the Arts Council for lottery funding had been deposited in the special bin the Arts Council appeared to reserve for R&R applications. The consistent argument of the Arts Council to a multiplicity of applications from the R&R for funding over the years has been the perfectly valid contention that it does not offer assistance to amateur companies. Given the number of voluntary/ amateur arts organisations in operation in Ireland that way lies madness.

The move to the National Concert Hall – where the society has made a loss on only one concert or production[79] – was necessitated by the R&R's obligation to its associate members to produce two shows annually, and the realisation that this could no longer happen at the Gaiety. Shows in South King Street became less frequent in the noughties. There were no R&R performances there in 2003 or 2007.[80] In 2006 the fortnightly rental for the theatre topped six figures for the first time, when *Fiddler on the Roof* played there. Increasingly the Gaiety shows were becoming 'loss leaders' and were being subsidised by the profits made from the less ambitious NCH events. The incessant touring of some of the most popular musicals and the extended Broadway and London runs of others, meant that the rights to potentially lucrative shows, like *Les Misérables* or *Cats* (or indeed most of the Lloyd Webber repertoire), were not being made available to amateur societies. This meant, of necessity, a diet of popular revivals in the noughties: *My Fair Lady* (2004), *Fiddler on the Roof* (2006) and *The Merry Widow* (2008). Total losses on all three came to an average of just over €30,000 per show. This was despite ticket sales for *My Fair Lady* topping a quarter of a million euro. *Gigi* (2005) was a far less popular revival and it lost around €60,000.[81] Fortunately cross-subsidisation from the November seasons in the NCH would have covered most of those deficits.[82] Nothing, however, could have prepared the society for what was going to happen in 2009.

The last show performed by the R&R at the Gaiety, up to the centenary production of *Hello, Dolly!*, was the Dublin premiere of *The Producers*. A Broadway musical, it was derived from the dark but hilarious 1968 Mel Brooks film of the same name, with music and lyrics by the multi-talented Brooks himself. The original movie, which boasted wonderfully tasteless choruses like 'Springtime for Hitler' and the immortal line 'If you've got it, flaunt it', had been adapted for Broadway in 2001. The stage version starred Nathan Lane as the crooked producer Max Bialystock, and Matthew Broderick as the timid accountant Leopold Bloom. It ran for over 2,500 performances and won twelve Tony awards.

In 2009, a year after a UK touring version finished its run, the amateur rights became available. There was some resistance in the R&R to taking on such a blatantly and exquisitely offensive piece of musical theatre. In certain quarters it was considered not to be 'an R&R show'. But it had the advantage of being a living, breathing original in a decade of R&R revivals. It was decided to risk alienating some of the more conservative members of the society's audience, with the spectacle of chorus members disporting themselves in Nazi uniforms, in favour of the prospect of attracting a newer, younger public.

The Producers, 2009. Garry Mountaine and the Usherettes – Aisling Sullivan, Victoria Clarke, Gina Condell and Lisa Collins – with Blind Fiddler Robbie Keogh.

Garry Mountaine was cast as the conniving Max Bialystock. Michael Evans, who had featured in the 2007 NCH production of *Anything Goes*, was Leopold Bloom, the man sent to examine Bialystock's accounts but who becomes his reluctant accomplice in a scam designed to make money from a theatrical disaster. Unfortunately, nature imitated art. The show, probably one of the best-ever staged by the R&R, was scheduled over the normally 'quiet' May bank holiday weekend. By the time word-of-mouth and some excellent reviews had alerted the Dublin public to the merits of the production, it was already too late. To make use of a technical expression peculiar to the world of theatre, it tanked. Although, as far as the vastly experienced Noel McDonough is concerned 'it's the best show we've ever done', the society sustained the greatest financial loss on a show in its one-hundred year history.

Conceived as the Celtic Tiger drew its dying breath, and launched into the world as the so-called Great Recession was beginning to bite (defunct banks had been bailed out the previous September but the IMF-EU-ECB troika would not arrive until the following year), the show was the most expensive ever staged by the R&R. The final bill (which included a rental fee of €122,000) was €333,000. This reflected the fact that the show includes twenty-eight scenes in thirteen different locations. The expenditure side would probably have paid for most of the first half-century of R&R productions. Unfortunately, as with the contemporary Irish property market, 2009 production prices were matched by 1995 box-office receipts. The show brought in only €175,000. The deficit almost completely wiped out financial reserves of around €200,000 built up over two decades.[83] A less well-endowed musical society would have folded immediately, after ninety-six years, leaving horrendous debts. Instead, after some panic and much soul-searching, in the words of Shay Gibson (who became general secretary shortly afterwards), 'We held our nerve.' The perilous financial situation was salvaged by the ever-dependent Gilbert and Sullivan (*Pinafore*, *Mikado*, *Pirates*) and two NCH concerts in March 2010 and 2011. Gradually a much-depleted show reserve was built up to a point where it was feasible to risk a return to the Gaiety for the all-important centenary presentation of *Hello, Dolly!* It was clear, however, that another financial disaster on the scale of *The Producers* would sink the R&R. Another Gaiety fiasco and the 2013 centenary would be the last significant anniversary ever celebrated by what had once been the oldest musical theatre society in the country.

. . . .

WHITHER THE R&R?

Back in 1913 none of the founder members of the Rathmines and Rathgar Musical Society gave a thought to whether or not the fruits of their labours would survive for a century. Their focus was on the next production, or the one beyond that. But as one gets on in life one's attention does tend more towards thoughts of morbidity and legacy. Today's active membership spends more time considering how much longer the society will survive than did their early twentieth-century equivalents. While conscious of its own worth, there is something of an air of internal puzzlement as to how the R&R has managed to avoid the fate of the Theatre Royal, the trams, the Dublin Metropolitan Police, the yo-yo and the Progressive Democrats. The society has, on occasion, come close enough to obliteration for the question to be asked: 'Will we be around to celebrate 125 years?'

Current president Pat Campbell offers no guarantees. Neither does general secretary Shay Gibson. Both have enough experience of the 'slings and arrows' of an outrageous amateur company trying their fortune in a highly professionalised world not to hazard a guess as to whether there will be any quasquicentennial celebration.

The society has changed radically in a hundred years. It has adapted and reinvented itself as required by circumstance and setback. It has remained resilient and tenacious. It has occasionally infuriated some of its more adventurous spirits with an innate conservatism and enraged its traditionalists with its intermittent spasms of radicalism. Along the way there has been more than one attempted *coup*. But the R&R has managed to survive and thrive. Its powers of regeneration would be the envy of Doctor Who.

But what exactly *is* the Rathmines and Rathgar Musical Society in 2013?

Is it merely a vehicle for a number of highly talented amateur performers? In the past that might, arguably, have been the case. From the 1960s to the 1990s, it was a clearly identifiable 'brand'. The R&R was an amateur repertory company with the same leading players appearing in most productions until they retired, died, wised up or wandered off to join the ranks of the permanently bewildered. It is clearly a different animal today. Many of the leading roles in the last twenty years have been taken by aspiring, professional singers.[84] Regina Nathan, now an experienced and sought-after soprano, played Gianetta in *The Gondoliers* in 1984. One of the three Celtic Tenors, Matthew Gilsenan, made his first significant stage appearance as Ralph Rackstraw in *H.M.S. Pinafore* in 1998. In the 2006 *Gondoliers* Gavan Ring and Nicola Mulligan took the parts of Giuseppe and Gianetta – both are now leading successful careers in the UK.[85] Brian Gilligan, winner of the Rathmines and Rathgar trophy at the 2013 Feis Ceoil, may well be destined to join this elite group. He has recently been cast in the London stage musical version of Roddy Doyle's *The Commitments*. A veteran of almost half a dozen R&R roles (in *Mikado*, *Oklahoma!*, *Pirates*, *Iolanthe* and *Pinafore*), he was the winner of the Best Male Singer award at the Buxton G&S Festival in 2008. Anna Brady, who played Laurey in *Oklahoma!* (2012) has taken a slightly different route. She has emulated Ria Mooney, following that great actor's 1924 journey to the Abbey Theatre, and taking part in the Frank McGuinness adaptation of James Joyce's *The Dead* in January 2013.

And there have been many more besides.[86] For all of them an engagement (albeit unpaid) with the R&R is a rite of passage, something almost mandatory for their CV. While this has the effect of maintaining standards and freshening up the society's frontline it also has a downside in terms of continuity and commitment. The casting committee can never be sure if the lead tenor or soprano in the autumn production of *Oklahoma!* will return to audition for *Hello, Dolly!* the following spring. Those intent on a professional career will probably have moved on. Some of the others may simply have moved elsewhere.

Nowadays gifted amateurs transfer from one society to another depending on the show, the venue, the producer, the choreographer or the colour of the wallpaper. Up and coming professionals usually get on with their careers after they have ticked the R&R box on their CVs. One of the few notable exceptions has been the gifted Irish tenor Paul Byrom, who, though an accomplished and much sought-after performer, retained his active membership of the society for a number of years. The only *quid pro quo* he

GENERATIONS OF G&S PLAYERS

Four secretaries: Shay Gibson, Camillus Mountaine, Pat Campbell and Peter Nolan.

Five Gianettas: Aisling Green-Madden (1991), Fionnuala Hough (1972), Nicola Mulligan (2006), Mary Brennan (1970) and Barbara Graham (1977).

The Merriest Fellows; Five Antonios: Paschal Walsh (1974), Denis Leahy (1991), David Scott (2006), Camillus Mountaine (1972) and Peter Lewis (1977, 1980, 1982 and 1984).

Five decades; five Ruths: Siobhán Fawsitt (1994), Glynis Casson (1984), Jackie Curran Olohan (2011), Lucy Lane (1977) and Anne Maria Smith (2002).

Five Inezs: Glynis Casson (1977), Dolores Barry (1972), Imelda Bradley (2006), Dodo O'Hagan (1980, 1982 and 1984) and Patricia Hough (1996).

Joe Lane (Luiz in 1959) gives Robert Vickers (Luiz in 2006) some pointers on drumming.

Joan Campbell (Kate in 1952) and Laura Murphy (Kate in 2011).

sought for his highly valued (unpaid) labours was a request that the names of performers be included on advertising fliers. *Plus ça change, plus c'est la même chose.* He first requested this minor concession in 2002.[87] He was forced to return to his theme in 2003.[88] He was still pressing his point in 2005. Byrom's petitioning finally bore fruit after he had departed the scene. The fliers for *Hello, Dolly!* in 2013, for example, carried the names of Rebecca Storm and Garry Mountaine.

So, if the society is not about its principal players (amateur, semi-professional or professional), is its primary purpose to service the needs of its active and associate members? Around forty people attend the annual general meetings of the R&R. On the face of it that is hardly a ringing endorsement of its activities by an enthusiastic membership. However, around forty people have *always* attended its annual general meetings. It now has fifty or so active and performing members when that figure was once closer to a hundred. At its height it had over 800 associate members, paying from a guinea to two pounds annually for the privilege of seats at its spring and autumn productions. Associate membership, an inspired notion dreamed up by the inaugural committee, contributed two vital elements to the society's good health: seed capital and a guaranteed audience. But associate membership had declined to 330 by the middle of 2002.[89] Today that number has shrunk to about 160 associates, paying €140 for the same privilege. Does this suggest an organisation in decline? Perhaps, but if a society can pack out the National Concert Hall for a week and withstand the loss of €150,000 on a failed production, reaching for the embalming fluid might be premature.

If you consult veteran members like Pat Campbell and Michael Forde, a former treasurer, you will be told emphatically that the R&R is about the chorus. The society continues in being able to cater to a hardworking group of individuals with modest ambitions.[90] Their very existence prompts a profoundly existential question. Why do thirty or more men and women give up at least two evenings a week for almost half the year to stand (or move vigorously, depending on the exigencies of the piece and the demands of the choreographer) in support of soloists who will still be counting their garlands when they (the chorus members) are on their way to the pub? Twice yearly, they are fashioned into a consummate ensemble capable of setting aside their jobs in Guinness and the ESB – most of the hundreds of members of the society appear to have worked for Guinness or the ESB at one time or another – and delight increasingly demanding audiences with the complex four-part harmonies of Sir Arthur Sullivan.

To their number we can add the unstoried multitudes, some of whom couldn't sing to save their lives, who have served on the various committees that shape the policy and decide the fate of the society. One of the manifest heroes of this volume has been Paddy Forde. Back in the 1930s he failed to impress T.H. Weaving at his audition and was not admitted to the chorus. Most aspiring amateur singers would, in the circumstances, have brought their vocal chords elsewhere or taken up chess.

Instead, Forde devoted the bulk of his leisure time, until his death in 1987, to the good of a society that would only permit him onstage as a non-singing juror in *Trial by Jury*, shielded from the audience by a newspaper. The Rathmines and Rathgar Musical Society owes its continued existence to Forde, Clem Ryan, Pat Campbell and many others of their ilk.

What of the future? The horizon looks as murky and uncertain at the dawn of the second century as it did at first light back in 1913. Production costs are escalating; viable and credible venues are in short supply; the stock of commercial, practicable, stage-able material is not being replenished; casting is not getting any easier; persuading newspapers to review shows is more challenging; and getting a slot on *The Late Late Show* has been far more problematic since the retirement of the society's unofficial cheerleader, Gay Byrne. As far back as 2001, then general secretary Camillus Mountaine observed at the annual general meeting that 'our casting committee is finding it increasingly difficult to cast the shows because many of the people competent to carry main parts prefer to use their talents where they will be financially rewarded'.[91] An obvious solution to that problem would be to offer payment where casting was proving difficult. However, notwithstanding the engagement of Rebecca Storm for *Hello, Dolly!* in April 2013, the current officers of the R&R are completely opposed to such creeping professionalisation. The R&R has always been, and will continue to be 'a platform for people to display their talents'.[92] For some, that can bring career benefits. To offer payment would also beg an obvious question: where do you draw the line? How many performers per production would be liable for compensation? In the context of rising budgets, payment of principals might limit the capacity of the society to continue to stage the high-quality work of the last 100 years. Sometime between now and 2038 (coincidentally, around the time Ireland Inc. will finish paying for the excesses of its banks) the R&R might succumb. But to do so, in the opinion of the current 'officer class', would be to jeopardise the chances of celebrating a 125th birthday.

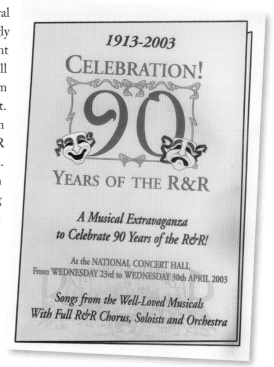

Celebration! 90 Years of the R&R, programme.

The issue of the paucity of new shows is not likely to disappear before 2038 either. Virtually none of, for example, the Andrew Lloyd Webber *oeuvre* is currently available for amateur production. The long-running *Les Misérables*,[93] finally turned into a film in 2013, is in the same category. It is far easier today to make an ascent of Mount Everest than it is to produce the most phenomenally successful musical of the late twentieth-century on the amateur stage. Perhaps by the time power generation from nuclear fusion becomes commonplace, the rights will have been made available. If that happens it is hard, at the moment, to envisage any other Irish amateur society being able to do it justice. It has been flagged by the R&R for a number of years now that, to put it at its starkest, 'there are no new suitable shows available'.[94] While the society regularly receives offers of untried shows from rights holders

General Secretary Shay Gibson and AIMS Representative Nora O'Rourke with AIMS President Richard Lavery at AIMS AGM 2013

like Weinbergers, they have been judged to be uncommercial in Dublin. Hence the constant recourse to the 'old reliables' likely to fill the Gaiety.

It could be argued, and has been argued within the ranks, that a more adventurous policy would help sustain the R&R; that a less expensive venue like the National Concert Hall is ideal for staging shows new to Dublin audiences; that the R&R can afford, given its reserves, to 'educate' its audience and attract a new generation of supporters by choosing works that have been popular and critically acclaimed elsewhere, without necessarily creating box-office records on Broadway or in the West End. It could also be argued, though this is not a point of view that finds widespread expression in the R&R itself, that the society has become the 'keeper of the flame' for Savoy operas and that its focus should be on preserving that tradition. A quarter of a century from now, if/when this work is updated, we will know what route has been followed. But, as the second century begins, it is far from clear what road will be taken.

R&R Committee, 2013. Back: Darren Johnson, Brendan Galvin, Edward O'Grady Walshe, Bernard Hurley, Victoria Clarke, David Cox, Michelle Foynes, Barney Gorman, John McCall. Front: Helen Hurley, Jackie Mountaine, Nora O'Rourke, Shay Gibson, Imelda Bradley, Gina Condell, Patricia Hough.

As regards a suitable venue for the performance of the productions of the R&R, the relationship with the National Concert Hall seems secure, while that with the Gaiety is awkward and uncertain. However, even a cursory assessment of the NCH as a permanent home for the society throws up questions and conundrums. The R&R is severely circumscribed in getting access to the NCH for even a six-night run. The current rehearsal requirements of the RTÉ Symphony Orchestra mean that, outside of its time-honoured week in November, the R&R cannot access the Concert Hall for six consecutive nights. This makes spring shows at the venue unsatisfactory. Will the R&R, like the Labour Party under Tony Blair, be forced to seek 'a third way'? Another question best left to whichever scribe is tasked with revising this current volume in 2038.

That the R&R has got this far is a minor miracle. Perhaps its golden years are behind it, perhaps they are yet to come, but the very fact of its survival for 100 years is its greatest single achievement, among many. Tastes have changed. Ireland is unrecognisable. But if Fitzgerald, O'Brien, Mulvin and the other pioneers were to return today, there are still things they would recognise about the society they brought into being before the onset of the Great War. One of those would be a compulsion, verging on the obsessive, towards the achievement of excellence. The founders would have a right to be proud of the standards their society has fought to maintain in the hundred years since 1913.

As a tentative course is set towards the next milestone, the horizon might glower or scowl with the threat of tempests yet to come, but one gets the feeling that the R&R would not have it any other way. Trying to do things correctly, efficiently and, at the same time, *con brio* has never been straightforward. One fears that if the Rathmines and Rathgar Musical Society were to sail off into a clear blue sky, towards a specific and discernible marker, there would be such confusion at this bizarre turn of events that the ship would quickly get lost and end up going around in circles.

Much better, really, to be heading into the unknown, just as it did in 1913.

If there is a sense of continuity between the R&R of today and that of 100 years ago, it is not just a continuity of excellence and achievement (though both are paramount), it is the continuity of glorious uncertainty. Musical theatre is a game of musical chairs. A century after its inception, the R&R always manages to hold onto its chair as the music stops.

The R&R is an institution, one with its own Pantheon. It houses the guiding spirits, those ghostly Rathmines and Rathgar Musical Societies from 1913, from the twenties, thirties and beyond – the ones that still exist through faded photographs, posters and extended family memories. The society began a century ago with a clean slate; today's inheritors of that proud and splendid tradition start each new year *tabula rasa*. It might be the best of years; it might be the worst of years. They've had both, and they've survived them.

We began with *The Mikado*, let us end the same way, with the entrance of the women's chorus and a song full of contradictory emotions, of the perturbed and optimistic trepidation of another guiding spirit, W.S. Gilbert.

Comes a train of little ladies
From scholastic trammels free,
Each a little bit afraid is
Wondering what the world can be!
Is it but a world of trouble–
Sadness set to song?
Is its beauty but a bubble
Bound to break ere long?
Are its palaces and pleasures
Fantasies that fade?
And the glory of its treasures
Shadow of a shade?
Schoolgirls we, eighteen and under,
From scholastic trammels free,
And we wonder–how we wonder!
What on earth the world can be!

CENTENARY YEAR

Launch of the R&R Centenary in the Mansion House, January 2013: Edith Lynch, Victoria Clarke, Lord Mayor Naoise Ó Muirí, Adam Lawlor, Pat Campbell, Jimmy Dixon, Sandra Kelly and Gay Byrne.

Lucy and Joe Lane: elected Life Members at The Gathering 2013.

Les Girls, The Gathering 2013.

RATHMINES & RATHGAR
MUSICAL SOCIETY

100
1913 2013

CENTENARY GALA CONCERT
14 JUNE 2013
THE NATIONAL CONCERT HALL

R&R CENTENARY GALA CONCERT, JUNE 14TH 2013, THE NATIONAL CONCERT HALL

PART 1

Overture	**YEOMEN OF THE GUARD**
	1914, 1915, 1923 (twice), 1927, 1936, 1939, 1941, 1944,
	1949, 1953, 1956, 1967, 1971, 1974, 1978, 1982, 1991,
	2004
Chorus	**If You Want to Know Who We Are**
	THE MIKADO
	1913,1914,1916,1922,1923,1926,1932,1936,1938,1941,
	1942, 1943, 1946, 1948, 1950, 1952, 1955, 1957, 1962,
	1983, 1966, 1968, 1970, 1971, 1973, 1976, 1979, 1981,
Chorus	1983, 1985, 1993, 2001, 2010
	French Military Marching Song
Paul & Sandra	*THE DESERT SONG* 1933, 1970
	Make Believe
	SHOWBOAT
Brian	1955, 1975, 1987, 1997
	Almost Like Being in Love
Lucy & Michael	*BRIGADOON* 1968
	Let's Do It!
Pádraig	*ANYTHING GOES* 1992, 2007
	When Britain Really Ruled the Waves
	IOLANTHE
	1915, 1916, 1924, 1932, 1935, 1940, 1942, 1944, 1947,
John	1950, 1956, 1959, 1965, 1968, 1975, 1978, 1985, 2008
	Leaning on a Lamppost
Chorus	*ME AND MY GIRL* 2002
	Stranger in Paradise
Lucy, Tara, Róisín	*KISMET* 1961
Garry	**Matchmaker**
	If I Were a Rich Man
	FIDDLER ON THE ROOF
Niamh	1972, 1988, 1998, 2006
	Vilia
	THE MERRY WIDOW
Róisín	1959, 1961, 1977, 2008
	Wouldn't it be Loverly.

Chorus	**Ascot Gavotte**
Arthur	**I'm Getting Married in the Morning**
	MY FAIR LADY
	1969 (twice,),1981, 1995, 2004

PART 2

Derek, Aisling	**When the Foeman Bares his Steel**
Tara, Jimmy	*THE PIRATES OF PENZANCE*
	1924, 1927, 1937,1940, 1948, 1952,1965, 1977, 1984, 1994,
Fred & Barbara	2002, 2011
	I Remember It Well
Sandra	*GIGI* 1978, 1986, 2005
Ciarán	**Wanting You**
	Stout Hearted Men
Jackie & Niamh	*THE NEW MOON* 1964
	The Wings of Sleep
Stuart	*THE DANCING YEARS* 1951, 1960, 1974
	Sit Down, You're Rocking the Boat
	GUYS & DOLLS
Aisling	1986, 1976, 2001, 2012
	We'll Gather Lilacs
Róisín & John	*PERCHANCE TO DREAM* 1954
	Anything You Can Do
Derek	*ANNIE GET YOUR GUN* 1956, 1983
	Some Enchanted Evening
Damien	*SOUTH PACIFIC* 1965, 1973, 1996
Jimmy & Michael	**Where is the Life that Late I Led?**
	Brush Up Your Shakespeare
Bryan	*KISS ME KATE* 1990
Chorus & Dancers	**Take a Pair of Sparking Eyes**
	Dance a Cachucha
	THE GONDOLIERS
	1916, 1923 (twice), 1926, 1935, 1938, 1939, 1941, 1942,
	1943, 1945, 1947, 1949, 1951, 1953, 1955, 1957, 1959,
	1962, 1965, 1967, 1970, 1972, 1974, 1977, 1980, 1982,
	1984, 1991, 1996, 2006

100 YEARS OF MUSICAL THEATRE

R&R SOLOISTS

Aisling Green Madden, Arthur McGauran, Barbara Graham, Bryan Hoey, Brian Gilligan, Ciarán Olohan, Damien Smith, Derek Ryan, Fred Graham, Garry Mountaine, John Mooney Jackie Curran Olohan, Lucy O'Byrne, Michael Evans, Niamh Murray, Paul Kelly, Pádraig O'Rourke, Róisín Sullivan, Sandra Kelly, Stuart Pollock, Tara McSwiney.

R&R CENTENARY CHORUS

Ann Gorman, Angela McBrien, Audrey Nolan, Andrea Olin, Caroline Keane, Deirdre Ryan, Deirdre Conolly, Eillen Gildea, Edith Lynch, Emma Mae West, Fiona Healy, Gail McGrath, Gina Condell, Joan Kavanagh, Joan Brittain, Joy Dolan, Kerrie Golden, Keara Jane Crawford, Liz Whelan, Lorraine Frewen, Michelle Foynes, Michelle Alison, Michelle Mulreany, Marian Megannely, Margaret Dickson, Margaret McAllister, Margaret Timoney, Nicole Hayden, Niamh O'Connor, Sara Louise Smith, Siobhán Hughes, Sophie Newell, Victoria Clarke, Wendy Thompson, Sally Young, Barney Gorman, Brendan Dempsey, Brendan Galvin, Camillus Mountaine, Darren Johnson, Denis Leahy, Donal Dixon, Eddie Corry, Fergal O'Sullivan, Hugh McBrien, Joe Griffin, Joe Swan, Kevin Hough, Ludo Martone, Ron Wainwright, Shay Gibson, Seamus Kearney, Paschal Walsh.

RTÉ CONCERT ORCHESTRA
MIA COOPER

LEADER:	
MUSICAL DIRECTOR	**GEARÓID GRANT**

ENTIRE PRODUCTION STAGED AND CHOREOGRAPHED BY
MARINA KEALY

CHORUS DIRECTOR:	**JACKIE CURRAN OLOHAN**
COMPERE:	**JIMMY DIXON**
PRODUCTION MANAGER:	NORA O'ROURKE
SCRIPT:	CATHAL MACCABE
	NIAMH MCDONOUGH
REPETITEUR:	PATRICIA GRANT
WARDROBE:	ASSISTED BY DYMPNA BEVAN & DYMPNA EGAR
LIGHTING:	NOEL MCDONOUGH
SOUND:	PAT O'BRIEN

Centenary concert, programme.

AFTERWORD

Serendipity – that's what it was, really. I first encountered the R&R way back in 1961 when, as a 17-year-old in love with the musicals, I took myself off to a Saturday matinee of *The Merry Widow* in the Gaiety. I was bowled over. That was where I wanted to be. The amazing Louise Studley; Lehar's music; the sheer glitz, glamour and exuberance of the company; it all knocked me out.

So the following March, during our production of *The Pirates of Penzance*, at St Paul's College, Raheny, I met Dodo [O'Hagan] and Noel Greene who had come out to assist us with makeup. On expressing my love of the musicals, Noel said that he would phone me in August, when the auditions were on and would take me to Rathmines. Wow!

August rolls around, when one afternoon the phone rings:

'Hi, Noel. This is Noel Greene.'

'Who?'

'Noel Greene from the R&R.'

'Oh, yes.'

'I'm sorry to leave it so late, Noel, but the auditions are this afternoon. Can you come with me?'

So, grabbing a score of *Yeomen*, we shot off to Rathmines on his motorbike. When we got there I was totally fearful and overawed. I gave a rendition of 'Is Life a Boon', with the marvellous Carmel Moore settling my nerves with her accompaniment. And I was in!

And so began my life with this wonderful society. Right from my first show, *Kismet*, with its magical music by Borodin and its 'Arabian Nights' tale, I was smitten. All through the 1960s I'm sure I spent more time in Rathmines and the Gaiety than at home.

We lived for theatre. Work was something you endured by day, before getting back to rehearsals and the camaraderie of the company. All that hard work! Each time, six weeks of music rehearsals were followed by increasingly intense floor rehearsals that gradually drew us into exotic worlds: Cockney London, the South Seas, Arthur's Camelot, Tevye's Russia and the wonderful topsy-turvy world of G&S. Each time we were transported far away from those cold Irish autumn nights.

Then those nerve-shredding dress rehearsals in the Gaiety, when nothing ever seemed to go right: 2am and still more to do...screaming tantrums and shouting matches...'Oh God, are we really opening *tonight*?'

What is it about arriving in through the stage door? 'Good evening, Harry!' You step up through the inner door, which makes a soft suction sound as if you are entering an airlock to a magical world and you are...backstage. The holy of holies. Inhale this atmosphere. There's nothing like it in the world: the musk of old canvas, paint, dust, seasoned wood, the afterglow of adrenalin rush, musty, ancient evenings, silent anticipation…Someone in the pit practises arpeggios on a flute, the notes riffling out over the empty stalls, spiralling away into the darkened auditorium like fairy dust. Who needs drugs? This is my opiate.

Then up the long stairs to Dressing Room No.9. The guys arrive. The craic begins. Sheer ribald, endorphin-releasing laughter. Into the costumes and the makeup is applied. Talc. 'Has anyone got the eyeliner?' Repartee and banter, the whole scene flooded in waves of golden light like an electric epiphany, cascading across the room from the phalanx of mirrors. A final check: all okay. Then those four little words that instil fear, anticipation, elation and dread: 'BEGINNERS ON STAGE, PLEASE!!!'

Then there are always the slip-ups, those unexpected mishaps that left us all smothering hysterical laughter. Pat Campbell's really quick change in *Fiddler* was one. He used to appear beside me, doing up his tunic just in the nick of time as we were about to walk on stage. Halfway through the second week, he strolls through the door: 'Well, I've made it on time for once – finally.' – 'That's great Pat. Minor problem: wrong costume.' Whereupon he does a fair impersonation of the Road Runner up the stairs and I have to walk onstage alone and somehow stifle the laughter!

There was a very different moment in November 1966 when I looked down at my onstage partner, saw those big amber eyes looking up at me and knew I was undone. Mary Walsh had arrived that season and, to cut a long story short, I guess I chased her 'til she caught me. We were engaged during the spring 1969 season of *My Fair Lady* and married in March 1970. Years later, in 1994, our daughter Karla joined the R&R. A proud moment.

And so, down the years we were blessed to have been part of those golden seasons, particularly in the late 1960s and early 1970s: *My Fair Lady, Fiddler, Camelot, South Pacific* and many more. I am of the R&R: I have been dipped in it like litmus paper. It is in my DNA; it is part of who I am. The best years of our lives.

So why did I start with 'serendipity'? Well, just suppose (and I've often pondered this myself) that on that distant summer afternoon in August 1961 when Noel Greene rang me about the auditions…well, just suppose I was out!

Thankfully I was there to take the call. I guess it was serendipity. You could call it fate. You could even call it *kismet*.

Noel Magee
Dublin, March 2013

APPENDIX 1

A Record of R&R Productions

1913	*The Mikado*		1927	*Trial by Jury*
1914	*The Yeomen of the Guard*		1927	*The Pirates of Penzance*
1914	*The Mikado*		1927	*The Yeomen of the Guard*
1915	*Les Cloches de Corneville*		1927	*Haddon Hall*
1915	*Iolanthe*		1928	*The Rose of Persia*
1915	*The Yeomen of the Guard*		1928	*The Geisha*
1916	*The Mikado*		1929	*San Toy*
1916	*The Gondoliers*		1929	*Patience*
1917	*Haddon Hall*		1929	*Cox and Box*
1917	*Ruddigore*		1929	*H.M.S. Pinafore*
1918	*Utopia Limited*		1930	*The Beloved Vagabond*
1918	*Haddon Hall*		1930	*A Country Girl*
1919	*A Princess of Kensington*		1931	*The Arcadians*
1919	*Merrie England*		1931	*A Waltz Dream*
1920	*Utopia Limited*		1932	*The Quaker Girl*
1921	*The Rose of Persia*		1932	*Monsieur Beaucaire*
1922	*Ruddigore*		1932	*Iolanthe*
1922	*The Mikado*		1932	*The Mikado*
1922	*Patience*		1933	*The Desert Song*
1923	*The Yeomen of the Guard*		1933	*Princess Charming*
1923	*The Gondoliers*		1934	*Florodora*
1923	*The Mikado*		1935	*Iolanthe*
1923	*The Yeomen of the Guard*		1935	*The Gondoliers*
1923	*Patience*		1936	*The Yeomen of the Guard*
1924	*Iolanthe*		1936	*The Mikado*
1924	*Trial by Jury*		1936	*Princess Ida*
1924	*The Pirates of Penzance*		1937	*The Pirates of Penzance*
1924	*The Duchess of Dantzic*		1937	*H.M.S. Pinafore*
1925	*Tom Jones*		1938	*Mercenary Mary*
1925	*Merrie England*		1938	*The Mikado*
1925	*The Duchess of Dantzic*		1938	*The Gondoliers*
1926	*Veronique*		1939	*The Yeomen of the Guard*
1926	*The Gondoliers*		1939	*The Gondoliers*
1926	*The Mikado*		1939	*Patience*

1939	*Trial by Jury*	1948	*Trial by Jury*
1939	*H.M.S. Pinafore*	1948	*The Pirates of Penzance*
1940	*Ruddigore*	1948	*The Mikado*
1940	*Cox and Box*	1949	*Wild Violets*
1940	*The Sorcerer*	1949	*The Gondoliers*
1940	*Trial by Jury*	1949	*Patience*
1940	*The Pirates of Penzance*	1949	*The Yeomen of the Guard*
1940	*Iolanthe*	1950	*Bless the Bride*
1941	*The Yeomen of the Guard*	1950	*The Mikado*
1941	*The Gondoliers*	1950	*Ruddigore*
1941	*Patience*	1950	*Iolanthe*
1941	*The Mikado*	1951	*The Dancing Years*
1941	*Princess Ida*	1951	*The Gondoliers*
1942	*The Mikado*	1951	*Trial by Jury*
1942	*The Gondoliers*	1951	*H.M.S. Pinafore*
1942	*Iolanthe*	1952	*Bitter Sweet*
1942	*Waltzes from Vienna*	1952	*The Mikado*
1942	*Utopia Limited*	1952	*Princess Ida*
1942	*The Impresario*	1952	*Cox and Box*
1942	*The Sorcerer*	1952	*The Pirates of Penzance*
1943	*The Student Prince*	1953	*La Vie Parisienne*
1943	*Wild Violets*	1953	*The Gondoliers*
1943	*The Mikado*	1953	*Patience*
1943	*The Gondoliers*	1953	*The Yeomen of the Guard*
1944	*Lilac Time*	1954	*Perchance to Dream*
1944	*Bitter Sweet*	1954	*Bless the Bride*
1944	*The Yeomen of the Guard*	1955	*Showboat*
1944	*Iolanthe*	1955	*The Gondoliers*
1945	*La Vie Parisienne*	1955	*The Mikado*
1945	*The Gondoliers*	1956	*Annie Get Your Gun*
1945	*Patience*	1956	*The Yeomen of the Guard*
1945	*Ruddigore*	1956	*Patience*
1946	*The Vagabond King*	1956	*Iolanthe*
1946	*The Mikado*	1957	*Oklahoma!*
1946	*Cox and Box*	1957	*The Gondoliers*
1946	*H.M.S. Pinafore*	1957	*The Mikado*
1947	*Gay Rosalinda*	1957	*Cox and Box*
1947	*Iolanthe*	1957	*H.M.S. Pinafore*
1947	*Princess Ida*	1958	*Love from Judy*
1947	*The Gondoliers*	1958	*Bitter Sweet*
1948	*The Student Prince*	1959	*The Merry Widow*

1959	*Ruddigore*		1972	*The Gondoliers*
1959	*Iolanthe*		1972	*Patience*
1959	*The Gondoliers*		1973	*South Pacific*
1960	*Naughty Marietta*		1973	*The Mikado*
1960	*The Dancing Years*		1973	*Princess Ida*
1961	*The Merry Widow*		1974	*The Dancing Years*
1961	*Kismet*		1974	*The Gondoliers*
1962	*Wild Violets*		1974	*The Yeomen of the Guard*
1962	*The Mikado*		1975	*Showboat*
1962	*The Gondoliers*		1975	*Iolanthe*
1963	*The Student Prince*		1975	*H.M.S. Pinafore*
1963	*The Yeomen of the Guard*		1975	*Trial by Jury*
1963	*Patience*		1976	*Guys and Dolls*
1963	*The Mikado*		1976	*Ruddigore*
1964	*The New Moon*		1976	*The Mikado*
1964	*Rose Marie*		1977	*Cox and Box*
1965	*Iolanthe*		1977	*The Gondoliers*
1965	*South Pacific*		1977	*The Pirates of Penzance*
1965	*The Gondoliers*		1977	*The Merry Widow*
1965	*The Pirates of Penzance*		1978	*Gigi*
1965	*Trial by Jury*		1978	*The Yeomen of the Guard*
1966	*Guys and Dolls*		1978	*Iolanthe*
1966	*Patience*		1979	*Sweet Charity*
1966	*The Mikado*		1979	*Patience*
1966	*Princess Ida*		1979	*The Mikado*
1967	*Bitter Sweet*		1980	*The King and I*
1967	*The Yeomen of the Guard*		1980	*H.M.S. Pinafore*
1967	*The Gondoliers*		1980	*The Gondoliers*
1967	*H.M.S. Pinafore*		1980	*Trial by Jury*
1968	*Brigadoon*		1981	*My Fair Lady*
1968	*The Mikado*		1981	*Princess Ida*
1968	*The Sorcerer*		1981	*The Mikado*
1968	*Iolanthe*		1982	*Oklahoma!*
1969	*My Fair Lady* (March and November)		1982	*The Yeomen of the Guard*
1970	*The Desert Song*		1982	*The Gondoliers*
1970	*The Mikado*		1983	*Annie Get Your Gun*
1970	*The Gondoliers*		1983	*The Sorcerer*
1971	*Camelot*		1983	*The Mikado*
1971	*The Mikado*		1984	*An Evening with Mr Gilbert & Mr Sullivan*
1971	*The Yeomen of the Guard*			
1972	*Fiddler on the Roof*		1984	*The Gondoliers*

1984	*Trial by Jury*	1999	*Romberg to Rodgers*
1984	*The Pirates of Penzance*	1999	*Oklahoma!*
1985	*Hans Andersen*	2000	*Celebration*
1985	*Iolanthe*	2000	*Carousel*
1985	*The Mikado*	2001	*The Mikado*
1986	*Rodgers & Hart and Rodgers & Hammerstein*	2001	*Guys and Dolls*
1986	*Gigi*	2002	*The Pirates of Penzance*
1987	*Romberg and Romance*	2002	*Me and My Girl*
1987	*Showboat*	2003	*90th Birthday Concert*
1988	*The Magic of Lerner & Loewe*	2003	*An Evening with Mr Gilbert & Mr Sullivan*
1988	*Fiddler on the Roof*	2004	*My Fair Lady*
1989	*I'll See You Again*	2004	*The Yeomen of the Guard*
1989	*Hello, Dolly!*	2005	*Gigi*
1990	*A Song to Sing O!*	2005	*Romberg to Rodgers*
1990	*Kiss Me, Kate*	2006	*Fiddler on the Roof*
1991	*The Yeomen of the Guard*	2006	*The Gondoliers*
1991	*The Gondoliers*	2007	*Let's Celebrate! The Magic of the Musicals*
1992	*Mad About Musicals*	2007	*Anything Goes*
1992	*Anything Goes*	2008	*The Merry Widow*
1993	*A Song For You*	2008	*Iolanthe*
1993	*The Mikado*	2009	*The Producers*
1994	*Hear Our Songs!*	2009	*H.M.S. Pinafore*
1994	*The Pirates of Penzance*	2010	*The Rodgers & Hammerstein Concert*
1995	*One Enchanted Evening*	2010	*The Mikado*
1995	*My Fair Lady*	2011	*Hear Our Songs!*
1996	*The Gondoliers*	2011	*The Pirates of Penzance*
1996	*South Pacific*	2012	*Guys and Dolls*
1997	*Show Business*	2012	*Oklahoma!*
1997	*Showboat*	2013	*Hello, Dolly!*
1998	*H.M.S. Pinafore*	2013	*Gala Centenary Concert*
1998	*Fiddler on the Roof*	2013	*The Mikado*

APPENDIX 2

Principal Officers of the Society

PRESIDENTS
- 1916–1919   William Martin Murphy
- 1919–1932   Sir Stanley Cochrane
- 1932–1943   Dr W. Lombard Murphy
- 1943–1953   Miss Eva Murphy
- 1953–1980   Michael J. Campbell
- 1980–1987   Patrick L. Forde
- 1987–1998   Clem P. Ryan
- 1999–2013   Patrick Campbell

HONORARY GENERAL SECRETARIES
- 1913–1915   W. Gerard Mulvin & Charles Jackson
- 1916–1934   Lionel A. Cranfield
- 1934–1944   Arthur V. Healy
- 1944–1947   Roderick Tierney
- 1947–1950   A.E. Glynn
- 1950–1953   P.A. Delany
- 1953–1974   Clem P. Ryan
- 1974–1987   Patrick Campbell
- 1987–1991   Stephen A. Faul
- 1991–1998   Joe Lane
- 1998–2007   Camillus Mountaine
- 2007–2008   Peter Nolan
- 2008–present Shay Gibson

HONORARY TREASURERS
- 1913–1916   J.A. Kelly
- 1917–1929   A.J. O'Farrell
- 1929–1937   Thomas Kane
- 1937–1950   Frederick Holland
- 1950–1960   C.P. Merry
- 1960–1975   Tom Murtagh
- 1975–1983   Michael Forde
- 1983–1987   Stephen A. Faul

- 1987–1991   Bernard Cullen
- 1991–1992   Michael Forde
- 1992–2006   Ig Lyons
- 2006–2009   Michael Clark
- 2009–2011   Wendy Thompson
- 2011–present   Bernard Hurley

Chair of Executive Committee

- 1913–1915   Edwin Lloyd
- 1915–1916   Lionel A. Cranfield
- 1916–1918   Edwin Lloyd
- 1918–1928   Minutes missing, but Chair occupied by W. Lewin, P.J. Heffernon, J.C. Chancellor and perhaps others
- 1928–1939   J.H. Hutchinson
- 1939–1969   Patrick L. Forde
- 1969–1974   Heather Hewson
- 1974–1981   Maurice O'Sullivan
- 1981–1984   Fred Graham
- 1984–1991   Stephen A. Faul
- 1991–2006   Oliver Hill
- 2006–2011   Lewis Clohessy
- 2011–present   Shay Gibson

Musical Directors

- 1913–1917   C.P. FitzGerald
- 1917–1952   T.H. Weaving
- 1953–1976   Terry O'Connor
- 1978–present   Gearóid Grant

APPENDIX 3

Life Members

Eileen Furlong
Paddy Delany
May Doyle
Roderick Tierney
Gladys MacNevin
Joe Flood
Terry O'Connor
Hilda White
Tommy O'Dwyer
Michael Campbell
Eithne Ryan
Tom Murtagh
Robert McCullagh
Kay Forde

Carmel Moore
Paddy Forde
Mida O'Brien
Clem Ryan
Pat Campbell
Maurice O'Sullivan
Dodo O'Hagan
Nora O'Rourke
Fred Graham
Barbara Graham
Joe Lane
Lucy Lane
Dympna Egar

NOTES

· ·

INTRODUCTION

[1] Lewis is a man of many parts, as is clearly illustrated by the reference to him in the minutes of 19 February 2007 as 'Louise Clohessy'.

· ·

CHAPTER 1 (PAGES 1-34)

[1] With 7,400 votes, 50.18 per cent, of the total poll: http://electionsireland.org/results/general/01dail.cfm.

[2] The R&R and the GAA are two of the few organisations from this period that are still in rude good health.

[3] http://www.crokepark.ie/gaa-museum/gaa-archive/gaa-museum-irish-times-articles/the-purchase-of-croke-park. An alternative site also considered was that of the 15 acres of Elm Park in Mount Merrion!

[4] This was a Catholic church, in a predominantly Protestant area, whose primary purpose was to supply the needs of Catholic domestic servants working in Rathgar.

[5] *The Irish Times*, 17 January 1961. *Irish Independent*, 17 January 1961. (Obituaries.)

[6] Minutes of the AGM, 24 September 1914.

[7] There had been one other notable departure from what became the norm. In 1914 the society staged a concert in the Town Hall in Rathmines. The programme was ambitious and the reaction was mixed; works by Wagner and others were included. The particular experiment was not repeated, although the society has a fine concert tradition. It did, however, have the effect of inaugurating another R&R tradition, that of offering a new production of some kind biannually (in spring and autumn), a pattern that persists to this day.

[8] Edwin's father, Owen Lloyd, was a noted harpist who taught violin, pipes and harp at Pearse's school in Rathfarnham, St Enda's. Owen was also a founder member of the Feis Ceoil Association. (Memo of Nora O'Rourke, *Jack O'Brien and the Early Years of the R&R*, 2012.)

[9] Myles Dungan, *No Great Shakes* (Dublin, 1982), pp.18–28. Mulvin, ever the democrat, was instrumental in the establishment of the Dublin Shakespeare Society around the time of his retirement from the civil service in 1935.

[10] Minutes of the AGM, 24 September 1914.

[11] *Freeman's Journal*, 3 February 1913.

[12] *Freeman's Journal*, 8 December 1913.

[13] Minutes of the AGM, 24 September 1914.

[14] Letter from Joy Hoyle, 24 November 2002. The daughter of Violet and Edgar, she wrote this account at the age of 88, pointing out that she and the R&R had been conceived at the same time.

[15] *Freeman's Journal*, 8 May 1913.

[16] *Freeman's Journal*, 11 November 1913.

[17] Minute Book 1913–19, 1 April 1914. For the next production, *The Yeoman of the Guard*, D'Oyly Carte agreed to a reduction to eight guineas per night (Minute Book, 13 May 1914). This had crept back up to almost £10 a night by December 1916 (Minute Book, 6 October 1916).

[18] *Freeman's Journal*, 3 June 1916. The other main venues in the city at that time included the Theatre Royal, the Olympia, the Tivoli and the Empire, whose fare would have been similar to that of the Queen's.

[19] *Irish Life*, 31 October 1913.

[20] It was a largely ceremonial role with no administrative functions other than chairing the AGM.

[21] Minute Book 1913–19, 24 September 1914.

[22] In general a sum of around £10 per production was allocated to advertising (Minute Book, 6 October 1916.)

[23] O'Brien was also described as 'stage manager', the terms being interchangeable at the time. Today he would likely be billed as 'director'.

[24] But only as far as the R&R was concerned: the partnership would be renewed when FitzGerald formed his own operatic ensemble.

25 Memo of Nora O'Rourke, *Jack O'Brien and the Early Years of the R&R*, 2012.

26 He attended a performance of *Iolanthe* on 26 December 1901 and retained a printed programme. (J.C. O'Brien scrapbook, in the possession of Joe and Lucy Lane.)

27 *Evening Telegraph*, 6 December 1913.

28 *Irish Independent*, 12 August 1913.

29 Kelly continued to play leading roles for a few years, before he stopped performing. In 1948 he miraculously re-emerged to share the role of Ko-Ko in *The Mikado* with Victor Leeson.

30 http://www.irishplayography.com/company.aspx?companyid=326.

31 *The Irish Times*, 9 December 1913.

32 *Freeman's Journal*, 9 December 1913.

33 *Irish Independent*, 9 December 1913.

34 Minutes of the AGM, 24 September 1914.

35 The first occasion on which details of the financial arrangements between the R&R and the Gaiety appear in minutes comes in February 1917, in relation to the proposed production of *Haddon Hall* for May 1917. The terms offered by the theatre related to the share of receipts.

Income under £450	R&R 45 per cent: Gaiety 55 per cent.
Income between £450–£600	R&R 50 per cent: Gaiety 50 per cent.
Income over £600	R&R 55 per cent: Gaiety 45 per cent.

36 Patrick F. Byrne, 'Fifty Years of Gaiety: Dublin's Gaiety Theatre, 1871–1921', *Dublin Historical Record*, 38/1 (December 1984), p.38.

37 http://diamond.boisestate.edu/gas/whowaswho/L/LucasArthur.htm. Lucas returned to London in 1928, continued his career there and died in 1973.

38 *Freeman's Journal*, 5 December 1914.

39 Minute Book 1913–19, 13 May 1914.

40 Minute Book 1913–19, 13 May 1914.

41 Minute Book 1913–19, 10 June 1914.

42 Letter from Joy Hoyle, 24 November 2002.

43 Minute Book 1913–19, 28 October 1914. They benefited to the tune of £10 each (26 January 1915).

44 John Redmond, Woodenbridge speech, *Freeman's Journal*, 21 September 1914.

45 Minute Book 1913–19, 28 October 1914. When the society moved its operations that year to Rathmines Town Hall, the Volunteers came along too (31 October 1914).

46 Memo of Nora O'Rourke, *Jack O'Brien and the Early Years of the R&R*, 2012.

47 *Haddon Hall*, first staged in May 1917, was written by Sullivan and Sidney Grundy.

48 Minute Book 1913–19, 11 October 1915.

49 Minute Book 1913–19, 27 October 1915.

50 *The Irish Times*, 9 December 1915.

51 Minute Book 1913–19, 31 August 1916. The premises were rented from Mr W. McBride 'at a yearly rent of £6 and a charge of 2/6 for light'.

52 Sean Dooney, 'The R&R 1913–1988' in *The Rathmines and Rathgar Musical Society: A Celebration of Seventy-Five Years, 1913–1988* (Dublin, 1988), p.5.

53 Patrick F. Byrne, 'Fifty Years of Gaiety: Dublin's Gaiety Theatre', p.43.

54 *The Irish Times*, 15 May 1916.

55 *Freeman's Journal*, 3 June 1916.

56 Minute Book 1913–19, 22 March 1917. The following year he was paid £30 for two weeks' work on a revival of *Haddon Hall* (Minute Book, 11 October 1918).

57 Minute Book 1913–19, 13 June 1917, AGM.

58 Minute Book 1913–19, 28 July 1917.

59 The potential penalty involved can be gauged by the receipts from a number of shows around that time. The R&R/Gaiety split would have been in the region of 50:50.

Dec 1916	*Iolanthe/Gondoliers*	£467
May 1917	*Haddon Hall*	£496
Dec 1917	*Ruddigore*	£489
May 1918	*Utopia Limited*	£473
Dec 1918	*Haddon Hall*	£511

60 Minute Book 1913–19, 20 August 1917.

61 *The Rathmines and Rathgar Musical Society: A Celebration of Seventy-Five Years, 1913–1988* (Dublin, 1988), p.10.

62 Minute Book 1913–19, Rules.

63 Minute Book 1913–19, 28 September 1917.

64 Minute Book 1913–19, 31 May 1918. Future D'Oyly Carte troupe member Arthur Lucas was one of the first to be paid. When he sought payment for playing the part of John Manners in the revival of *Haddon Hall* in December 1918, the committee prevaricated until the new musical director T.H. Weaving informed them that a new member, William Lewin, was capable of taking the role. A 'Dear John' letter of regret

was immediately despatched to Lucas. In 1919 May Doyle was paid five guineas for missing a potential engagement with the Carlow Operatic Society.

65 Minute Book 1913–19, 28 April 1919.

66 http://www.imdb.com/name/nm0331064/.

67 Whose best-known work, *The Geisha*, was produced by the R&R in 1928.

68 *The Irish Times*, 8 October 1919.

69 Minute Book 1913–19, 15 November 1917.

70 Lloyd, who had resumed the chair in 1918, resigned after writing a number of letters protesting against breaches in lines of demarcation by the honorary secretary.

71 *The Irish Times*, 3 May 1932. 'Souvenir of Twentieth Anniversary Performances, 1932' cited in Nora O'Rourke memo.

72 Minute Book 1913–19, 28 September 1917.

73 To date the R&R has had only four musical directors: FitzGerald, Weaving, Terry O'Connor and Gearóid Grant. As FitzGerald was gone by 1917 the latter three have, in reality, divided most of the century between them.

74 *The Irish Times*, 28 January 1966. (Obituary.)

75 http://bRoadwayworld.com/article/The_Rose_of_Persia_Sullivan_Without_Gilbert_20070114.

76 J.P. Wearing, *The London Stage 1890–1899: A Calendar of Plays and Players, Volume 2: 1897–1899* (London, 1976), p.844.

77 Address by Lionel Cranfield to the Dublin Rotary Club, 2 May 1932. (*The Irish Times*, 3 May 1932.)

78 Society minutes reflect no interest whatsoever in the Anglo–Irish conflict. The only vaguely intriguing entry is a 1919 reference to the payment of 18/– to the Café Cairo for 'screens supplied for dance'. The Cairo would become a haven for senior British military and intelligence officers. The latter acquired the nickname of 'the Cairo gang'. A number of them fell victim to the infamous 'Squad' led by Michael Collins on the morning of 21 November 1920 (Bloody Sunday).

79 *Irish Independent*, 18 November 1963.

80 British Pathé newsreel film exists of the R&R performing scenes from *The Rose of Persia* for the Cancer Research Fund in 1921.

81 The Minute Book for the period 1919–24 is missing, as was Cochrane from the AGMs of 1925, 1926, 1927, 1928, 1929 and 1931, 1932 and 1934. There were no AGMs in 1930 or 1933.

82 *The Irish Times*, 1 May 1922.

83 *The Irish Times*, 1 May 1922.

84 *Freeman's Journal*, 4 December 1915. In this instance, Lord Wimborne – but from 1913–15, Lord Aberdeen.

85 *Freeman's Journal*, 3 December 1924. *The Irish Times*, 27 April 1926.

86 Minute Book 1925–29, 14 July 1927.

87 *The Irish Times*, 29 September 1924. The newspaper expressed the hope that the R&R 'will do some choral work in addition to their operatic enterprises' and might step into the breach left by the Dublin Oratorio Society. While the company did attempt choral works from time to time, including a contribution to an ambitious 500-voice *Messiah* in 1921 (*The Irish Times*, 19 December 1921), it was never allowed to interfere with 'their operatic enterprises'.

88 Bouch's role became even more pivotal in the 1930s. In fact, after the highly successful production of *The Arcadians* in May 1931, such had his influence been that Weaving's normal fee was reduced from £40 to £30 and Bouch, though very much the society member and enthusiastic amateur, was voted £20 for his services. There had been minor rumblings of discontent at Weaving's level of commitment. He had had no part in the selection of *The Arcadians*, so that might have prompted a certain ennui on his part. At the ever-conciliatory Bouch's instigation, Weaving's normal fee was restored and Bouch himself was paid ten guineas for his pains. (Minute Book 1929–32, 18 May 1931.)

89 *The Irish Times*, 1 October 1924. This policy was repeated by Rupert D'Oyly Carte in 1927 (Minute Book 1925–29, 21 April 1927) prompting a plebiscite of members and Gaiety patrons at the spring 1927 production, which resulted in *Haddon Hall* being produced in December 1927.

90 http://diamond.boisestate.edu/gas/whowaswho/M/MooneySamuel.htm.

91 James P. McGlone, *Ria Mooney: The Life and Times of the Artistic Director of the Abbey* (North Carolina, 2002), p.11.

92 *The Irish Times*, 6 December 1922.

93 *The Irish Times*, 2 December 1924. When she reprised the role in her final appearance for the R&R in December 1925, the newspaper praised her 'artistry and vivacity' (*The Irish Times*, 8 December 1925).

94 *Irish Independent*, 1 December 1925.

95 James P. McGlone, *Ria Mooney*, p.13.

96 Barbara Leaming, *Orson Welles: A Biography* (New York, 1985), p.45.

97 http://theatricalia.com/person/ptm/betty-chancellor.

98 http://www.imdb.com/name/nm1641192/bio.

99 *Freeman's Journal*, 19 March 1921; *The Irish Times*, 19 March 1921. As it transpired, that production fell victim to an extension of the military curfew and was never staged (*Freeman's Journal*, 21 March 1921).

100 She was also subjected to a wide range of inventive misprints of her name in newspaper reviews in the following decade. Appearing as 'Holmes', 'Howe' and 'Horne' at different times.

101 *The Irish Times*, 17 December 1923.

102 *The Irish Times*, 17 December 1923.

103 By Edward German, A.M. Thompson and Robert Courtneidge.

104 *The Irish Times*, 2 December 1924.

105 *The Irish Times*, 7 December 1923.

106 *The Arcadians*, *Irish Independent*, 26 May 1931.

107 *Ruddigore*, *The Irish Times*, 2 May 1922.

108 *The Desert Song*, *The Irish Press*, 23 May 1933.

109 By Andre Messager and Frederick Lonsdale.

110 *The Irish Times*, 21 June 1932.

111 Robert McCullagh, 'Seventy-Five Years of the Rathmines and Rathgar Musical Society', *Dublin Historical Record,* 45/2 (Autumn 1992), p.113.

112 Selby [Gaiety Theatre London manager] to Cranfield, quoted in Minute Book 1929–34, 4 October 1932.

113 *The Irish Times*, 16 June 1932.

114 *Irish Independent*, 8 May 1931.

115 Minute Book 1929–34, 13 September 1929.

116 For a period in the 1920s Rupert d'Oyly Carte had constructively denied performing rights to the society by insisting that any profits made by the production of Gilbert and Sullivan operas by amateur companies should be 'handed to some *bona fide* charity' (Minute Book 1925–29, 7 August 1926). Although the R&R had good relationships with a number of '*bona fide*' charities, to have handed their entire surplus over to those organisations would have been commercial suicide.

117 Minute Book 1929–34, 26 May 1930, *The Beloved Vagabond*, £425. Minute Book 1929–32, 30 December 1930, *A Country Girl*, £633. Contrast that with the December 1932 run of *Iolanthe* and *Mikado* at £920 (Minute Book 1929–34, 19 December 1932) or *The Desert Song* in May 1933 at £937 (Minute Book 1929–34, 18 May 1933).

118 Minute Book 1929–34, 16 December 1930.

119 *The Irish Times*, 3 October 1933.

120 Minute Book 1929–34, 17 April 1934.

121 Minute Book 1929–34, 29 December 1933.

122 Minute Book 1929–34, 23 January 1934.

123 Minute Book 1929–34, 15 February 1934.

124 Minute Book 1929–34, 26 March 1934.

125 Minute Book 1929–34, 17 April 1934.

126 *The Irish Times*, 10 December 1934.

CHAPTER 2 (PAGES 35-72)

1 Minutes of the AGM, 24 February 1935.

2 Minutes of the AGM, 24 February 1935. The critics tended to agree with this assessment, the *Irish Independent* describing the production as 'worthy of the traditions of the society' (4 December 1934). *The Irish Times* noted that 'all the splendid old traditions are preserved' (4 December 1934).

3 Minutes of the AGM, 24 February 1935. The members in question, according to the 1963 fiftieth anniversary publication, were Arthur Healy, Joe Bouch, Fred Holland, Eddie Marsden and Sam Donaldson. The date given in the booklet, probably erroneously, is 1937.

4 Minutes, 11 March 1937.

5 *The Irish Times*, 8 December 1936.

6 *The Irish Press*, 8 December 1936.

7 Minutes, 11 March 1937.

8 *The Irish Times*, 8 December 1936.

9 Minutes, 11 March 1937.

10 Minutes of the AGM, 31 March 1937.

11 Minutes, 31 August 1937.

12 Robert McCullagh, 'Seventy-Five Years of the Rathmines and Rathgar Musical Society', *Dublin Historical Record,* 45/2 (Autumn 1992), p.116.

13 *The Irish Times*, 17 May 1938.

14 *Irish Independent*, 17 May 1938.

15   Minutes, 25 April 1938.

16   Minutes, 11 March 1938.

17   Minutes, 28 May 1938.

18   Amateur licences were withdrawn in 1943, the next occasion on which the society wished to launch a production (Minutes, 14 January 1943).

19   Minutes of the AGM, 18 July 1938.

20   *The Irish Times*, 2 February 1937.

21   The 'Irishman's Diary' in *The Irish Times* commented: 'I cannot call to mind any previous occasion when Gilbert and Sullivan has been presented twice nightly.' (*The Irish Times*, 5 November 1937.)

22   Minutes, 16 November 1939.

23   John Cronin, 'Brother of the More Famous Flann: Ciaran O'Nuallain', *New Hibernia Review*, 3/4 (Winter, 1999), p.15.

24   Flann O'Brien, *At Swim-Two-Birds* (London, 1967), p.94.

25   As it happens the R&R had produced the show as far back as 1915.

26   *The Irish Times*, 8 November 1944.

27   *The Irish Times*, 3 November 1950.

28   *The Irish Times*, 10 August 1955.

29   Associates, as opposed to 'active' members, were non-performing. They were a vital ingredient in the survival of the R&R. Their subscriptions, for which they received tickets for performances, committee representation and AGM voting rights, were often vital in covering losses on shows. Forde was a long-time representative on the committee of the associate members.

30   Minutes, 12 August 1940.

31   Healy was a civil servant working in Customs and Excise who, according to Robert McCullagh, 'could use his knowledge on behalf of the society to get costumes rapidly through Customs difficulties' (Robert McCullagh, 'Seventy-Five Years of the Rathmines and Rathgar Musical Society', *Dublin Historical Record*, 45/2 (Autumn 1992), p.113). Healy was an accomplished stage actor who had played at the Gate and the Abbey as well as a playwright whose drama, *Rejected Loyalty*, was staged at the Abbey in 1931. On the sporting field he won an All-Ireland football medal with Dublin.

32   Minutes, 4 December 1940.

33   Minutes, 18 December 1940.

34   Minutes, 4 December 1940.

35   Minutes, 27 and 29 January 1941.

36   Niamh McDonough, 'Ethna Barror: Profile of a Successful Conductor' (M.Phil thesis, Dublin Institute of Technology, December 2008), p.12. Ethna had probably been encouraged to join the OBMS by her future husband, Cecil Barror, who had an uneasy relationship with the R&R from early 1939 when J.J. Bouch had admonished him for talking in the wings of the Gaiety during a performance after which he 'took every advantage in his dressing room in the Gaiety Theatre to generally belittle the efforts of the Society' (Minutes, 14 August 1939). Cecil Barror appeared opposite Ethna Barror as the Lord Chancellor in the OBMS production.

37   Minutes, 12 December 1940.

38   Minutes, 18 November 1940.

39   *The Irish Press*, 15 May 1942.

40   Minutes, 22 December 1941.

41   Minutes, 5 March 1942.

42   http://www.guardian.co.uk/uk/2000/apr/22/books.booksnews.

43   Apparently he was utterly wrong. According to an article in *The Guardian*, 'behind his bumbling tweedy front, Betjeman was an exceedingly good spy' (*The Guardian*, 22 April 2000).

44   The poem, written in 1937, three years before the Blitz, begins:
'Come friendly bombs and fall on Slough!
It isn't fit for humans now,
There isn't grass to graze a cow.
Swarm over, Death!'

45   Minutes, 23 March 1942.

46   Minutes, 5 March 1942. Lionel Cranfield died in February 1948.

47   Minutes, 23 March 1942.

48   Tierney played in fifty productions over a period of thirty-one years. Perhaps his outstanding performance was as Alfred P. Doolittle in *My Fair Lady* in 1969.

49   *Irish Independent*, 26 April 1943.

50   *The Irish Press*, 18 November 1963.

51   My thanks to Nora O'Rourke for this information.

52   *The Irish Press*, 27 May 1945.

53   There is a romantic story about the arrival of the Elliman family in Ireland, possibly apocryphal. This suggests that Louis Elliman's parents had booked passage from eastern Europe to the USA but had been cheated by their agent and booked only as far as Dublin. They had chosen to settle in the city and took the name Elliman from a hoarding advertising for Elliman's Embrocation.

54 *The Irish Times*, 8 November 1945. Whether or not this is actually the case, the fact is the opera had not appeared in the D'Oyly Carte repertoire for thirty years before the 1917 revival (*The Irish Times*, 2 November 1945).

55 *The Irish Times*, 2 November 1945.

56 Minutes of the AGM, 28 June 1946.

57 Both the R&R and the Belvederians were described by Myles na gCopaleen in a 'Cruiskeen Lawn' column as 'neo-Lutheran lodge(s)'.

58 *The Irish Times*, 21 February 1949.

59 As Quidnunc once observed in 'An Irishman's Diary': 'It is difficult to find a member of the Rathmines and Rathgar Musical Society who lives in Rathmines or Rathgar (*The Irish Times*, 2 November 1945).

60 Minutes, 23 January 1943. The process was repeated in 1944 (*The Irish Press*, 11 September 1944).

61 *The Irish Times*, 30 April 1959.

62 Minutes, 27 July 1942.

63 Minutes, 27 December 1941.

64 Minutes, 2 February 1942.

65 Minutes, 23 January 1943.

66 Minutes, 2 February 1942.

67 Minutes, 6 September 1945. The R&R was prepared to swap Gaiety dates in November with the Old Belvedere Musical Society but was, ultimately, not required to do so.

68 Minutes, 10 September 1939.

69 Minutes, 21 September 1939.

70 Minutes, 18 November 1941.

71 Minutes, 28 November 1940.

72 Minutes, 30 June 1942.

73 Minutes, 23 January 1943.

74 Minutes, 8 February 1943. Flood was not cast in *The Student Prince* that spring but returned to play Nanki-Poo in November, a part he had first played in 1932!

75 Midgley, a prominent Mason, who worked for the Dunlop company, was also a governor of the Royal Irish Academy of Music (*The Irish Times*, 3 June 1957).

76 Minutes, 8 and 24 February 1943.

77 Between December 1913 and November 1955 the role of Katisha was shared between Mabel Home and Eileen Furlong. Furlong first played the part in the inaugural R&R production and went on to play it eight times in all. In 1966 Mabel Home's daughter, Heather Hewson, took over the part and made it her own until 1979 when Lucy Lane took over for two productions.

78 Minutes, 16 July 1945. The committee agreed 'that this point would have to be borne in mind by the sub-committee who would caste [*sic*] the forthcoming shows'.

79 Minutes, 8 October 1945.

80 Minutes, 5 January 1947, 3 February 1948 and 31 May 1948.

81 Minutes, 14 December 1959.

82 *The Irish Times*, 7 April 1947.

83 Minutes of the AGM, 11 June 1948.

84 Minutes of the AGM, 28 June 1958.

85 *The Irish Times*, 1 November 1952.

86 *Irish Independent*, 17 April 1951.

87 *The Irish Times*, 7 November 1951.

88 *The Irish Press*, 28 October 1966.

89 *Irish Independent*, 10 March 1959.

90 *The Irish Times*, 6 November 1953.

91 *The Irish Press*, 28 October 1966.

92 *The Irish Times*, 10 March 1956; *The Irish Press*, 23 March 1956.

93 *The Irish Times*, 8 March 1956.

94 *The Irish Press*, 28 May 1957.

95 She re-appeared briefly in 1989 to take the lead in *Hello, Dolly!*, a production dealt with elsewhere.

96 *The Irish Times*, 1 April 1960.

97 *The Irish Times*, 7 May 1954. Apparently the two were inseparable.

98 One critic wrote of Bruton, a gifted comic actor, an optician by trade and a qualified pilot: 'Bruton may excel in Gilbert if not in Sullivan' (*The Irish Times* Pictorial, 5 March 1949).

99 Henry once sang an entire encore of 'A Policeman's Lot is Not a Happy One' in Irish (*Irish Independent*, 8 November 1952).

100 A brother of long-time Labour party leader Brendan Corish.

101 *The Irish Times*, 14 November 1963.

[102] *The Irish Press*, 13 November 1957.

[103] *The Irish Times*, 6 November 1954. The previous year Studley had taken a lead role in *The Belle of New York* for the Dublin Musical Society immediately after appearing as Elsie in *The Yeomen of the Guard*.

[104] The current writer has some small insight into the affairs of T.P. McKenna, since they were second cousins.

[105] http://tpmckabbey.blogspot.ie.

[106] Minutes, 27 July 1953.

[107] Minutes, 28 August 1953.

[108] Minutes, 29 November 1952. Grave dissatisfaction was voiced over the performance of the Gaiety Orchestra during the G&S season.

[109] *The Irish Times*, 5 November 1952.

[110] *The Irish Times*, 5 November 1952.

[111] Minutes, 31 May 1956.

[112] For accounts of the lives, careers and professional relationships of Gilbert, Sullivan and D'Oyly Carte, see Michael Ainger, *Gilbert and Sullivan: A Dual Biography* (Oxford, 2002); Arthur Jacobs, *Arthur Sullivan: a Victorian Musician* (Oxford, 1984); and Jane Stedman, *W.S. Gilbert: A Classic Victorian and his Theatre* (Oxford, 1996). The film *Topsy Turvy*, written and directed by Mike Leigh, is an engaging examination of the relationship of composer and librettist during the production of *The Mikado*.

[113] Minutes, 10 January 1940. Carte was also reported as being willing to lend scenery for *Ruddigore*.

[114] Minutes of the AGM, 16 June 1949.

[115] Francois Cellier and Cunningham Bridgeman, *Gilbert and Sullivan and Their Operas: With Recollections and Anecdotes of D'Oyly Carte & Other Famous Savoyards* (London, 1914), pp.394–6. Something of the order of 200 amateur companies gave over 1,000 performances of Savoy operas in 1914.

[116] The condolences of the R&R were conveyed in a letter in September 1948 (Minutes, 14 September 1948).

[117] Minutes, 8 December 1938.

[118] Internal and external criticisms of inadequate articulation were not confined to the 1950s. In 1973 *Irish Times* critic David Nowlan, while commenting that the transmission of Gilbert's lyrics 'demands greater exactitude and more discipline than is required by almost any other form of theatre', shredded the diction of chorus and principals in the sixtieth anniversary *Mikado*, remarking that 'one needed to know the book in advance to determine what was going on' (*The Irish Times*, 20 November 1973).

[119] Minutes, 10 January 1950.

[120] *Irish Independent*, 4 November 1952.

[121] Minutes, 1 December 1949.

[122] Minutes, 8 December 1949.

[123] Minutes, 10 January 1950. The minutes also noted that: 'recordings of *Patience* had been made during the Hospital show by Victor Leeson and by Brother Wilfred of St John of God, both had however given their word to wipe out the recording soon afterwards'.

[124] Minutes, 7 February 1951.

[125] Elliman is to be seen getting married to Ettie Robinson in footage shot in March 1930 at the Adelaide Road synagogue [http://www.britishpathe.com/video/pretty-dublin-wedding].

[126] Kevin Rockett, Luke Gibbons and John Hill, *Cinema and Ireland* (London, 1987), p.97.

[127] *The Irish Times*, 15 April 1950.

[128] Minutes, 8 July 1949.

[129] Minutes, 23 June 1951.

[130] A loss of £800 was announced in 1954 alone after the disastrous box-office performance of Ivor Novello's elaborate and expensive *Perchance to Dream*.

[131] To put this figure in perspective, based on a calculation of www.measuringworth.com, that would have amounted to over £20,000 in 2010.

[132] Minutes, 11 June 1956.

[133] Minutes, 7 March 1957.

[134] *The Irish Press*, 11 October 1955; *The Irish Times* Pictorial, 22 October 1955.

[135] *Irish Independent*, 29 October 1959.

[136] Stephen Watt, Eileen Marie Morgan, Shakir M. Mustafa, *A Century of Irish Drama: Widening the Stage* (Indiana, 2001), p.128.

[137] Minutes, 30 November 1959. The other objectors were Ray Joyce and Sean Dooney.

Chapter 3 (pages 73-106)

1   Echoing, whether knowingly or not, the sentiments of the founders who in a circular to prospective associates in late 1916 declared: 'and it is hoped in time to build up an organisation worthy to rank with the Opera Comique of Paris'.

2   Ignoring the pedantic assertions that the sixties didn't officially begin until 1 January 1961. If we can celebrate the dawn of the new millennium on 1 January 2000, then custom and practice trumps exactitude.

3   Minutes of the AGM, 7 June 1960.

4   Minutes, 13 June 1960.

5   Minutes, 15 January 1962.

6   Minutes, 11 September 1962.

7   http://www.prii.ie/show_content.aspx?idcategory=1&idsubcategory=38.

8   *The Irish Times*, 10 May 1995.

9   My thanks to Nora O'Rourke for this information.

10 For example, was the normally sensible Paddy Henry being disingenuous at the 1959 AGM when he claimed that: 'the starring of principals was a departure from the established practice. Such a system could be construed as a reflection *on the chorus* [my italics].' The suggestion was rejected by Paddy Forde who pointed out that, in the past, advertising had often carried the names of principals (Minutes of the AGM, 9 June 1959).

11 Minutes, 14 March 1960.

12 This vow of anonymity extended to advertising as well. Paid-for newspaper notices were to refer merely to the R&R 'with no names mentioned' (Minutes, 15 March 1960).

13 *The Irish Times*, 10 May 1995.

14 *The Irish Times*, 7 March 1960.

15 *Irish Independent*, 12 February 1970; *The Irish Press*, 18 September 1970.

16 *The Irish Times*, 29 October 1962. Patricia Dolan playing Katisha in the *Mikado*.

17 *The Irish Press*, 30 October 1970 and 18 November 1972.

18 *Irish Independent*, 22 September 1970.

19 *The Irish Times*, 23 March 1982.

20 *The Irish Times*, 3 April 1973.

21 http://www2.ul.ie/web/WWW/Administration/Ceremonies/Honorary_Conferrings/Honoured_by_UL/Recipients/Terry per cent.20Wogan.

22 *The Irish Times*, 24 November 1982.

23 The cricket eleven was, highly democratically for the time, open to both men and women; Heather Hewson and Dodo O'Hagan are seated in the lotus position in the front row of the photograph.

24 *The Irish Times*, 29 March 1960.

25 *The Irish Press*, 29 March 1960.

26 Seventy-fifth anniversary booklet.

27 http://www.feisceoil.ie/about/history.asp.

28 *Freeman's Journal*, 14 May 1924.

29 'Isidore Myers' appears to be a pseudonym for one Laurence Michael Phillips. In the copious files of Nora O'Rourke there exists a letter from him (under both names) to Gladys MacNevin — written in 1969.

30 Minutes of the AGM, 3 June 1927.

31 Maurice O'Sullivan note to Gladys MacNevin in 1972.

32 McCullagh went on to become treasurer of the Feis Ceoil for two decades and president of the organisation in the 1990s (*The Irish Times*, 11 April 2001).

33 Minutes, 2 July 1945.

34 Minutes, 16 July 1945.

35 Minutes of the AGM, 28 June 1946.

36 Minutes, 3 November 1947.

37 Minutes, 9 June 1950.

38 *The Irish Times*, 14 May 1952.

39 Minutes, 26 May 1952.

40 Minutes, 25 June 1952.

41 *The Irish Times*, 15 May 1955. Neary won again in 1960.

42 Minutes, 5 October 1964.

43 *Irish Independent*, 5 November 1963.

44 Ryan's point was reiterated in 1977 by Maurice O'Sullivan when compèring a benefit concert for the Feis hosted by the R&R in the John Player

Theatre. He observed that: 'The R&R, dating from 1913, is one of the Feis's "earliest offshoots"… It is the Feis which is the main channel of entry to keep the R&R recruiting new members.' (*The Irish Times*, 29 September 1977.)

45 John Conroy returned the cup to the R&R and it is on display in the society's premises in Rathmines.

46 *The Irish Press*, 5 November 1963.

47 *Irish Independent*, 11 February 1965.

48 Minutes, 6 December 1965.

49 *The Irish Times*, 31 March 1973.

50 Minutes, 12 December 1966.

51 The Taylors were long-serving members: Cynthia was Wardrobe Mistress; Fred was a performer and later Booking Secretary. He also represented the R&R in AIMS (Association of Irish Musical Societies) and served as National Treasurer and later National President of AIMS in the 1970s.

52 The first prize, of £1,500, was won by Nyle Wolfe.

53 The Feis was, however, cancelled in 1916 and also fell victim to a 2011 'foot and mouth' scare.

54 Minutes, 25 November 1946.

55 Minutes, 16 December 1946.

56 Minutes, 8 January 1963.

57 The R&R has a direct connection to Shaw through Glynis Casson. Shaw wrote *St Joan* for her grandmother, the distinguished actress Dame Sybil Thorndyke.

58 Minutes, 9 December 1968.

59 Minutes, 6 September 1970. Decision taken that there was to be no hospital show that year.

60 Minutes, 2 December 1958.

61 The production itself was highly successful, generating a total gross of £5,198 in box-office receipts.

62 Photographed at the 'press conference' to announce the event was Gerry Jones, complete with distinctive eye-patch. Jones, a member of the hospital's executive committee, never seemed to have been far from the side of Charles J. Haughey at his trial for arms importation in 1971 (*The Irish Times*, 9 November 1973).

63 *The Irish Press*, 5 November 1962.

64 *Irish Independent*, 13 March 1980.

65 *The Irish Times*, 15 November 1977.

66 Minutes, 17 January 1961.

67 *The Irish Times*, 14 November 1963.

68 Minutes, 1 July 1963.

69 Minutes, 15 July 1963.

70 *The Irish Times*, 14 November 1963.

71 *The Irish Times*, 14 November 1963.

72 *Irish Independent*, 12 November 1963.

73 This nugget was communicated by Kitty Forde to Lucy Lane and thence to Nora O'Rourke (26 November 2012).

74 *The Irish Times*, 6 December 1963.

75 *The Irish Times*, 19 November 1982.

76 *The Irish Times*, 14 November 1962.

77 Taking 1971 and 1972 as examples, the winter G&S made £273 and £1,208 respectively, while *Camelot* (1971) and *Fiddler on the Roof* (1972) showed significant losses despite being well-received. *Camelot* lost the society £1,800 (Minutes of the AGM, 28 June 1971 and 26 June 1972).

78 A well-known, and expensive, London costumier.

79 Minutes, 10 May 1962.

80 Minutes, 18 June 1962.

81 *The Irish Times*, 6 November 1962.

82 *The Irish Press*, 18 November 1976.

83 *The Rathmines and Rathgar Musical Society: A Celebration of Seventy-Five Years, 1913–1988* (Dublin, 1988).

84 *The Irish Times*, 4 November 1970.

85 Pearson staged *Pirates* and *Pinafore*, the scores of which were orchestrated by one Bill Whelan, who later made a bit of theatrical history of his own with *Riverdance* (http://www.taramusic.com/press/pr3030.htm).

86 *The Irish Press*, 18 November 1976. Johnston was reviewing that year's R&R production of *Ruddigore*.

87 *The Irish Times*, 31 October 1962.

88 *The Irish Times*, 14 November 1962.

89 *Irish Independent*, 13 November 1962.

90 Minutes, 8 December 1949.

91 Minutes, 26 May 1952.

92 Minutes, 18 December 1967.

93 Minutes, 22 April 1968.

94 Soon to become part of the Allied Irish Banks group.

95 Minutes, 7 August 1969.

96 Minutes, 24 June 1969.

97 Minutes, 1 July 1969.

98 Minutes, 28 July 1969.

99 Minutes, 7 August 1969.

100 Minutes, 25 August 1969.

101 Minutes, 29 September 1969.

102 Minutes, 30 June 1970.

103 Minutes of the AGM, 28 June 1971.

104 Minutes, 21 February 1972.

105 Minutes of the AGM, 26 June 1972.

106 *The Irish Times,* 9 January 2010.

107 Minutes, 10 August 1972.

108 Minutes, 18 September 1972.

109 Minutes, 8 January 1973.

110 Minutes, 22 January 1973.

111 Minutes, 29 July 1987.

112 Minutes, 8 March 1988.

113 *The Irish Times,* 3 December 1985.

114 Minutes of the AGM, 27 June 1988.

115 Pedants might well argue about whether he could, strictly speaking, be categorised as a 'performer' even on that single occasion.

116 Minutes of the AGM, 27 June 1988.

117 *The Irish Press,* 26 September 1989.

118 *The Irish Press,* 11 October 1989.

119 *The Irish Times,* 11 October 1989.

120 Minutes, 25 September 1961.

121 *The Irish Times,* 2 February 1960.

122 *The Irish Times,* 24 November 1977.

123 Minutes, 11 January 1965.

124 *The Irish Press,* 24 November 1979.

125 Minutes, 8 August 1966.

126 *The Irish Press,* 28 October 1981.

127 *The Irish Times,* 25 December 1981.

128 He didn't return to the fold until *H.M.S. Pinafore* at the Gaiety in 1985. He famously lost his Major Porter on that occasion when a 'tired and emotional' Alan Devlin walked offstage muttering to himself and retreated to the pub.

129 *The Irish Times,* 18 December 1981.

130 *The Irish Times,* 24 November 1981.

131 *The Irish Times,* 24 November 1981.

132 *The Irish Times,* 14 November 1962.

133 *The Irish Times,* 30 March 1965.

134 *The Irish Times,* 18 November 1965 and 15 November 1966.

135 Minutes, 9 December 1974.

136 Gearóid Grant interview, 26 January 2012. All such quotes, unless otherwise indicated, are taken from this interview.

137 The current incumbent is Niamh McDonough.

138 *The Irish Times,* 8 July 1975.

139 *The Irish Times,* 30 October 1986.

140 *The Irish Times,* 17 February 1978.

141 *The Irish Times,* 7 March 1978.

142 *The Irish Times,* 21 November 1978.

143 *The Irish Press,* 22 November 1979.

144 Grant's work with the Cross Border Orchestra, since 1996, goes some way towards fulfilling T.H. Weaving's aspiration from 1922: 'that on the foundation of art could be built up as their only hope a really united Ireland'.

145 Hewson was more challenged by the constant lack of male chorus members than she was by the self-confident young north-sider. In an *Irish Times* interview with Maev Kennedy in 1983 she kept returning to the theme. 'Getting soubrettes is no problem. Getting enough young men

for two shows, neatly divided into basses and tenors, and more or less preferably all of a height, is a perennial problem.' (*The Irish Times*, 19 November 1983.)

[146] Interview with Noel McDonough, 4 February 2012.

[147] He was permitted to retain his day job.

[148] *The Irish Times*, 29 November 1988.

[149] *The Irish Times*, 8 January 1988.

[150] *The Rathmines and Rathgar Musical Society: A Celebration of Seventy-Five Years, 1913–1988* (Dublin, 1988).

[151] *The Irish Times*, 23 August 1988.

[152] *The Irish Times*, 19 November 1988.

[153] My thanks to Nora O'Rourke for this reference.

[154] One of the 'realities' of *Fiddler on the Roof* was that it was costing £80,000 to mount the show (*The Irish Times*, 19 November 1988).

. . . .

CHAPTER 4 (PAGES 107-58)

[1] *The Irish Press*, 11 November 1967.

[2] Christopher Morash, *A History of Irish Theatre 1601–2000* (Cambridge, 2004), p.221.

[3] Minutes, 25 September 1964. Typed report.

[4] *The Irish Times*, 16 November 1965.

[5] *The Irish Times*, 13 September 1965.

[6] In fact the R&R winter 1965 and spring 1966 productions went ahead in the theatre as scheduled.

[7] Minutes, 28 June 1965.

[8] *The Irish Times*, 21 May 1966.

[9] *The Irish Times*, 24 May 1966.

[10] http://www.independent.ie/business/irish/joseph-murphy-jnr-469470.html. http://www.supremecourt.ie/supremecourt/sclibrary3.nsf/(WebF iles)/77A646EB8E876F2B8025770E0034BDA4/$FILE/Murphy per cent.201.pdf.

[11] Minutes, 20 June 1966.

[12] Minutes, 4 July 1966.

[13] Minutes, 2 August and 20 November 1966.

[14] *The Irish Times*, 24 September 1966.

[15] Forde to Ryan, 12 June 1967 [copy in Minute Book].

[16] Minutes, 19 June 1967.

[17] [Minutes, 12 December 1967.] The production did not go ahead and two years later the R&R staged the Irish premiere on the Gaiety stage to critical acclaim. There is, occasionally, some justice in a cruel world.

[18] Minutes, 20 May 1968.

[19] Minutes, 19 August 1968.

[20] *The Irish Times*, 8 November 1971. Interview with Joe and Lucy Lane [McCarthy].

[21] Later it metamorphosed from the RTÉLO caterpillar into the butterfly that is the RTÉ Concert Orchestra. It is lovingly referred to in RTÉ as the 'Number 2 Works Band', the Symphony Orchestra being the 'Number 1 Works Band'.

[22] *The Irish Times*, 29 October 1971.

[23] *Irish Independent*, 28 October 1971.

[24] This was reduced to 5 per cent in the 1984 budget (*The Irish Times*, 27 January 1984).

[25] *The Irish Times*, 7 October 1983.

[26] *The Irish Press*, 7 October 1983.

[27] One of the directors of the holding company that owned the theatre, Gaiety Theatre (Dublin) Ltd, was one James Gogarty, whose relationship with his employers, Joseph Murphy Senior & Junior, deteriorated somewhat when he gave evidence to the Flood/Mahon Tribunal that they had bribed Fianna Fáil Minister Ray Burke.

[28] *The Irish Press*, 11 November 1983.

29 *The Irish Times,* 22 October 1983.

30 Technically it was Eamonn Andrews Studios that went into receivership, but the receiver, Bernard Somers, had control of the assets of Eamonn Andrews Productions. Later EAP went into liquidation. It emerged that some of the recent EAP Gaiety productions had lost a total of £200,000 and that even long-running shows like *Annie* and *Joseph and his Amazing Technicolour Dreamcoat* had been loss-makers (*The Irish Times,* 14 January 1984).

31 *The Irish Times,* 21 January 1984.

32 *The Irish Times,* 26 January 1984.

33 *The Irish Press*, 26 January 1984.

34 *The Irish Press*, 27 October 1984.

35 *The Irish Times*, 20 October 1984.

36 *The Irish Times*, 7 September 1984.

37 Minutes, 14 December 1992.

38 Minutes, 15 February 1993.

39 Minutes, 1 March 1993.

40 *The Irish Times,* 8 May 1993.

41 *The Irish Times,* 13 May 1993.

42 *The Irish Times,* 19 January 1996.

43 *The Irish Times,* 19 February 1999.

44 Minutes, 12 December 1994.

45 Minutes, 20 February 1995.

46 *The Irish Times,* 26 November 2009.

47 We can probably assume that O'Donovan was not referring to the NCH when he wrote of the R&R committees in the 1988 seventy-fifth anniversary publication: 'they have seen managements come and go and I am sure they will see many more'.

48 Minutes, 6 May 1950.

49 Minutes, 17 December 1987. I am basing the gross on an R&R net of around £13,000.

50 http://www.bankofengland.co.uk/education/Pages/inflation/calculator/flash/default.aspx.

51 Hilda's son, Eoin O'Brien, went on to play leading roles with the society, among them Jack Point and Ko-Ko, while Mida's children – Clodagh and Colm – were also prominent members.

52 *Irish Independent*, 26 May 1931.

53 *The Irish Times,* 26 May 1931.

54 *Irish Independent*, 10 April 1944.

55 *The Irish Press*, 10 April 1944.

56 *Irish Independent*, 30 April 1946.

57 *Irish Independent,* 30 April 1946.

58 *The Irish Press*, 30 April 1946.

59 *The Irish Times,* 30 April 1946.

60 *The Irish Times,* 30 April 1946.

61 *Irish Independent,* 30 April 1946.

62 *Irish Independent,* 30 April 1946.

63 Cowering somewhere in the male chorus line was a young R&R debutant, one Patrick Campbell, later to become president of the R&R. From acorns to mighty oaks…

64 This song is to the R&R what 'The Sash' is to the Orange Order or 'There Is an Isle' is to Munster rugby supporters. It has become an anthem. It is usually sung at the end of social engagements, so renditions might not always be up to the R&R's customary impeccable standards.

65 http://www.guidetomusicaltheatre.com: a useful source of information of all kinds on musical theatre.

66 *The Irish Times,* 14 April 1952.

67 *The Irish Press,* 14 April 1952.

68 Minutes, 26 May 1952.

69 *The Irish Press*, 6 May 1958.

70 *The Irish Times*, 6 May 1958.

71 £5,198 as opposed to £2,520.

72 Minutes of the AGM, 9 June 1959.

73 Minutes, 7 June 1960.

74 *The Irish Press,* 10 March 1961.

75 *The Irish Times,* 8 March 1961.

76 Interview with Jackie Curran Olohan, 8 March 2012.

77 *The Irish Times,* 14 March 1961.

78 Joe stood down as Londis MD in 1991, after twenty-five years.

79 Interview with Joe and Lucy Lane, 20 March 2012.
80 *The Irish Times,* 14 March 1961.
81 Minutes, 29 April 1963.
82 *The Irish Times,* 14 November 1963.
83 *Irish Independent*, 13 November 1963.
84 *Irish Independent*, 12 November 1963.
85 *Irish Independent*, 23 March 1966.
86 *The Irish Times,* 23 March 1966.
87 Minutes, 10 May 1967.
88 Minutes, 29 May 1967.
89 Minutes, 19 June 1967.
90 Minutes, 12 December 1967.
91 Minutes, 20 May 1968.
92 Minutes, 4 December 1968.
93 http://www.belchamber.me.uk/68043.html.
94 Minutes, 17 December 1968.
95 Minutes, 29 January 1969.
96 *Irish Independent,* 12 March 1969.
97 *The Irish Times,* 12 March 1969.
98 *The Irish Press* 5 November 1969.
99 My thanks to Nora O'Rourke for this information.
100 For example, *The Irish Press,* 22 November 1979.
101 Campbell, as a child, had seen the great Henry Lytton play the role in a D'Oyly Carte production in the Gaiety (*The Irish Times,* 11 November 1971).
102 Interview with Camillus Mountaine, 20 March 2012.
103 *The Irish Times,* 15 November 1977.
104 *The Irish Times,* 15 November 1971.
105 Minutes of the AGM, 28 June 1971.
106 Minutes, 20 September 1971.
107 Minutes, 14 December 1971.
108 *The Irish Times,* 24 April 1972.
109 *The Irish Times,* 26 April 1972.
110 Interview with Camillus Mountaine.
111 *The Irish Times,* 26 April 1972.
112 *Irish Independent,* 28 February 1978.
113 *The Irish Times,* 11 March 1978.
114 *The Irish Times,* 7 March 1978.
115 *The Irish Press*, 8 March 1978.
116 *The Irish Press*, 20 March 1980.
117 *Irish Independent*, 20 March 1980.
118 *The Irish Times,* 19 March 1980.
119 *The Irish Times,* 31 March 1981.
120 Interview with Noel McDonough, 4 February 2012.
121 Since 2000 the Rogers and Hammerstein organisation, which owns the rights to the show, has stipulated that licences will only be issued where black performers are used for the African American roles.
122 *The Irish Press*, 16 November 1987.
123 *The Irish Times,* 12 March 1975.
124 *The Irish Times*, 18 November 1987.
125 Minutes, 17 December 1987.
126 Minutes, 13 January 1987.
127 http://randr.ie/programme-archive-1990-1999/. Programmes from 1990 to the present day are reproduced. These include full cast-lists and biographies of leading performers.
128 *The Irish Times,* 14 November 1991.
129 *Irish Independent*, 14 November 1991.
130 Minutes of the AGM, 31 May 1997.
131 http://randr.ie/programme-archive-1990-1999/.

132 *The Irish Times,* 7 November 1996.

133 Rita Kealy (1995–2000) and Marina Kealy (2005–) have taken charge of concert productions at the NCH.

134 *The Irish Times,* 28 October 1998.

135 His first significant contribution to an AGM was in 1949 when he suggested, after Mida O'Brien, Eileen Clancy and Joe Flood had been producing (of necessity) for the previous few years, that it might be advisable to engage 'a D'Oyly Carte producer for G&S shows in the future, that we were inclined to play these shows in a musical comedy fashion and were losing some of the "quaintness"' (Minutes of the AGM, 16 June 1949).

136 Nora O'Rourke profile of Chris Bruton.

137 http://randr.ie/demo-issuu/.

138 http://www.sondheimguide.com/sideby.html.

139 Abject apologies if I have misrepresented his preferences.

140 *The Irish Times,* 19 October 2001.

141 http://www.paulbyrom.ie.

142 *The Irish Times,* 25 March 2004.

143 As, for example, in 1953, when the committee decided that 'laxity and casualness' were creeping into the company 'and that we should take steps to tighten up discipline'. Such eruptions were as regular as Stromboli.

144 Information from Nora O'Rourke.

145 Minutes, 6 May 1953.

146 *The Irish Press,* 12 March 1970.

147 Acton did add generously, however, that he often found himself 'judging professionals by the R&R, weighing them in the balance against the R&R and finding them wanting'.

148 *The Irish Times,* 20 November 1973.

149 *The Irish Times,* 28 March 1974.

150 *The Irish Times,* 19 November 1975. The *Irish Press* critic, Robert Johnston, was well pleased with both productions. Nowlan's review of *Iolanthe,* appearing in rep with *Pinafore,* was much more positive.

151 *Irish Independent,* 27 March 1974.

152 *The Irish Times,* 28 March 1974.

153 Interview with Noel McDonough.

154 *The Irish Press,* 28 March 1979.

155 *The Irish Times,* 12 April 1985.

156 Interview with Camillus Mountaine.

157 Interview with Gearóid Grant.

CHAPTER 5 (PAGES 159-202)

1 Minutes, 6 March 1990.

2 Minutes, 8 January 1990.

3 Minutes, 23 April 1990.

4 Minutes, 23 July 1990.

5 The results can be heard in 30-second iTunes-type snatches on http://www.muziekweb.nl/Link/HFX2729.

6 Minutes of the AGM, 25 June 1990.

7 At any rate, it could hardly be described, given the circumstances, as 'non-performing'.

8 Minutes of the AGM, 21 June 1990.

9 *The Irish Times,* 8 September 1990; 15 September 1990.

10 Programme notes, *Anything Goes.*

11 Minutes, 3 February 1992.

12 Minutes, 2 November 1992.

13 *Irish Independent,* 12 November 1992.

14 *The Irish Press*, 11 November 1992.

15 Minutes of the AGM, 28 June 1992.

16 Minutes, 30 November 1992.

17 Minutes of the AGM, 28 June 1992.

18 These were the eightieth anniversary concerts with the RTÉCO, the eightieth anniversary gala concert *Hear our Songs* and *One Enchanted Evening*. The G&S shows were *The Mikado* (1993) and *The Pirates of Penzance* (1994).

19 Minutes, 7 April 1993.

20 Minutes of the AGM, 28 June 1999.

21 Information from Nora O'Rourke.

22 *The Irish Times*, 17 April 1951.

23 *The Irish Times*, 17 April 1951.

24 Minutes, 4 June 1956.

25 *The Irish Press*, 28 May 1957.

26 *The Irish Press*, 17 November 1965.

27 *The Irish Times*, 27 March 1968.

28 *Irish Independent*, 23 March 1966.

29 R&R choreographers are obliged to be warriors.

30 I am indebted to Nora O'Rourke, herself an accomplished stage manager and production manager, for most of the information in this section.

31 Minutes, 14 December 1960.

32 Glynn, who was honorary secretary from 1947–9 also played Lord Dramaleigh (Lord Chamberlain) and Phantis (Judge of the Utopian Supreme Court) in *Utopia Limited* and Jack Point in *Yeomen*, but never managed Ko-Ko in *The Mikado*.

33 Pat Campbell's natural successor, both in the G&S canon as the Major General, Duke of Plaza Toro and Sir Joseph Porter, and as a suave and debonair presenter and MC of NCH Concerts, is Jimmy Dixon, who first appeared in *Showboat* in 1987.

34 Interview with Stephen Faul.

35 *The Irish Press*, 28 August 1972 (SFX Hall) and 10 January 1983 (RDS).

36 *The Irish Times*, 31 March 1987. He was writing about *Romberg and Romance*.

37 Minutes, 2 July 2001.

38 Minutes of the AGM, 2 July 2001.

39 Minutes of the AGM, 26 June 1989.

40 The selling-out of a significant percentage of seats in advance is largely down to the creation in 1974 of the position of booking secretary who chased group bookings. The position was first held by Fred Taylor and more recently by Barney Gorman.

41 Minutes, 9 April 2001.

42 Pat Farrell to Nora O'Rourke, 31 October 2000.

43 Minutes, 22 January 2001.

44 Minutes, 14 November 2001.

45 *The Rathmines and Rathgar Musical Society: A Celebration of Seventy-Five Years, 1913–1988* (Dublin, 1988).

46 Minutes, 26 September 1989.

47 Interview with Stephen Faul.

48 Minutes of the AGM, 25 June 1990.

49 Interview with Shay Gibson, 3 February 2013.

50 Interview with Pat Campbell, 31 January 2013.

51 Interview with Nora O'Rourke, 25 January 2013.

52 Dympna and her family are R&R 'lifers'. Her maternal uncle, Gerald O'Byrne, was in the 1913 *Mikado* and her paternal aunt, Julie O'Callaghan, joined in 1916 and made her debut in the *Mikado* of that year. Both continued in the chorus for many years. Dympna Egar herself has been in the society since 1960 and is now a life member; her brother, Commandant Fred O'Callaghan acted as musical director in the brief interregnum between Terry O'Connor and Gearóid Grant; her granddaughter played Peep-Bo in *The Mikado* (2010) and her grandson was in *Oklahoma!* (2012).

53 A shout of 'level zero, level zero' from the producer to the assembly doubles as a genial instruction that reduces the hall to a focused silence and allows the work to continue without fuss.

54 Interview with Nora O'Rourke, 25 January 2013.

55 The *Hello Dolly!* sets can be seen on the Scenic Projects website: http://www.scenicprojects.co.uk/Shows/hello-dolly.aspx.

56 For the *Hello Dolly!* Costumes, see http://www.utopiacostumes.com/shows.html.

57 Josef Weinberger brochure.

58 Interview with Brendan Galvin, 2 March 2012.

59 http://www.chernobyl-international.com/about-us/our-history.

60 The first was at a Gilbert and Sullivan invitation concert in the more traditional surroundings of the Albert Hall.

61 Minutes, 27 September 1999.

62 http://www.thedramateacher.com/how-much-does-it-cost-to-mount-a-bRoadway-musical/.

63 http://www.aims.ie/societies.php?r=e.

64 *The Irish Times,* 14 November 1969.

65 *The Irish Times,* 8 December 1973.

66 *The Irish Times*, 17 November 1979.

67 *The Irish Times*, 31 March 1981.

68 Minutes of the AGM, 23 June 1969.

69 More startling is the fact that this was based on a 78 per cent seat occupancy figure.

70 *The Irish Times,* 12 March 1969.

71 Minutes, 9 December 1974.

72 *The Irish Times,* 22 March 1982.

73 *Irish Independent*, 28 August 1978.

74 *The Irish Times,* 17 November 1981.

75 *The Irish Times,* 22 March 1982. Kevin Myers in 'An Irishman's Diary' reported that £48,000 would be spent on *Oklahoma!*

76 Minutes, 6 March 1990. This was for a run of one week only.

77 Minutes of the AGM, 31 July 2006. The higher figure was applied to the 2005 production of *Fiddler on the Roof.*

78 Report of business secretary, 5 June 1990.

79 An otherwise well-received production of *The Yeomen of the Guard* in 2004.

80 Though the latter can be accounted for by the closure of the Gaiety from February to May for refurbishment (Minutes of the AGM, 31 July 2006).

81 Minutes of the AGM, 25 July 2005.

82 Figures for expenditure, rental costs and sales income supplied by Nora O'Rourke.

83 The last year for which figures are available, 2006, saw the 'Show Reserve' at €189,000 (Minutes of the AGM, 31 July 2006).

84 Many of those talented ingénues have been channelled towards the society by two of the great Dublin singing teachers, Veronica Dunne and Mary Brennan – the latter a distinguished former member.

85 And were due to marry in 2013.

86 Obviously it is only possible to mention some of the more prominent performers in a 100-year history. However, thanks to an ongoing project it is now possible to access programmes, for the entire century, online at www.randr.ie.

87 Minutes of the AGM, 1 July 2002.

88 Minutes of the AGM, 7 July 2003.

89 Minutes, 27 May 2002.

90 Interview with Michael Forde, 31 January 2013.

91 Minutes of the AGM, 2 July 2001.

92 Camillus Mountaine, Minutes of the AGM, 1 July 2002.

93 The R&R's Robert Vickers is currently understudy to Alfie Boe in the London production.

94 Minutes of the AGM, 2 July 2001.

Note: Photographs and illustrations are indicated by page numbers in **bold**

233

Irish Volunteers 16–17, 19
Irishman's Diary (*Irish Times*) 65, 77–8, 79
Ivanhoe (Sullivan) 18

Jackpot (TV show) 79
Jackson, Charles 5, **9**
Jacob's 71
James H. North (auctioneers) 111
Jennings, Anna 163
Jessop, George H. 21
Jew Suss (Kornfeld) 27
John Bull's Other Island (Shaw) 12
Johnston, Denis 28
Johnston, Mary Todd 81–2
Johnston, Robert
    Gondoliers, The 1965, review of 167
    and Grant, Gearóid, views on 103
    King and I, The, review of 142
    and Meadmore, Norman, views on 93
    My Fair Lady 1969, review of 131
    and R&R, views on 136, 153
    Sweet Charity 1979, review of 156
Jones, Frances **118**
Jones, Paddy 169
Jones, Sidney 21, 33
Jordan, Helen 156
Josef Weinberger Ltd 181, 200
Jourdan, Louis 140
Joyce, James 42, 80, 195
Joyce, Ray **79**

Kaye, Danny 156
Kealy, Marina (choreographer) 146, **167**, 168, 179
Kealy, Rita (choreographer) 146, 148, 167–8, **167**
Keane, Caroline **118**
Kearns, Joe, manager Gaiety Theatre 111–12
Kelleher, Claire **72**, **137**
Kelly, Brian 79
Kelly, David 50–51
Kelly, Grace **72**
Kelly, Lisa 148

Kelly, Marie 179
Kelly, Muriel (choreographer) 166
Kelly, Paul 145, **192**
Kelly, Sandra 150, **203**
Kelly, Seamus 65, 99, 187
Kelly, Wilson **2**, **9**, 12, 14, **17**, 215n29
Kennedy, John F. 128
Kenny, Pat 79
Kern, Jerome 41, 143
Kester, Max 110
King and I, The (Rodgers and Hammerstein) (1980) 86, 141–2, **142**, 150, 167
Kirwan, Patrick 81, 123
Kismet (1963) 63
Kiss Me Kate (Porter) (1990) 167
Kissane, Brian 86, 124, 126
Knowles, Eileen **47**, 82, 102–3, 122, 123
Knox, Walter **9**
Korngold, E.W. 58

Land of Heart's Desire, The (Yeats) 26
Lane, Joseph (Joe) 126–7, 164, **197**, **203**
    and Gaiety Theatre discussions 119
    review of 127
    South Pacific 1996, views on 145
Lane, Lucy **197**, **203**
    review of 127
    roles **102**, 137, **137**, 145
    soloist 105, 173
    and Wogan, Terry 79
Lane, Nathan 193
Larchet, J.F. 23
Larkin, Jim 8
Late Late Show 199
Lavery, Richard (AIMS) **200**
Lawlor, Adam **203**
Lawlor, Pat **89**
Leahy, Denis **197**
Leaming, Barbara 27–8
Leeson, Victor 62, **62**, **111**
Lehar, Franz 126
Leigh, Vivienne 78
Lerner, Alan Jay and Loewe,

Frederick 130, 140, 151
Lewin, William 215n64
Lewis, Peter 105, 162, **196**
Lilac Time (1944) 122
Lily of Killarney (1960) 99
Little, Ita **76**
Littler, Emile 75
Lloyd, Edwin 5, **5**, **10**, 12, **21**, 214n8
Lloyd Webber, Andrew 192, 199
Loesser, Frank 128
Long, Betty 169
Lost Chords and Discords (Brahms) 48
Love from Judy (Littler) (1958) 75, 79, 125–6, 167
Lucas, Arthur 14, 17, 215n64
Lunar Records 161–2
Lynch, Edith **203**
Lynch, Irvine **9**, 12, 21, 28
Lyons, Ig, treasurer 118, 119, **175**
Lyric Opera Productions 151, 178

McAleese, Mary **147**, 149
McAnally, Ray 62, 64
McAuliffe, Catherine 83
MacBride, John 19
MacCabe, Cathal **117**, 136, 144, 167, 177
McCabe, Leo 110
McCall, John, advertising and PR 182–3
McCambridge, Malcolm 96
McCann, Mary **126**
McCarthy, Justin Huntly 123
McCarthy, Lucy (later Lane) 83, 126–7
McConnells Advertising 71
McCormack, John 80
McCullagh, Robert
    awards 81
    and DGOS 54
    lecture on R&R 105
    remuneration 56, 58
    review of 30
    roles 30, 39, **49**, 56, 57, 124
    scholarship in honour of 84, 163
McCutcheon, J. **55**
MacDonagh, Thomas 19, 51

Mountaine, Camillus, review of 138
My Fair Lady 1981, review of 190
Pirates of Penzance, 1977, review of 86–7
and R&R, views on 154, 161
Showboat 1987, review of 144

O2 (Point Theatre) 164, 186, 190
O'Brien, Eoin **79**, **88**, 126, 150, 225n51
O'Brien, Flann *see* O'Nolan, Brian
O'Brien, Frank 105
O'Brien, Jack **8**, **11**
  casting difficulties 1915 17–18
  Cranfield's omission of 21
  departure from R&R 19–20
  as Jack Point **15**, 18
  Mikado, The, 1913, producer of 8, 12
  reviews of 12, 18
O'Brien, Mida
  committee 1942 **47**
  executive committee 1950 **60**
  inhouse producer 60, 67, 127
  review of 39
  roles **29**, 122, 123
O'Callaghan, Fred 102, 228n52
O'Callaghan, Mary 83, **83**, 129
O'Connor, Hubert **88**
O'Connor, Jack
  cartoon of **58**
  and Dublin Musical Society 63
  and Irish Festival Singers **72**
  remuneration 58
  reviews of 123, 128
  roles 62, 122, 123, 124, 125
  and Wogan, Terry 79
O'Connor, Kevin 95
O'Connor, Loreto 150
O'Connor, Terry **64**, **77**, **101**
  as conductor 58, 64
  and Feis Ceoil R&R Cup 82
  and Glasnevin Musical Society 99, 101
  as musical director 64, 65, 153

professional career 64
retirement from R&R 101–2
O'Dea, Jimmy 70, 110
O'Donoghue, John 169
O'Donovan, Fred 69–70, 113, 118, 120, 152
Offenbach, Jacques 152
O'Gorman, May **9**
O'Hagan, Dodo, 206
  assistant treasurer 103, 104, 162, **163**
  Cricket XI **79**
  roles **102**, **197**
Ó hAnnracháin, Fachtna 75
O'Herlihy, Bill 182
O'Herlihy Communications 182
O'Herlihy, Jill 182–3
O'Higgins, Brigid Mary 25
O'Higgins, Kevin 25
Oklahoma! (Rodgers and Hammerstein) 61
  (1957) 83, 143, 167
  (1982) 143, 191
  (1999) 165
  (2012) 174–5, 176, 195
Old Belvedere Musical Society 46, 48, 53, 54, 218n36
Olohan, Ciaran 174
Olohan, Jackie Curran
  casting committee 179
  chorus director 104, 126, 146, 166, 179
  roles 174, **197**
O'Loughlin, Una 15
Olympia Theatre 32, 33, 40, 57, 62, 68, 110
O'Mahony, Synan, dress designer 188
Ó Muirí, Naoise **203**
O'Neill, Joseph **22**, 60
O'Neill, Seamus, stage manager 168–9
O'Nolan, Brian 42–3
  views on Gilbert and Sullivan 43–4
Opportunity Knocks (ITV) 145
O'Rattigan, Madame 94
O'Reilly, Anthony (Tony) 105
O'Reilly, Gerry 118, 119, 164
O'Rourke, Nora 178, 181

AIMS representative **200**
committee **200**
production manager 186
stage manager 149, 169, **169**, 170, **172**, 180–81
O'Shea, Milo 61–2
O'Sullivan, Eileen 146
O'Sullivan, Maurice 62, **85**, 162, 169
  roles 131, 143, **160**
O'Sullivan, Proinsias **77**
O'Toole, Peter 118

Palace Theatre (London) 58
Papp, Joseph 100
Parnell, Charles Stewart 25, 123
Pat McGann Productions 181
Patience (G&S)
  (1922) 26–7
  (1923) 29
  (1929) 18, 32
  (1941) 45
  (1945) 52
  (1948) cast members **55**
  (1963) **89**, 127–8
  (1966) **36**, 83, **111**
Patrick, F.W. 29
Pavarotti, Luciano 161, 163
Payne, Fred 33
Pearse, Colman 114
Pearse, Patrick 19, 51
Pearson, Noel 93, 100, 222n85
Perchance to Dream (Novello)
  (1954) 62, 220n130
Phillips, Laurence Michael *see* Myers, Isidore
Pioneer Orchestral Society 20
Pirates of Penzance, The (G&S)
  (1937) 76
  (1940) 44
  (1952) 65, 67
  (1977) 86
  (1984) **117**
  (1994) **188**
  (2002) 151
  (2011) **189**
  choruses at Gaiety re-opening 118
  and Clontarf Musical Society 100

241

and R&R CDs 161
RTÉ Concert Orchestra 104,
188, 224n21
RTÉ Light Orchestra 114,
224n21
RTÉ Symphony Orchestra 104,
201, 224n21
Ruddigore (G&S) 20, **28**
(1922) **24**, 81
(1945) 52
(1976) **101**
Runyon, Damon 128, 150
Russell, Willy 178
Ryan, Clem **61**, **90**
at US Embassy **106**
centenary of Gaiety **115**
and dancing group 167
death of 148
and Elliman 110
executive committee 1950 **60**
and Feis Ceoil winners 83
and Gaiety Theatre 71, 113
Guthrie, discussions with
91–2
management of R&R 70,
126
president **97**, **98**, **162**
and R&R competitors 100
and Radio Éireann 75
75th anniversary of R&R
105
Ryan, Eithne **90**, 95, **95**, **106**, **162**
Ryan, Jonathan 103, 140, 141,
141, 156
Ryan, Paula 169
Ryan, Ted 105, 157

St James's Gate Musical Society
62
San Toy (Jones and Morton)
(1929) 33
Sardou, Victorien 27
Savoy Theatre 12, 26, 31
Scally, Siobhan 103, 140, **141**
Scanlon, Josephine 126
Scenic Projects 181, 182, 228n55
Schubert, Franz 122–3
Scott, David **196**
Scott, Michael 146
Selby, Mr [London agent] 33, 40

sets
building costs 186
delivery 'window' 169, 182
Gaiety, provision of sets 168
Gondoliers 2006 at NCH 187
hire of 38, 180–81
Mikado, The 1913 8
mishaps with viii, 157,
169–70
and NCH 169
and O'Donoghue, John 169
'Seventy-Five Years of the R&R'
(McCullagh) 105
Shane, Lisa *see* Yeomans, Hazel
Shannon, William **106**
Shaw, George Bernard 12–13, 21,
85, 130, 222n57
Shea, Queenie 30
Shelbourne Hotel 19, 23, 88
Shields, William 27
Showboat (Kern) 41
(1955) 61
(1975) **171**, 190
(1987) **120**, 121, 143–4, 167,
191, 226n121
(1997) 148, 165
Shumate, Anne 143
Side by Side by Sondheim 150
Silverthorn Investments 119
Simmons and Company (London)
8
Sinatra, Frank 59, **72**, 128
Singin' in the Rain (film) 177–8
Sinn Féin 3
Smith, Anne Maria 144, 162, **197**
Smith, Billy Blood 138
Smith, Damian 143
Smith, Ken **55**, **60**
Smyth, Elizabeth 83
Sondheim, Stephen 178
South Pacific (Rodgers and
Hammerstein)
(1965) 83
(1973) 78, **83**
(1996) 145–6, 165
Spong, Jon **162**, 163
stage management 168–9
see also Bruton, Chris;
O'Rourke, Nora; sets
Staveley, Eva **101**, **126**

Stewart, Michael 176
Storm, Rebecca 119, 178, 179,
180, 182, 183, 198, 199
Strauss, Johann 46, 47, 48
Strauss, Oscar 21, 32
Streisand, Barbra 62, 177
Strife (Galsworthy) 12
Strumpet City (Plunkett) 51
Student Prince, The
(1943) 50, 57
(1948) 59
(1963) **89**
Studley, Louise
Dancing Years, The 124, 155
and Dublin Musical Society
61, 63, 220n103
film roles 61
King and I, The 142, **142**
Merry Widow, The vii, 61, **61**,
86, 126
My Fair Lady vii, **74**, 131,
131, **132**, 169, 190
reviews of 60–61, 131, 155
at Shaw Bequest 85
Yeomen of the Guard 88
Sullivan, Sir Arthur 4, 18, 19, 22,
27, 66, 198
Sullivan, Roisin 151
Sweeney, Maxwell 37
Sweeney, Tony **173**
Sweet Charity (1979) **155**, 156,
187
Swift, Jonathan 118

Talbot, Howard 32, 121
Tanner, James 32
Tarisio (*nom de plume*) 6
Tate, Sir Robert 23–4, 25
tax, abolition on 'live' theatre 32
Taylor, Cynthia **84**, 222n51
Taylor, Fred **79**, **84**, **115**, 222n51,
228n40
Te Kanawa, Kiri 161, 163, 164
Tennyson, Alfred, Baron 59
Theatre Council 71
Theatre Royal 53, 70, 167
Theatre Royal (Norwich) 117
Theatrical Costume Hire 181
Thorndike, Sybil, Dame 140,
222n57

Carousel, 2000

The Magic of Lerner & Loewe, 1988

The King and I, 1980

Fiddler on the Roof, 2006